ETERNITY IS NOW IN SESSION

PARTICIPANT'S
GUIDE

ETERNITY IS NOW IN SESSION

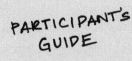

A RADICAL ~~~~~~~~~ HAT JESUS
REALLY ~~~~~~~~ ATION,
ETERNITY, A ~~~~~~~~ OOD PLACE

PARTICIPANT'S GUIDE

JOHN ORTBERG
& GARY MOON

TYNDALE
MOMENTUM®

The nonfiction imprint of
Tyndale House Publishers, Inc.

Visit Tyndale online at www.tyndale.com.

Visit Tyndale Momentum online at www.tyndalemomentum.com.

TYNDALE, *Tyndale Momentum,* and Tyndale's quill logo are registered trademarks of Tyndale House Publishers, Inc. The Tyndale Momentum logo is a trademark of Tyndale House Publishers, Inc. Tyndale Momentum is the nonfiction imprint of Tyndale House Publishers, Inc., Carol Stream, Illinois.

Eternity Is Now in Session Participant's Guide: A Radical Rediscovery of What Jesus Really Taught about Salvation, Eternity, and Getting to the Good Place

Designed by Jennifer Phelps

Edited by Jonathan Schindler

For information about special discounts for bulk purchases, please contact Tyndale House Publishers at csresponse@tyndale.com, or call 1-800-323-9400.

ISBN 978-1-4964-3169-1

Printed in the United States of America

24	23	22	21	20	19	18
7	6	5	4	3	2	1

CONTENTS

INTRODUCTION

Thank you for choosing to use *Eternity Is Now in Session* for your group. This participant's guide is designed to accompany the *Eternity Is Now in Session DVD Experience* and the book *Eternity Is Now in Session* by John Ortberg. This study guide is five sessions long and will help participants grow closer to God as they rediscover "what Jesus really taught about salvation, eternity, and getting to the good place." The sessions will show participants what it means to follow Jesus in discipleship through the stages of awakening, purgation, illumination, and union.

Each session follows a similar format: there is a video with teaching from John Ortberg, discussion questions for group reflection, and a key activity that invites participants to go deeper into the topic studied. There are also suggestions for ways that participants can engage this study throughout the week (including reading corresponding chapters in the book *Eternity Is Now in Session*) and Scripture passages that follow the theme of the session.

Your group should have a leader who is responsible for

starting the video, prompting participants with the discussion questions, and directing the key activity. The leader should also monitor the time and can adjust the session's activities and discussion accordingly. (See "Leader Tips" on page xi.)

John writes, "God is not waiting for eternity to begin. God lives in it right now. It is the interactive fellowship and joy that exists between Father, Son, and Holy Spirit. Eternity is rolling right along, and we are invited to be part of it—*now*." Are you ready to join in?

Eternity is now in session!

MATERIALS NEEDED

This *Eternity Is Now in Session Participant's Guide* is intended to accompany the *Eternity Is Now in Session DVD Experience* and the *Eternity Is Now in Session* book. Each session of this curriculum is intended to last sixty to ninety minutes. In order to get the most out of this study, we recommend that you have the following materials present at your meetings:

- One copy of the *Eternity Is Now in Session DVD Experience* for the group
- A copy of the *Eternity Is Now in Session* book and this participant's guide for each person
- A DVD player and TV or a computer (to watch the video component for each session)
- A clock (to monitor time)
- A pen or pencil for each person (to take notes during the video and for use in each session's key activity)
- A Bible for each person

LEADER TIPS

The following are some tips that will help you as you lead your group through the *Eternity Is Now in Session* study:

BEFORE THE SESSION
- Watch the video (if possible) and look over the study notes, discussion questions, and activities in the participant's guide in advance of the meeting.
- Pray by name for each person who will be at the session and ask that God would open new avenues for intimacy with this person through the study.
- Consider preparing (or appointing someone to prepare) a snack for the session. Snacks can loosen an atmosphere and make people more comfortable with sharing.
- Make sure the materials needed (page ix) are present at every session. It's a good idea to arrive early in case of problems.
- Encourage study participants to read the chapters in *Eternity Is Now in Session* in advance of your meetings. While reading the chapters isn't necessary to use the

participant's guide or DVD, participants will get the most out of the experience by following along in the book.

AT THE SESSION

- Be sure to welcome each person to the group when they arrive, and carry that spirit of welcome throughout the session.
- Try to encourage each person to speak during the discussion.
- Don't be afraid to adapt the material provided in this study—cutting questions or lingering on a topic—to provide the best experience for your group.
- Be mindful of participants' time, and do your best to keep the study within the parameters you've set for the group. That being said, if the Holy Spirit is moving, do what you can to allow extra time and space to minister.
- Remind participants of the homework activities that accompany each session, which can be accomplished throughout the week. Highlight one or more of these activities and request reports at your next session.
- Consider taking prayer requests at the close of your session or breaking into smaller groups for prayer.

Session 1

ARE WE THERE YET?

WELCOME

Welcome to session 1 of the *Eternity Is Now in Session DVD Experience*. Each of the five sessions in this study is designed to be completed in 60 to 90 minutes, with additional activities that you can do at home.

This session accompanies chapters 1–3 of the *Eternity Is Now in Session* book (pages 11–63). Watch the video, discuss the questions, and complete the key activity as a group as time allows.

VIDEO NOTES

As you watch the video, use the space below to take notes. We've included some key points to get you started.

Jesus—and the entire New Testament, for that matter—defines eternal life only once, with great precision, and in a way that has been largely lost in our day.

> This is eternal life, that they may know you, the only true God, and Jesus Christ whom you have sent.
>
> JOHN 17:3, NRSV

To know God means to know what Paul called "the power of his resurrection" (Philippians 3:10) in the details and tasks and challenges of my daily, ordinary life.

God is not waiting for eternity to begin. God lives in it right now. Eternity is now in session.

> The New Testament is a book about disciples,
> by disciples, and for disciples of Jesus Christ.
>
> DALLAS WILLARD

Discipleship is a journey—a lifelong journey in which we learn to live the life that Jesus offers. For many centuries, that journey was described using certain stages:

- **Awakening:** I become aware of God's extraordinary presence in my ordinary days. I wake up to love, gratitude, wonder, and responsibility.
- **Purgation:** I confess my character defects. I humbly ask God to remove them. I engage in practices that can help free me from them.
- **Illumination:** I begin to change at the level of my automatic perceptions and beliefs. My "mental map" of how things are begins to look like Jesus' mental map.
- **Union:** I begin to experience the life that Jesus invited us into when he said, "Abide in me, and I will abide in you" (see John 15:4).

DISCUSSION QUESTIONS

1. In John 17:3 Jesus defines eternal life as *knowing* God.
    What does it mean to know God? How does this differ
    from knowing *about* God?

2. What is the significance of eternity being in session right
    now?

3. What are any barriers you may have to experiencing
    Jesus as your "shepherd" or "your very good friend"
    as you go through each day? Why are these things in
    the way?

4. How would you define *discipleship* to a friend?

5. Without looking at the notes above, how many movements from John's description of the journey of discipleship can you name? Which do you think best characterizes your walk with Jesus now? Explain.

6. How would you live differently if it were organized around living in an interactive relationship with the Trinity? What specifically would change?

KEY ACTIVITY: KNOWING GOD

BELIEF VS. KNOWLEDGE

Belief and *knowledge* are two very different words. We can believe something even if it is false. We can believe, for example, that the moon is made of cheese or that the universe sprang from nothingness without assistance. Jesus knew that even the demons in hell believed he was the Son of God. But, as Dallas Willard has written, "We have knowledge of something when we are representing it (thinking about it, speaking of it, treating it) as it actually is, on an appropriate basis of thought and experience."[1] Knowledge is truth based on adequate evidence.

So when John states that "eternal life = knowing God," he is talking about stepping into a belief. We can believe that a chair can support our bodies. We know this is true when we trust the chair with our weight. Eternal living means trusting our lives to what is real, present, and right here. Knowledge takes belief to a new and experiential level.

- If knowing God through living *with* the Trinity is the key to understanding who we are, and why we are here, what are some practical ways you can live more moments of your life "with" God?

---

[1] Dallas Willard. *Knowing Christ Today: Why We Can Trust Spiritual Knowledge* (New York: HarperOne, 2009), 15.

DISCERNING GOD'S VOICE

As you live in more active conversation with your good friend Jesus, you may want to consider the following questions to help you recognize the voice of God.

1. **Does it sound like God?** Does what you heard sound like something God would say? Is it consistent with God as you know him through Scripture?

2. **Does it sound like Jesus Christ?** Does it sound like something Jesus would say? Is it consistent with Jesus as you see him revealed in the pages of the New Testament?

3. **Does it help you be conformed to the image of Christ?** The glory of God is our transformation into Christlikeness (see 2 Corinthians 3:18).

4. **Is it consistent with a previous experience you have had that you now know was from God?** We can take advantage of the 20/20 vision of hindsight.

5. **Is it consistent with the fruit of the Spirit, and does it promote the growth of Christ's character in us?** The fruit of the Spirit is the character of Christ.

6. **Is it consistent with the witness of what the saints and devotion masters have had to say about God?** Do I get a witness from those who have won the race?

7. **Do my closest friends and spiritual mentors believe it was from God?** Do I get a witness from those I trust?

8. **Is it consistent with the overarching themes of Scripture?** God's spoken word will not contradict his written Word.

What questions would you add to this list?

HOMEWORK: RECOGNIZE AND RESPOND

Before the next session, read chapter 4, "Awakening" (pages 75–98), in the *Eternity Is Now in Session* book. Consider also completing the following activity:

FRANK LAUBACH AND THE "GAME WITH MINUTES"

Frank Laubach is a great example of a person who got to know God and lived his life very differently based on that knowledge.[2]

---

[2] This discussion of Frank Laubach is adapted from Gary Moon, *Falling for God: Saying Yes to His Extravagant Proposal* (Colorado Springs: WaterBrook, 2004), 89–92. Used by permission of the publisher.

On March 23, 1930, Laubach wrote in his diary, "Can we have contact with God all the time? All the time awake, fall asleep in his arms, and awaken in His presence, can we attain that? Can we do His will all the time? Can we think His thoughts all the time?"

When he posed these questions, forty-five-year-old Laubach was laboring under a cloud of profound dissatisfaction, despite his academic achievements—a BA from Princeton, a graduate degree from Union Theological Seminary, and an MA and PhD in sociology from Columbia University—and his success as a missionary to the Philippines. For fifteen years he had won praise as a teacher, writer, and administrator.

Laubach's sterling achievements make it doubly puzzling when we read the self-assessment he made at the halftime of his life: "As for me, I never lived, I was half dead; I was a rotting tree."

Even as his churches filled with converts, his heart was becoming crowded with loneliness, discouragement, and mild depression. Even after planting a seminary in the Philippines to train missionaries, he confessed that he had learned nothing of surrender and joy in Christ.

How can that be? Frank Laubach spoke of God daily. He had a devoted wife and family and all the trappings of success. Why was he so weighed down with doubt and despair?

Like Augustine's, Laubach's soul would forever feel restless and alone until nestled into the arms of God; it would forever feel lonely until awake to constant companionship with God. He was waiting for something more.

Laubach determined to do something about his miserable

condition and decided to make the rest of his life a continuous inner conversation with God, in perfect responsiveness to God's will so that his own life could become rich with God's presence.

All he could do was throw himself open to God. All he could do was raise the windows and unlock the doors of his soul. But he also knew that these simple acts of the will were very important and so he resolved to spend as many moments as possible in listening and determined sensitivity to God's presence.

He invented something he called a "game with minutes." Laubach's "game" is a method of calling God to mind at least one second of each minute for the purpose of awareness and conversation.

As he began to live moment by moment in attentiveness to God's presence, Laubach experienced a remarkable change. By the end of the first month of his experiment with the game, he had gained a sense of being carried along by God through the hours of cooperation with him in little things.

When Laubach began his experiment he was living among the fierce Moros, an anti-Christian, Islamic tribe on Mindanao. Not long after he began to keep constant company with God, the Moros began to notice the difference. Two of the leading Muslim leaders began telling people that Laubach could help them know God. And even though he never pretended to be anything other than a follower of Jesus, the Moros began to take Laubach into their hearts and lives, loving, trusting, and helping him without regard to their cultural and religious differences.

Laubach lived the second half of his life as God's constant companion. His life is a picture of the path of real change. He took the *time* to be with God, was *honest* about the condition of his heart, and trusted that God *desired* the same intimate relationship that he craved.

GAME WITH MINUTES IDEAS

Make a list of some ways you might become more aware of God's presence as you go through your day. We'll start you with a few ideas from Laubach's "game with minutes."

1. Wake up and greet God with a warm "good morning" and listen for his response.

2. Read favorite portions of Scripture as faded love letters— listening for the voice of the Author as you read.

3. Recognize the long line at the grocery store as an opportunity for a few deep breaths and a time to listen for the voice of God.

4. Make sure your day planner has at least one appointment with God that is written in indelible ink. Close the door. Offer him an empty chair. Then be quiet, be patient, and lean in.

5. See each person you meet as a new opportunity to show love to the *imago dei* (the image of God inside them). God's reflection is on every face.

6. Make hugging your close family or friends a sacrament of communicating love to God.

7. When you turn the light out, ask God if he enjoyed spending the day together and listen for his response.

SCRIPTURE FOR REFLECTION

The following passages of Scripture focus on *knowing* God.

> This is eternal life, that they may know you, the only
> true God, and Jesus Christ whom you have sent.
> JOHN 17:3, NRSV

> We proclaim to you the one who existed from the
> beginning, whom we have heard and seen. We saw
> him with our own eyes and touched him with our
> own hands. He is the Word of life. This one who is
> life itself was revealed to us, and we have seen him.
> And now we testify and proclaim to you that he is the
> one who is eternal life. He was with the Father, and
> then he was revealed to us. We proclaim to you what
> we ourselves have actually seen and heard so that you
> may have fellowship with us. And our fellowship is
> with the Father and with his Son, Jesus Christ. We
> are writing these things so that you may fully share
> our joy.
>   This is the message we heard from Jesus and now
> declare to you: God is light, and there is no darkness in
> him at all.
> 1 JOHN 1:1-5, NLT

> We know that we have come to know him if we keep
> his commands.
> 1 JOHN 2:3

Dear friends, let us love one another, for love comes
from God. Everyone who loves has been born of God
and knows God. Whoever does not love does not know
God, because God is love. . . . This is how we know
that we live in him and he in us: He has given us of
his Spirit.

1 JOHN 4:7-8, 13

I want to know Christ—yes, to know the power of
his resurrection and participation in his sufferings,
becoming like him in his death.

PHILIPPIANS 3:10

That is why I am suffering as I am. Yet this is no cause
for shame, because I know whom I have believed, and
am convinced that he is able to guard what I have
entrusted to him until that day.

2 TIMOTHY 1:12

His divine power has given us everything needed for
life and godliness, through the knowledge of him who
called us by his own glory and goodness. Thus he has
given us, through these things, his precious and very
great promises, so that through them you may escape
from the corruption that is in the world because of lust,
and may become participants of the divine nature.

2 PETER 1:3-4, NRSV

Session 2

AWAKENING

WELCOME

Welcome to session 2 of the *Eternity Is Now in Session DVD Experience*. Each of the five sessions in this study is designed to be completed in 60 to 90 minutes, with additional activities that you can do at home.

This session accompanies chapter 4 of the *Eternity Is Now in Session* book (pages 75–98). Watch the video, discuss the questions, and complete the key activity as a group as time allows.

VIDEO NOTES

As you watch the video, use the space below to take notes. We've included some key points to get you started.

Immanuel means "God with us." God wants to have an intimate relationship with us.

"What Jesus wants—what God wants—is for your home, your school, your office, your neighborhood, your Starbucks to become 'holy land,' because it becomes the place where you and Jesus walk together."

For Jesus to be *with* his apprentices meant he was to become their intimate friend, humble and transparent.

> When they saw the courage of Peter and John and realized that they were unschooled, ordinary men, they were astonished and they took note that these men had been with Jesus.
>
> ACTS 4:13

Dallas Willard said that life is mostly made up of experiences. That is why we treasure them so much. Intimacy is shared experience. Every time we invite God into our lives, we are sharing experiences and increasing intimacy. To love someone means that you are interested in her or his experiences.

> When Jacob awoke from his sleep, he thought,
> "Surely the LORD is in this place,
> and I was not aware of it."
>
> GENESIS 28:16

Jesus said, "You are the light of the world. . . . Let your light shine before others, that they may see your good deeds and glorify your Father in heaven" (Matthew 5:14-16).

It takes two things to experience greater intimacy with God: time and honesty.

DISCUSSION QUESTIONS

1. How can you make your home, office, or Starbucks "holy land"? What has worked for you?

2. Dallas Willard said that persons are mostly made up of experiences. Intimacy is shared experience. What are some ways we can learn more about what God experiences? What are some ways God can learn more about your experiences? What does it look like to share experience with God?

3. What does it look like to listen to Jesus? When should we listen? Where should we listen? How should we listen?

4. In the video, John says that it takes time and honesty to
    live a life of more intimacy with God. Do you agree? Why
    or why not? How essential are time and honesty in human
    relationships?

5. What does it mean that "when you come before the real
    God and you bring the real self . . . and you're in the
    presence of Jesus, someday you're gonna glow"? Have you
    ever known someone so radiant with the love of God that
    they "glow"? If so, what qualities seemed to make that
    person glow? What might "glowing" like Jesus look like?

KEY ACTIVITY: UP THE MOUNTAIN / DOWN THE MOUNTAIN—IN EVERYDAY LIFE

As John beautifully describes, Jesus' three closest friends accompanied him up the mountain to see who he and his Father truly are. This reached a crescendo as they fell to the earth—perhaps symbolic of their death to old ways of thinking. And then they got up, resurrected so to speak, into a new way of living and followed Jesus down the mountain, back into everyday life.

Perhaps for Christians each day should include a rhythm of going "up the mountain" to sit in the radiance of God's identity and then going "down the mountain" to live more and more moments of each day in awareness of God's presence.

Take some time to brainstorm ideas for going up and down the mountain with God each day.

UP THE MOUNTAIN IDEAS

Things that will help you to have a sense of soaking in God's presence. (Hint: most ideas will involve either time or honesty.) Here are some ideas to get you started:

- Put fifteen minutes into your calendar each day for sitting with God.
- Listen to a song that causes you to feel lost in God's presence while spending this time with God.
- Memorize a few verses of Scripture that speak of God's desire to be with you.
- Read Bible verses that record the things Jesus did and said.
- Be real and transparent with God—no more hiding; just you coming before God exactly as you are.

DOWN THE MOUNTAIN IDEAS

Things that will help you to live more moments each day with God:

- Rename your alarm clock a "resurrection" clock.
- Before getting out of bed, invite God to go through the day with you.
- Imagine that Jesus is standing beside you when you greet people.
- Thank God for what you are eating, not only before you eat but constantly during the meal.
- Change the way you commute to work, giving thanks for the miracle of transportation and the time your commute provides for honest conversation with God about your day.
- Invite Jesus to sit beside you as you work.
- Invite the Trinity into your problems and ask for ideas.
- Have a conversation with God about your day as the last thing you do before going to sleep.

HOMEWORK: RECOGNIZE AND RESPOND

Before the next session, read chapter 5, "Purgation" (pages 99–124) in the *Eternity Is Now in Session* book. Consider also completing the following activities:

1. WHAT IS YOUR VISION FOR YOUR LIFE WITH GOD?

Write out a page or so on your vision for what your life would be like if transformed by God so that you are living more and more moments aware of his presence and as his intimate friend. Note: The sign of an adequate vision is that it releases your deepest desire.

2. REFLECTION ON FRIENDSHIP

Reflect on the best friendships you have had throughout your life and compare them to your relationship with God. What is the impact of this exercise on your desire for intimacy with God?

3. CHILD OF LIGHT EXERCISE

Rate yourself on how each of the components of you are progressing in their own transfiguration. We'll use what Dallas Willard had to say about a person becoming a "child of light."

- *Thoughts*: Children of light think constantly about God, dwelling upon his greatness and loveliness.
- *Feelings*: Love is the dominant emotion of children of light.
- *Will (spirit, heart)*: They are habitually devoted to doing what is good and right. The will is habitually attuned to surrender and obey.

- *Body*: Their body is constantly poised to do what is right and good.
- *Social Relations*: Children of light are completely transparent in their relations with others.
- *Soul*: All of the above is not just at the surface; these things are deep and effortless.

4. RECOGNIZE AND RESPOND

Ignatius of Loyola, the founder of the Society of Jesus, observed that the best way we can live is in a constant state of recognizing and responding to God's presence with us in all of the mundane and glorious moments of the day. Take a moment to reread the outline, questions, and exercises above and construct a list of things you can do each day to help you recognize and respond to the astounding gift of God's friendship.

SCRIPTURE FOR REFLECTION

You are my friends if you do what I command. I no longer call you servants, because a servant does not know his master's business. Instead, I have called you friends, for everything that I learned from my Father I have made known to you.

JOHN 15:14-15

Was not our father Abraham considered righteous for what he did when he offered his son Isaac on the altar? You see that his faith and his actions were working together, and his faith was made complete by what he did. And the scripture was fulfilled that says, "Abraham believed God, and it was credited to him as righteousness," and he was called God's friend.

JAMES 2:21-23

Session 3

PURGATION

WELCOME

Welcome to session 3 of the *Eternity Is Now in Session DVD Experience*. Each of the five sessions in this study is designed to be completed in 60 to 90 minutes, with additional activities that you can do at home.

This session accompanies chapter 5 of the *Eternity Is Now in Session* book (pages 99–124). Watch the video, discuss the questions, and complete the key activity as a group as time allows.

VIDEO NOTES

As you watch the video, use the space below to take notes. We've included some key points to get you started.

Jesus begins teaching from the Word of God. He loves people, so he's giving them wisdom about how to live. The people are so hungry for these words that Jesus has to finish his talk from a boat. He sits down and continues teaching.

> Simon answered, "Master, we've worked hard all night and haven't caught anything. But because you say so, I will let down the nets."
>
> LUKE 5:5

Peter doesn't see what Jesus sees, but he is willing to do what Jesus says; that is enough to be a disciple, to be part of a "because you say so" community.

> When Simon Peter saw this, he fell at Jesus' knees and said, "Go away from me, Lord; I am a sinful man!"
>
> LUKE 5:8

Peter sees Jesus' full identity, and he becomes fully aware of his own identity as being separate and apart from Jesus—a sinner. He becomes aware of his own sinfulness and brokenness.

We are all in the same situation as Peter. We are on the same boat, but it can be the Jesus boat. Church is to be a place for messed-up people, a hospital for souls. Nobody's perfect, but everyone is welcome and nothing is impossible with Jesus.

DISCUSSION QUESTIONS

1. What do you most identify with in this story about a lake, a man, and a boat? Why does this part of the story speak to you?

2. What are some of the barriers you face to becoming a habitual "because you say so" type of Christ follower? What causes these barriers? How might you overcome them?

3. Have you ever had an experience with another person where you expected condemnation but instead received unexpected love? What was your reaction?

4. What do the words *repentance* and *confession* mean? What do you think of when you hear these words? Why are they important to our own spiritual healing?

5. If you were to call 1-800-GOT-JUNK, what is some of the spiritual junk that you might ask to be hauled off? How would this affect your intimacy with God?

KEY ACTIVITY: MOVING TOWARD OR AWAY FROM GOD

James Martin, SJ, in his book *The Jesuit Guide to (Almost) Everything: A Spirituality for Real Life*, presents a modification of Ignatius of Loyola's classic exercise the examen, which is a review of the day. What follows is a slight modification of Martin's modification.[3]

THE EXAMEN IN FIVE STEPS

This prayer can be practiced at any set time of the day, but many enjoy using it in the evening, just before going to bed, as a way of reviewing the day. It is good to remind yourself both that you are in the presence of God and that the aim of this examination is to become progressively more aware of that presence and available friendship as you go through each day. Walk through these five steps as a group.

1. *Gratitude*: Recall events from your day that made you smile with gratefulness. Enjoy the memory, and then breathe a "thanks" to God.

2. *Review*: Recall events from the day where you felt most aware of God's presence and the desire to move toward and with him.

3. *Sorrow*: Recall times during the day when you felt distracted from God's presence and intimacy, times when you felt you were away from God and running your life on your own.

---

3 See James Martin, *The Jesuit Guide to (Almost) Everything: A Spirituality for Real Life* (New York: HarperCollins, 2010), 97.

4. *Forgiveness*: Like Peter at Jesus' feet, humbly ask God to forgive your times of distraction from his presence, especially if during those times you may have caused hurt to anyone, including yourself.

5. *Grace*: Ask God for the grace you need to live more moments tomorrow with the ability to feel the reality of God's presence and love more clearly.

HOMEWORK: RECOGNIZE AND RESPOND

Before the next session, read chapter 6, "Illumination" (pages 125–145), in the *Eternity Is Now in Session* book. Consider also completing the following activities:

1. DAILY EXAMEN

Resolve to set aside time each day to walk through the five steps of the examen as presented above.

2. 1-800-GOT-JUNK

John reminds us that our goal of living more and more moments pursuing intimacy with God (shared experience) takes effort. There are consistent barriers that get in the way of our intimacy with God. Both two thousand years ago and today, there are the same number of hours in the day and a very similar list of distractions from living in awareness of God's presence. Very common barriers are busyness, fear, ambition, guilt, shame, and the consequential tendency to be distracted from the reality of divine presence and love and to move away from instead of toward God. Two thousand years ago and today, we need the same things to overcome the barriers to healing friendship: deep self-awareness, confession, and ongoing examination and repentance.

Take a few minutes and write out your schedule for a typical weekday. What activities are you most likely to be engaged in?

Now, go back over the events of a typical day and label each with either "MT" (activities that are helping you *move toward* God, becoming more aware of divine presence and love) or "MA" (activities that are causing you to *move away* from God, being less aware of divine presence and love).

Use this schedule and talk to God about how you might redeem your time.

3. CONFESSION WITH A PSALM

Read Psalm 51 (see pages 39–41) as a confession to God at least one time this week.

4. CONFESSION WITH AN EMPTY CHAIR

During one of Dallas Willard's last public appearances he said, "Sin always splits the self to some degree, yes. You know that you have harmed yourself and others, but you probably are not going to come to terms with that because you're carrying on a charade of righteousness, even if you don't believe it. So confession is very deep in the process of discovering the soul."[4]

There are several things necessary for giving a good confession: 1) an examination of conscience: inviting God to show us when we are moving away from his Kingdom and into the kingdom of our ego and self-will; 2) sorrow: like Peter, falling to the bottom of the boat with deep regret and abhorrence; 3) determination to stop the movements away from intimacy with God; and 4) avoidance of nongodly sorrow. (Note: godly sorrow leads to a restoration of relationship and lightness of being. Nongodly sorrow can lead to self-condemnation, despair, pity, and self-indulgence.)

---

4 Dallas Willard, *Living in Christ's Presence: Final Words on Heaven and the Kingdom of God* (Downers Grove, IL: InterVarsity Press, 2014), 133.

Place an empty chair near you so that if a person were in that chair, they would be facing you, close enough to reach out and touch your knee.

Now imagine God is sitting in the chair. Read aloud the descriptions on page 24 of a person who is becoming a "child of light." Then confess to God where you are in terms of this being a description of you. If these are good descriptions of your current level of intimacy with God, wonderful; it is a cause for celebration. If they sound more like aspirational statements than descriptions of present reality, then turn the time into a confession.

SCRIPTURE FOR REFLECTION

Here are some passages to help you reflect on coming clean with God.

> Since you have been raised to new life with Christ, set your sights on the realities of heaven, where Christ sits in the place of honor at God's right hand. Think about the things of heaven, not the things of earth. For you died to this life, and your real life is hidden with Christ in God. And when Christ, who is your life, is revealed to the whole world, you will share in all his glory.
>
> So put to death the sinful, earthly things lurking within you. Have nothing to do with sexual immorality, impurity, lust, and evil desires. Don't be greedy, for a greedy person is an idolater, worshiping the things of this world. Because of these sins, the anger of God is coming. You used to do these things when your life was still part of this world. But now is the time to get rid of anger, rage, malicious behavior, slander, and dirty language. Don't lie to each other, for you have stripped off your old sinful nature and all its wicked deeds. Put on your new nature, and be renewed as you learn to know your Creator and become like him. In this new life, it doesn't matter if you are a Jew or a Gentile, circumcised or uncircumcised, barbaric, uncivilized, slave, or free. Christ is all that matters, and he lives in all of us.

Since God chose you to be the holy people he loves, you must clothe yourselves with tenderhearted mercy, kindness, humility, gentleness, and patience. Make allowance for each other's faults, and forgive anyone who offends you. Remember, the Lord forgave you, so you must forgive others. Above all, clothe yourselves with love, which binds us all together in perfect harmony. And let the peace that comes from Christ rule in your hearts. For as members of one body you are called to live in peace. And always be thankful.

Let the message about Christ, in all its richness, fill your lives. Teach and counsel each other with all the wisdom he gives. Sing psalms and hymns and spiritual songs to God with thankful hearts. And whatever you do or say, do it as a representative of the Lord Jesus, giving thanks through him to God the Father.

COLOSSIANS 3:1-17, NLT

Have mercy on me, O God,
    because of your unfailing love.
Because of your great compassion,
    blot out the stain of my sins.
Wash me clean from my guilt.
    Purify me from my sin.
For I recognize my rebellion;
    it haunts me day and night.
Against you, and you alone, have I sinned;
    I have done what is evil in your sight.
You will be proved right in what you say,

and your judgment against me is just.
For I was born a sinner—
    yes, from the moment my mother conceived me.
But you desire honesty from the womb,
    teaching me wisdom even there.

Purify me from my sins, and I will be clean;
    wash me, and I will be whiter than snow.
Oh, give me back my joy again;
    you have broken me—
    now let me rejoice.
Don't keep looking at my sins.
    Remove the stain of my guilt.
Create in me a clean heart, O God.
    Renew a loyal spirit within me.
Do not banish me from your presence,
    and don't take your Holy Spirit from me.

Restore to me the joy of your salvation,
    and make me willing to obey you.
Then I will teach your ways to rebels,
    and they will return to you.
Forgive me for shedding blood, O God who saves;
    then I will joyfully sing of your forgiveness.
Unseal my lips, O Lord,
    that my mouth may praise you.

You do not desire a sacrifice, or I would offer one.
    You do not want a burnt offering.

The sacrifice you desire is a broken spirit.
> You will not reject a broken and repentant heart,
>> O God.
Look with favor on Zion and help her;
> rebuild the walls of Jerusalem.
Then you will be pleased with sacrifices offered in the
>> right spirit—
> with burnt offerings and whole burnt offerings.
> Then bulls will again be sacrificed on your altar.

PSALM 51, NLT

ILLUMINATION

WELCOME

Welcome to session 4 of the *Eternity Is Now in Session DVD Experience*. Each of the five sessions in this study is designed to be completed in 60 to 90 minutes, with additional activities that you can do at home.

This session accompanies chapter 6 of the *Eternity Is Now in Session* book (pages 125–145). Watch the video, discuss the questions, and complete the key activity as a group as time allows.

VIDEO NOTES

As you watch the video, use the space below to take notes. We've included some key points to get you started.

Jesus' most famous pop quiz has just one question on it: "Who do you say that I am?"

Caesarea Philippi was on the northernmost border of Israel. In ancient times so much water gushed out, they couldn't measure the depth of the pool. In the ancient world where water was sacred, this became a center for religious shrines.

Apparently, back at the beginning of their relationship, Jesus didn't say, "Believe the right things about me and you can be my disciples." He said, "Follow me, and you'll be my disciples." The idea that first you believe the right things about Jesus did not come from Jesus.

Jesus replied, "Blessed are you, Simon son of Jonah, for this was not revealed to you by flesh and blood, but by my Father in heaven. And I tell you that you are Peter, and on this rock I will build my church, and the gates of Hades will not overcome it."

MATTHEW 16:17-18

Jesus' main vehicle on earth is going to be the church. Jesus' main problem on earth is going to be the church. You can get the right answers and still become the wrong person.

> If anyone would come after me, he must deny himself and take up his cross and follow me. For whoever wants to save his life will lose it, but whoever loses his life for me will find it.
>
> MATTHEW 16:24-25

Jesus doesn't want people whose main goal and identity is that they give right religious answers. Those are the people who are going to kill him. He doesn't want answer givers; he wants life givers.

Arise, shine, for your light has come,
and the glory of the LORD rises upon you.

ISAIAH 60:1

DISCUSSION QUESTIONS

1. Why had Jesus not already told the disciples the right answer for the "pop quiz"? Why did he choose Caesarea Philippi as the backdrop for this teaching?

2. How would you describe, in practical, day-to-day terms, what it is like to be "blessed" by being in a living relationship with "Christ, the son of the God who is alive"?

3. What does it mean to pick up your cross and follow Jesus? How does that change your identity as a Christ-follower?

4. Are you in school to become a "child of light"? Why or why not? What is your curriculum like?

5. Over the past couple of weeks, what were your most spiritually high and spiritually low moments? When have you felt affirmed by God? When have you felt corrected?

KEY ASSESSMENT: WHO AM I—WHAT IS MY TRUEST IDENTITY?

In this teaching, Jesus focuses on identity, first his own and then that of Peter. He does this against the backdrop of Caesarea Philippi and its display of a massive wall of idols—nonliving gods. He offers this spiritual life lesson near a deep spring of water that is a primary source of the Jordan River—the place where John the Baptist offered baptism into a new identity. With baptism, there is a rethinking and a letting go of false sources of security and intimacy.

ASSESSMENT 1: IDOL IDENTIFICATION QUOTIENT

What is your IIQ (Idol Identification Quotient)? Take a moment to rate yourself on some of the common idols that John lists. As Tim Keller has said, an idol is a good thing that only becomes a bad thing if we try to make it into the ultimate thing.[5] To what extent is each of the following a potential substitute for your full identity being an intimate friend to Jesus?

	Not a Problem "with Jesus"	Absolutely a Major Idol
1. Money	1——2——3——4——5——6——7——8——9——10	
2. Sex	1——2——3——4——5——6——7——8——9——10	
3. Power	1——2——3——4——5——6——7——8——9——10	
4. Position	1——2——3——4——5——6——7——8——9——10	
5. Relationship	1——2——3——4——5——6——7——8——9——10	
6. [You Name It]	1——2——3——4——5——6——7——8——9——10	

---

[5] Timothy Keller, *Counterfeit Gods: The Empty Promises of Money, Sex, and Power, and the Only Hope That Matters* (New York: Penguin Books, 2016).

ASSESSMENT 2: TRUE IDENTITY

What does intimacy with Jesus look like? It means both freedom from the idols that would otherwise demand intimacy with our hearts, and it means honesty about our true identity with Jesus. Continuing with raw honesty in assessing your IIQ, use the following scales to rate your identity as a stranger, acquaintance, admirer, follower, or intimate friend of Jesus.

	No Way This Describes Our Relationship								This Is a Good Word for Where We Are
1. Stranger	1—2—3—4—5—6—7—8—9—10
2. Acquaintance	1—2—3—4—5—6—7—8—9—10
3. Admirer	1—2—3—4—5—6—7—8—9—10
4. Follower	1—2—3—4—5—6—7—8—9—10
5. Intimate Friend	1—2—3—4—5—6—7—8—9—10
6. [You Name It]	1—2—3—4—5—6—7—8—9—10

To the extent that you are comfortable, share your results and your feelings about those results with others in the group. Consider the following questions individually and as a group:

- Are you happy with your results?
- In what areas can you grow in your relationship with Jesus?
- In what ways can the group support you in your growing relationship with Jesus?

You may also want to consider this question as a group: What is your old name and what would you like your new name to be? See Revelation 2:17 (on page 55).

HOMEWORK: RECOGNIZE AND RESPOND

Before the next session, read chapter 7, "Union" (pages 147–173), in the *Eternity Is Now in Session* book. Consider also completing the following activities:

1. DAILY SCRIPTURE STUDY ON IDENTITY

God created each of us with unique characteristics and purpose and to walk with him in an interactive, transforming friendship. We discover both our individual identity (the one no one else has) and our identity that we share with others (friends of Jesus). Consider a slow reading of each of the following Bible verses this week to understand more about our identity in Christ and how to not lose sight of who we are destined to be.

- Sunday: 1 John 3:1-2 (children of God); Revelation 2:17 (given a new name)
- Monday: Genesis 1:27 (created in the image of God)
- Tuesday: John 1:12 (a child of God)
- Wednesday: Romans 6:6 (no longer a slave to sin)
- Thursday: 1 Corinthians 6:19-20 (temple of the Holy Spirit)
- Friday: Ephesians 1:5 (adopted into God's family)
- Saturday: 1 Peter 2:9 (God's special possession, called into the light)

2. CHILD OF LIGHT EXERCISE REVISITED

How is it going on your journey into a new identity? Take a few minutes and rate yourself again on how each of the components of you are progressing in their own transfiguration. Again, we'll use what Dallas Willard had to say about a person becoming a "child of light":

- *Thoughts*: Children of light think constantly about God, dwelling upon his greatness and loveliness.
- *Feelings*: Love is the dominant emotion of children of light.
- *Will (spirit, heart)*: They are habitually devoted to doing what is good and right. The will is habitually attuned to surrender and obey.
- *Body*: Their body is constantly poised to do what is right and good.
- *Social Relations*: Children of light are completely transparent in their relations with others.
- *Soul*: All of the above is not just at the surface; these things are deep and effortless.

SCRIPTURE FOR REFLECTION

Imitate God, therefore, in everything you do, because you are his dear children. Live a life filled with love, following the example of Christ. He loved us and offered himself as a sacrifice for us, a pleasing aroma to God.

Let there be no sexual immorality, impurity, or greed among you. Such sins have no place among God's people. Obscene stories, foolish talk, and coarse jokes—these are not for you. Instead, let there be thankfulness to God. You can be sure that no immoral, impure, or greedy person will inherit the Kingdom of Christ and of God. For a greedy person is an idolater, worshiping the things of this world.

Don't be fooled by those who try to excuse these sins, for the anger of God will fall on all who disobey him. Don't participate in the things these people do. For once you were full of darkness, but now you have light from the Lord. So live as people of light! For this light within you produces only what is good and right and true.

Carefully determine what pleases the Lord. Take no part in the worthless deeds of evil and darkness; instead, expose them. It is shameful even to talk about the things that ungodly people do in secret. But their evil intentions will be exposed when the light shines on them, for the light makes everything visible. This is why it is said,

"Awake, O sleeper,
> rise up from the dead,
> and Christ will give you light."

EPHESIANS 5:1-14, NLT

Anyone with ears to hear must listen to the Spirit
and understand what he is saying to the churches.
To everyone who is victorious I will give some of the
manna that has been hidden away in heaven. And I
will give to each one a white stone, and on the stone
will be engraved a new name that no one understands
except the one who receives it.

REVELATION 2:17, NLT

Session 5

UNION

WELCOME

Welcome to the final session of the *Eternity Is Now in Session DVD Experience*. Each of the five sessions in this study is designed to be completed in 60 to 90 minutes, with additional activities that you can do at home.

This session accompanies chapter 7 of the *Eternity Is Now in Session* book (pages 147–173). Watch the video, discuss the questions, and complete the key activity as a group as time allows.

VIDEO NOTES

As you watch the video, use the space below to take notes. We've included some key points to get you started.

Jesus offers you a picture and an invitation: I am the vine, you are the branches. Abide in me.

Living in connection with God is not about where; it's about how.

> I am the vine, you are the branches. Those
> who abide in me and I in them bear much fruit,
> because apart from me you can do nothing.
>
> JOHN 15:5, NRSV

If you understand the picture, if you accept the invitation, Jesus says you can have an intimate relationship of love with God.

What is abiding? When you abide, you make a home in a place, you linger there, and your inner person—your spirit—gets shaped by your abode. You can abide in fear. You can abide in ambition. You can abide in anger. You can abide in lust. Or you can abide in God. God wants to make your heart his home. God wants to make his heart your home.

The branch's job is not to produce fruit. The branch's job is to learn to continually receive life from the vine. The fruit is a by-product of abiding.

We will never produce the right fruit by trying to produce the right fruit. It is the inside of the branch that must change. The automatic flow of thoughts and desires and intentions must change from being ego centered and conflicted and greedy and fearful, to confident and grateful and humble and joyful and always ready to love.

> Abide in me as I abide in you. Just as the branch cannot bear fruit by itself unless it abides in the vine, neither can you unless you abide in me.
>
> JOHN 15:4, NRSV

Your job is not to try to generate more God-pleasing actions by greater willpower. Your job is to abide.

DISCUSSION QUESTIONS

1. If the branch's job is not to produce fruit, what is the job description for a branch? How does John describe the "fruit" that branches are to produce? What must change for the "fruit of the Spirit," the very character of Christ, to be produced in your life?

2. What are your primary obstacles to abiding in God through the day as a branch that is connected to a vine? What are possible ways to overcome these obstacles?

3. How do spiritual disciplines help with living in friendship with Jesus? What spiritual disciplines have you tried? Which do you think would be most effective for you?

4. What does it mean that the thoughts are the roots of your spirit? How do your thoughts affect your life on the vine?

5. How do you usually react when you mess up? As a branch on the vine, how should you react? What would change if you consistently reacted this way?

KEY ASSESSMENT: THE ABC'S OF THOUGHT

Take a look at the following illustration. On the table is a pool cue that is labeled A. The pool cue is about to strike a ball (labeled B) that will in turn strike a second ball (C), and if the rules of physics are properly applied, C will drop into the pocket of the table—a successful shot.

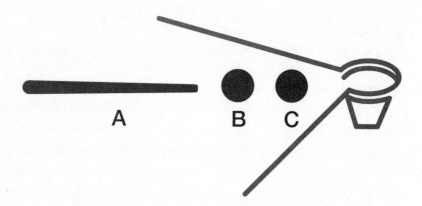

This pool diagram represents the role your thoughts play in other aspects of your life—particularly your emotions. The pool cue represents an event from your day—any event. Let's say you are at work, and your boss says, "I would like to see you later today." This brief contact with your boss is an A, which stands for "activating event."

B in this scenario represents your "immediate belief"—that is, the first thought or thoughts that pass through your mind. If your thought is, *Oh, no! I'm going to be fired*, you will probably have a pretty bad day, with emotions (that's the C, "emotional consequence") of anxiety and dread.

But on the other hand, if your first thoughts are *This is*

wonderful; I'm finally going to get that promotion!, then your emotions will be drastically different: excited anticipation.

It is important to note that the pool cue (activating event) did not change. In both cases it was an ambiguous encounter with your boss, who said, "I want to see you later today." What changed? The thoughts that played in your head like CDs in a jukebox (or a random iTunes shuffle of your top 25 playlist). The radically different thoughts produced radically different emotions.

Let's look at one more "A-B-C" example. Imagine you are driving in your car. A light you were hoping to catch while still green turns red. That's A, the "activating event." The "emotional consequence" (C) of the red light will not be caused by the light but by the thoughts and beliefs (B) that flash through your mind. If you think, *Oh great! I bet I'll catch every one now. I'll be late for my hair appointment and will probably miss it*, that type of B will cause some pretty unpleasant C.

But if the light changes (A) and you think (B), *This is great! I needed a sixty-second vacation. I'll take three or four deep, slow breaths and relax*, well, your C will be very different: gratitude for the mini-vacation.

By changing our thoughts (and it is quite possible to do so), we can change more than our emotions; we can participate in the process of authentic spiritual transformation. To a large extent, our thoughts are under our control. We can set out to change them, and the results can be not only different emotional consequences but also changes in our will, behavior, and social interactions.

EXERCISE

Take a few minutes to unplug and take a few deep and slow breaths. Then ask yourself the question, *What is the most common thought I have about myself?* Whether that thought is good, bad, or neutral, breathe it in and out for a while. Then note how you are feeling.

Now, breathe this thought for a while: *I am an eternal spiritual being in whom God dwells and delights.* Breathe that thought for a while as you allow yourself to sink into the truth that your very existence is in an ocean of divine love. Then note again: How are you feeling? What changed? Only the primary thought in your mind.

HOMEWORK: RECOGNIZE AND RESPOND

This is the final session of the *Eternity Is Now in Session* curriculum, but the experience needn't end here. These are some activities you can complete in the next week:

1. DAILY SCRIPTURE STUDY ON UNION AS A *LECTIO DIVINA* PRAYER

Lectio divina is a slow, contemplative way of praying the Scriptures that enables the Word of God to become a means of union with God. It is one classic way of allowing the Word and presence of Christ to penetrate to the center of our being and begin a process of transforming us from the inside out.

There are four movements contained within this method of praying Scripture. The first movement is called "reading" or "listening." The practice of *lectio divina* begins with cultivating the ability to listen deeply, to hear "with the ear of our hearts," as St. Benedict describes in the prologue of his Rule. It is a way of being more sensitive to the still, small voice of God (see 1 Kings 19:12), the "faint murmuring sound" that is God's word for us, his voice touching our hearts.

The reading or listening step in *lectio divina* is very different from the speed reading you may be used to applying to magazines or novels. *Lectio* is reverential listening, listening in a spirit both of silence and of awe. In *lectio* we read slowly and attentively, gently listening to hear a word or phrase that is God's communication for us this day.

The second phase of *lectio* is meditation. Once through "listening," if we have found a word, passage, or image in the Scripture that speaks to us in a personal way, we must take it in and ruminate on it. We ponder it in our hearts. We do this by gently repeating a key word or phrase, allowing it to interact with our thoughts, hopes, memories, and desires. Through this phase we allow the word from God to become his word *for us*, a word that touches us at our deepest levels.

The third step is prayer: prayer understood both as dialogue with God (that is, as loving conversation with the one who has invited us into his embrace) and as consecration (that is, as the priestly offering to God of parts of ourselves that we have not previously believed God wants). Here we allow the word that we have taken in and on which we are pondering to touch and change our deepest selves.

The final step is to rest in the presence of the one who has used his Word as a means of inviting us to accept his transforming embrace. It is the phase called "contemplation," where there are moments when words are unnecessary. Contemplation is wordless, quiet rest in the presence of the one who loves us.

In the practice of *lectio divina*, you will choose a text of Scripture that you wish to pray. Let's start with Psalm 1 (see page 72).

Here is what to do next:

- Place yourself in a comfortable position and allow yourself to become silent.
- *Read/Listen:* Turn to the text and read it slowly, gently. Savor each portion of the reading, constantly listening for the "still, small voice" of a word or phrase that somehow says, "I am for you today."

- *Meditate*: Next, take the word or phrase into yourself. Memorize it and slowly repeat it to yourself, allowing it to interact with your inner world of concerns, memories, and ideas. Do not be afraid of distractions. Memories or thoughts are simply parts of you. Don't try to chase them away; just return to the word you are pondering.
- *Converse*: Then, speak to God. Whether you use words, ideas, images, or all three is not important. Interact with God as you would with one who you know loves and accepts you. Give to God what you have discovered in yourself during your experience.
- *Rest*: Finally, simply rest in God's embrace. Enjoy his presence. And when he invites you to return to your pondering of his Word or to your inner dialogue with him, do so. Rejoice in the knowledge that God is with you in both words and silence.

You've started with Psalm 1. Sometime this week, try this practice again with John 15:4-15 and Philippians 4:8-9 and then with another passage of your choosing.

2. LIVING PLUGGED IN

Make a game out of keeping plugged into God this week, remaining in his presence. Try some of these, or your own, ideas:

- Memorize either the Twenty-third Psalm or the Lord's Prayer. Before getting out of bed each morning, breathe the verses as a prayer.

- Set a clock or timer (such as your smartphone or Fitbit) to remind you—morning, noon, and evening—to stop and pray.
- During one of those pauses, breathe the Nicene Creed.
- During another pause, allow love for others to flow out into intercession.
- Take time to step into a passage of Scripture using *lectio divina*.
- When you are in conversation and see the eyes of the person you are with, be reminded that Christ lives inside that person.
- Every time you glance at a watch, clock, or phone to check the time, be prompted to pray internally, *Lord, Jesus Christ, have mercy on me.*
- Take the time to admire the beauty of a plant, tree, or flower and then admire the Designer.
- Leave an empty chair at each meal as a reminder that you are not alone.
- Leave an empty chair by your computer as both a reminder and accountability check that you are not alone.
- Perform an act of service for another person (in secret, if possible) as an act of love for God.
- End the day with the examen (for a refresher, see page 33). Reflect on the times when you felt most close to and most distant from God.

SCRIPTURE FOR REFLECTION

Remain in me, and I will remain in you. For a branch cannot produce fruit if it is severed from the vine, and you cannot be fruitful unless you remain in me.

Yes, I am the vine; you are the branches. Those who remain in me, and I in them, will produce much fruit. For apart from me you can do nothing. Anyone who does not remain in me is thrown away like a useless branch and withers. Such branches are gathered into a pile to be burned. But if you remain in me and my words remain in you, you may ask for anything you want, and it will be granted! When you produce much fruit, you are my true disciples. This brings great glory to my Father.

I have loved you even as the Father has loved me. Remain in my love. When you obey my commandments, you remain in my love, just as I obey my Father's commandments and remain in his love. I have told you these things so that you will be filled with my joy. Yes, your joy will overflow! This is my commandment: Love each other in the same way I have loved you. There is no greater love than to lay down one's life for one's friends. You are my friends if you do what I command. I no longer call you slaves, because a master doesn't confide in his slaves. Now you are my friends, since I have told you everything the Father told me.

JOHN 15:4-15, NLT

Oh, the joys of those who do not
    follow the advice of the wicked,
    or stand around with sinners,
    or join in with mockers.
But they delight in the law of the LORD,
    meditating on it day and night.
They are like trees planted along the riverbank,
    bearing fruit each season.
Their leaves never wither,
    and they prosper in all they do.

But not the wicked!
    They are like worthless chaff, scattered by the wind.
They will be condemned at the time of judgment.
    Sinners will have no place among the godly.
For the LORD watches over the path of the godly,
    but the path of the wicked leads to destruction.

PSALM 1, NLT

ABOUT THE AUTHORS

John Ortberg is an author, a speaker, and the senior pastor of Menlo Church in the San Francisco Bay Area. A consistent theme of John's teaching is how to follow a Jesus way of life—that is, how faith in Christ can affect our everyday lives with God. His books include *All the Places to Go . . . How Will You Know?*; *Soul Keeping*; *Who Is This Man?*; *The Life You've Always Wanted*; *Faith and Doubt*; and *If You Want to Walk on Water, You've Got to Get Out of the Boat*. John teaches around the world at conferences and churches.

Born and raised in Rockford, Illinois, John graduated from Wheaton College. He holds a master's of divinity and a doctorate in clinical psychology from Fuller Seminary, and he did postgraduate work at the University of Aberdeen, Scotland.

John is a member of the board of trustees at Fuller Seminary, where he has also served as an adjunct faculty member. He is on the board of the Dallas Willard Center for Christian Spiritual Formation and has served in the past on the board of Christianity Today International.

Now that their children are grown, John and his wife, Nancy, enjoy surfing in the Pacific to help care for their souls. He can be followed on Twitter @johnortberg.

Gary W. Moon (PhD, Fuller Theological Seminary) is director of the Martin Family Institute and the Dallas Willard Center for Christian Spiritual Formation at Westmont College in Santa Barbara, California. He is also codirector of Fuller's doctor of ministry degree program in spiritual direction, which blends ancient Christian spirituality, Ignatian spirituality, and spiritual formation insights from Dallas Willard. He served as distinguished professor of psychology and Christian spirituality at Richmont Graduate University, editor in chief for the journal *Conversations*, and the director of the Renovaré International Institute for Christian Spiritual Formation. His books include *Apprenticeship with Jesus* and *Falling for God*.

WHAT DID JESUS REALLY TEACH ABOUT SALVATION?

LEARN MORE WITH THESE RESOURCES

< *Eternity Is Now in Session*
Discover what it means to live
eternally with God here and now.

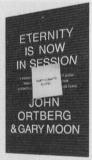

Eternity Is Now in Session Participant's Guide
Great for small-group or
individual Bible study.

Eternity Is Now in Session DVD Experience
DVD to accompany
the participant's guide,
with teaching from
John Ortberg.

How Do I Know If I'm Really Saved?
Uncover what it really
means to be a disciple.

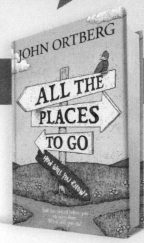

MARTIN INSTITUTE
for Christianity and Culture
WESTMONT COLLEGE

The Martin Institute for Christianity and Culture is dedicated to placing an enduring emphasis on spiritual formation with a particular focus on the path of authentic transformation as an interactive, loving relationship with Jesus Christ. As part of that quest, we hope to honor the legacy of Dallas Willard while placing his work in the context of other thought and praxis leaders who have developed methods for authentic Christian formation that have stood the test of time.

The Goals:

The goals of the Martin Institute for Christianity and Culture are to 1) support a new generation of thought leaders in the area of Christian spiritual formation and 2) help establish this discipline as a domain of public knowledge that is open to research and pedagogy of the highest order.

The Centers:

Dallas Willard Research Center: Supports and engages in Christian spiritual formation research and writing efforts through 1) maintaining and offering access to the books and papers of Dallas Willard's personal library, including online availability for many of these resources; 2) a senior fellows program; 3) annual book and research awards programs; and 4) providing faculty research retreats.

Conversatio Divina: A Center for Spiritual Renewal: Creates and offers resources for both "pilgrims" and "guides." Specific activities include 1) academic course development for pastors, church leaders, spiritual directors, and mental health professionals; 2) development of small group curriculum projects in the area of spiritual formation; 3) a variety of writing efforts; and 4) continuing education and retreat offerings for ministry leaders.

Westmont Center for Spiritual Formation: Offers spiritual formation opportunities for the Westmont community through providing a retreat space and programming along with partnerships across campus. Specific offerings include small group development, residence-life-based spiritual formation coordinators, and support for Augustinian Scholars and chapel programs.

For more information, visit www.dallaswillardcenter.com.

Praise for

ARCHIPELAGO

"*Archipelago* is beautifully done. There's a warmth to it, an exuberance and a wisdom. It's funny and sometimes bitingly poignant. Monique Roffey writes the male central character so well, and as for the little girl at the center of the story, it's one of the most vivid and charming portraits of a young child I can remember reading in years. A brilliant piece of storytelling."

—Andrew Miller, author of *Pure*, winner of the Costa Book of the Year Award

"An adventure blazing with a lust for life . . . Monique Roffey has established herself as a fearless writer with her choices of subject and her visceral style. . . . *Archipelago* travels to new, intoxicating latitudes. . . . Roffey excels equally at the hands-on descriptions of yachting, the intricacies of island navigation, the beauty and terror of the sea, and the inner life of her rudderless protagonist. The girl is captured with pitch-perfect empathy. . . . [A] big-hearted *Moby-Dick* story for our times."

—Kapka Kassabova, *The Guardian* (London)

"Arresting . . . Strikingly vivid . . . *Archipelago* beautifully evokes the pared-back rawness of being adrift, at the mercy of nature, first by accident and then by design."

—Maria Crawford, *Financial Times*

"Engrossing . . . [*Archipelago*] washes over the reader's imagination with the force of a tidal wave as its protagonists embark on a perilous journey along the Caribbean Sea. . . . A haunting portrayal of the dangers and delights, trials and tribulations, of surviving in an archipelago. Roffey evocatively conjures the life and landscape of the Caribbean islands. . . . Roffey here creates an incrementally po study of a father-daughter relationship, with a compelling account of climate change and a transformative journey. . . . The novel shows what remains in the heart when we have lost what we love, and the inner resources needed to rebuild a life from its ruins."   —Anita Sethi, *The Independent* (London)

"[*Archipelago* shows] the finesse Roffey reveals in her understanding of men in extremis. . . . As a writer, Roffey meets the challenge confidently, structuring her narrative adeptly and holding the reader's attention throughout. . . . It's a powerful story of endurance and triumph in the face of adversity, and one that also offers answers to questions of how we might respond in a rapidly changing world when things start to go wrong."   —Jim Ferguson, *The Scotsman*

"Compelling . . . Roffey, herself from Port of Spain, writes like one who knows these waters well, their beauty and their capacity to cleanse, but also their volatility. The writing is studded with striking images—the dog's nose is as pink as a scrap of ballet shoe—and there's a real sense of momentum. . . . Roffey is adept at conveying wonder."

—*The Observer* (London)

"A man's family home is destroyed by flood in Trinidad, but after it is rebuilt the nightmare continues. Roffey's lyrical style won her accolades for *The White Woman on the Green Bicycle*; this is just as enchanting."   —*Elle* (UK)

"Read this novel by Monique Roffey for its craft, its intense, elemental optimism, and for the lyricism of a joyful girl-child's discovering of the different faces of an archipelago."
     —Earl Lovelace, author of *Is Just a Movie* and *Salt*, winner
          of the Commonwealth Writers' Prize

"Islands are everywhere in this stunningly rendered novel, reminding or teaching us anew about our individual selves against their history-mired backdrops. The long arm of human injustice, greed, and excess runs on no shorter a leash here, as Gavin, Océan, and Suzy dock in multiple ports to discover. Beachcombing through the sea's washed-up treasures on one of the Los Roques islands, Gavin muses on the disturbing assortment of plastic debris and shattered coral, thinking, too, of how oil swallows up life around them, oil destroying nature. Nothing seems clear about human progress: it all glimmers, like the *Sea Empress* tourist ship, 'grotesque and a spectacle in its own right.' *Archipelago*'s trajectory reminds the reader in both subtle and unapologetic flourishes that through our best-laid plans for Nature, Nature herself persists. The novel is replete with achingly beautiful descriptions of the world that frames these seafarers."

—Shivanee Ramlochan, *The Trinidad Guardian*

"[*Archipelago*] is lovely: a novel full of sensual, elemental description, soaked in loss and damage and softly haunted by the Caribbean's bloody history of slavery."

—Claire Allfree, *Metro* (UK)

"A stirring narrative . . . Roffey captures the impotence of man in the face of the extremes of nature quite superbly."

—*Scotland on Sunday*

"Most people dream of escaping *to* the Caribbean; the hero of Roffey's novel is mad keen to escape *from* Trinidad after his house is destroyed by a flood. He returns to rebuild his home with his six-year-old daughter, but memories of the flood haunt him and he takes to his boat. You can feel the sea breeze on your face and you'll be itching to dive into 'the green and turquoise leopard print sea.'"

—Sebastian Shakespeare, *Tatler* (London)

THE WHITE WOMAN ON THE GREEN BICYCLE
ORANGE PRIZE FINALIST

"Roffey's explorations of longtime marriages, race, and the lingering effects of colonialism are insightful and often painful to read. . . . The true main character in this novel is Trinidad itself: its people, its customs, and its contradictions."

—Nancy Pearl, National Public Radio

"Engaging . . . A firebomb of a book, revealing a slowly disintegrating marriage, a country betrayed, and a searing racism that erupts in terrible violence. . . . This is a stunning book, and its depiction of an aspect of Caribbean life is well worth contemplating." —*The Cleveland Plain Dealer*

"Roffey succeeds wonderfully in writing an informative and deeply moving novel about her homeland. . . . She writes realistically enough to make readers feel that they have visited the island. Deservedly a finalist for the Orange Prize; Roffey is a fantastic talent who, one hopes, will keep writing for years to come." —*Library Journal* (starred review)

"Heartrending and thought-provoking, you will never again see the Caribbean as just another holiday destination." —*Elle*

"Few novels capture the postcolonial culture with such searing honesty as this Caribbean story told through the alternating viewpoints of a white British couple over the last fifty years. . . . The pitch-perfect voices capture the colonials' racism and sense of entitlement." —*Booklist*

"A rich and highly engaging novel." —*The Guardian* (London)

"Roffey's evocation of Trinidad is extraordinarily vivid, the central relationship beautifully observed."

—*The Times* (London)

"Roffey is a writer of verve, vibrancy, and compassion, and her work is always a joy to read."

—Sarah Hall, author of *How to Paint a Dead Man*

"Equal love and attention go into the marriage and the country at the heart of this Orange Prize shortlisted novel. . . . It's a book packed with meaty themes, from racism to corruption to passion and loyalty." —*Seven*, *The Sunday Telegraph* (London)

"Roffey's Orange Prize–nominated book is a brilliant, brutal study of a marriage overcast by too much mutual compromise." —*The Independent* (London)

"A searing account of the bitter disappointment suffered by Trinidadians on securing their independence from British colonial rule and of the mixed feelings felt by a white couple who decide to stay on. An earthy, full-blooded piece of writing, steaming with West Indian heat."

—*London Evening Standard*

"[Roffey's] plot engages the reader through a gradual revelation of the past—slowly forming a melancholy whole."

—*Financial Times*

"From its opening pages, I was entranced by the world of this novel. Monique Roffey's Trinidad is full of strife and languor, violence and also hushed moments of peace, so beautifully and lushly evoked that while I was reading Trinidad became more real for me than my own neighborhood. What a vibrant, provocative, satisfying novel—I can't stop thinking about it."

—Suzanne Berne, Orange Prize–winning author of
A Ghost at the Table

Also by Monique Roffey:

ARCHIPELAGO

A Novel

MONIQUE ROFFEY

PENGUIN BOOKS

PENGUIN BOOKS
Published by the Penguin Group
Penguin Group (USA) Inc., 375 Hudson Street,
New York, New York 10014, USA

(Ⓟ)

USA / Canada / UK / Ireland / Australia
New Zealand / India / South Africa / China
Penguin Books Ltd, Registered Offices: 80 Strand, London WC2R 0RL, England
For more information about the Penguin Group visit penguin.com

First published in Great Britain by Simon & Schuster UK Ltd 2012
Published in Penguin Books 2013

Grateful acknowledgment is made for permission to reprint excerpts
from the following copyrighted works:
"Zero Circle" by Rumi from *Rumi: The Big Red Book* by Coleman Barks (HarperOne,
2010). Copyright © Coleman Barks, 2010. Used by permission of Coleman Barks.
"Islands" from *Collected Poems, 1948–1984* by Derek Walcott. Copyright © 1986 by
Derek Walcott. Reprinted by permission of Farrar, Straus and Giroux, LLC.

LIBRARY OF CONGRESS CATALOGING-IN-PUBLICATION DATA
Roffey, Monique.
Archipelago : a novel / Monique Roffey.
pages cm
ISBN 978-0-14-312256-2
1. Fathers and daughters—Fiction.   I. Title.
PR6118.O37A73 2013
823'.92—dc23
2012043549

Printed in the United States of America
1 3 5 7 9 10 8 6 4 2

Set in Palatino

ALWAYS LEARNING   PEARSON

For my brother, Nigel Roffey, a sailor man

But islands can only exist
If we have loved in them.

"Islands," Derek Walcott

Yes, as everyone knows,
meditation and water are
wedded forever.

Moby-Dick, Herman Melville

THE VOYAGE OF *ROMANY*

Ora

CARIBBEAN SEA

Cartagena

San Blas
Archipelago

Colon

PANAMA

COLOMBIA

To Galapagos Islands

PACIFIC
OCEAN

GALAPAGOS ISLANDS

Isla Pinta

*Isla
Marchena*

*Isla
Genovesa*

Isla Santiago

*Isla Santa
Cruz*

*Isla
Fernandina*

*Puerto
Ayora*

*Isla
Isabela*

*Isla San
Cristobal*

*Isla
Santa Maria*

*Isla
Espanola*

PACIFIC OCEAN

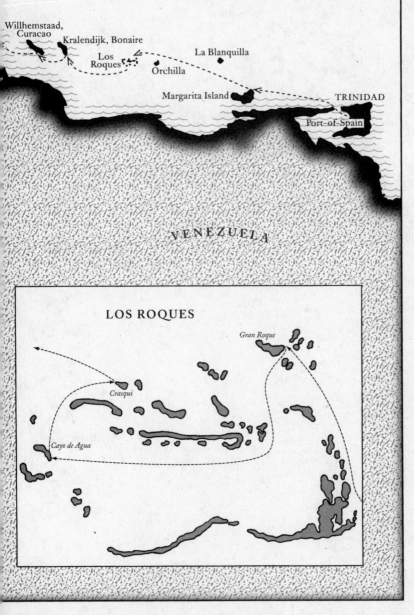

ARCHIPELAGO

THE PINK HOUSE

CHAPTER ONE

RAIN

The dog mumbles something under her breath.

What now, Gavin replies, as he goes about the kitchen in an aimless fashion. 7 p.m. Dinner should be on the table and she's trying to remind him. Animals have a keen sense of time.

Okay, okay, he says. The dog sits in the middle of the kitchen, trying not to slump over. Her chest is robust, yet she sits in a manner which suggests her stiff front legs are propping her up. Her triangular eyes are narrowed to slits; her tongue hangs from her dark mouth. She's making sure everything is all right, that they'll get through for the time being. She mumbles long and loud, a sound not dissimilar to his stomach when he's hungry.

Good girl, he says to her, not knowing if he needs or loves this dog any more.

Maccy cheese and chicken Vienna sausages will be their meal tonight. This is what his daughter likes.

They've eaten it the last three nights; very little else will tempt her. Maybe he'll add a tin of peas. She's lying in the huge double bed in the bedroom, like a mermaid on a raft, watching *Casper the Friendly Ghost*. November and it's still raining, popcorn rain, almost every day, short dense showers, ten minutes of a mauve downpour and then nothing. It falls from the mountains all around, unbidden, and makes him feel like he's done something wrong, like he's been in an argument and was the one to say all the stupid things.

He opens the tin of chicken sausages and winces at the stink. Like the innards of a gym shoe, a stale acid smell. He spills the brine out into the sink.

Here, have one of these, he says to the dog. He prongs a short brownpink sausage and holds it close to the dog's muzzle. She sniffs it but doesn't take a bite.

Go *on*, try it, he cajoles.

She sniffs again and puts her snout to the sausage. She nibbles it like a Japanese lady might nibble on a rose petal.

Oh, for God's sakes.

She takes the sausage carefully in her mouth and then slides to the floor and drops it on the lino. She looks up at him and mumbles.

Jesus Christ.

To be this close to collapse is a soft feeling. All his inner fibre, all his strength is ungluing and stretching and he can feel himself going stringy, like he could just come apart. It will be a tender experience, like falling in love. Yes, surely dying, losing, failing, giving up, are similar to all the great uplifting feelings; surely dying is like being born.

He fills the saucepan with a jet of water, sits it on the hob and watches the ring turn candy red. The water is cloudy from the tap. As he watches it clear he puts his hand on his chest to check his heart. He scratches his beard. Black flies flit to the stove and he grabs the electric flyswatter, shaped like a small tennis racket. He swats one, *smack,* and the fly fries on the lines. It sizzles and forms a small black lump.

Ha, ha, *see,* he says to the dog. I'm still dangerous.

He swats another fly, smacking the racket down on the counter top. Another good shot, another sizzling sound. The racket smokes.

Smack, smack. Two more flies get mashed and charred. He picks at his T-shirt, and fans it against his stomach; a small sweat has broken out. Maybe he, Gavin Weald, isn't dying, after all. Maybe he is Godzilla, the Great Ape; maybe he will destroy and conquer all.

Daddy?

The dog looks round at the little girl in the hallway.

He looks at her too.

Yes, dou dou.

What's for dinner?

It's a surprise, he says, hiding the racket behind his back. He towers over her, and yet he feels her strength; she can make louder sounds than he can. She can sob for a whole night, not eat for days, throw tantrums which spin themselves from nowhere. Or spin themselves from her new fear, the rain which bounds down from the hills. She is six and small and oh, so powerful.

I don't want a surprise.

You'll like this surprise, guaranteed.

She shakes her head which makes her blonde hair sway around her face.

What then?

Pizza.

Pizza? Since when did you prefer pizza?

With anchovies please.

You don't even know what an anchovy is.

Yes I do.

He drops to his knees. He holds the flyswatter like a real tennis racket, across his shoulder, affecting the style of a pro, forgetting the charred lumps.

What is an anchovy, then?

It's a fish.

Oh, he nods. This is unexpected. When did she learn about anchovies? Captain Nemo, yes, but an anchovy?

A fish? You mean like a whale?

Nooooo, she shrieks at his stupidity. They're tiny, like a shrimp.

A shrimp?

She laughs and her face glows. The dog's tail thumps the ground.

Océan, I'm sorry, but we don't have anchovies. Nor whales, nor any kind of fish, and anyway, anchovies taste horrible.

I love anchovies.

You've never even tried one!

Yes I have.

Look, we're having your favourite tonight, maccy cheese and . . . He looks at the sausage on the lino still between the dog's paws . . . And then we are having ice cream with peas. That was the surprise; I wasn't supposed to tell you. It's a secret recipe. Now go away – and leave me to cook.

Ha. She's outfoxed. Her face is pensive, trying to work out what to do next. He's losing his marbles and the one good thing about it is that he can now defuse a pre-tantrum six-year-old.

Go on now. She turns and he paddles her behind with the racket full of burnt flies.

She wanders back to the bedroom and the TV.

The water in the pan bubbles furiously and he opens a packet and throws the pasta in to boil and waits, stirring and stabbing it with a wooden spoon. When it's soft, he drains the tubes, throws them back in the pan. He takes the sachet of macaroni cheese mix and tears it open, sprinkling it in. The grey powder dissolves in a puff and the pasta coagulates into a stiff mess at the bottom. He pours in milk, adds a knob of butter. He prods and stirs, prising the pasta into separate pieces and the powder starts to become thinner and lighter in texture, like a miracle; it even starts to smell like cheese.

They eat together at the table. He doesn't attempt conversation for fear of where it might lead. Anchovies, rain. Mummy. Cheesy steam lifts from the pot of macaroni, sedating them. Next to it, a bowl of grated cheddar, slices of bread and butter. He scoops some macaroni into her bowl and her eyes grow wide and dilated at the sight of the starchy goo.

Yum, yum, he says and means it. He sprinkles the real cheese on top and puts the bowl down in front of her. She holds her fork like a trident and gazes into the bowl, inhaling deeply. One day she'll fall asleep into her macaroni.

Yum, yum, he says again to himself, as he scoops a triple helping and takes a fistful of cheddar.

They both hum while eating their food. She sucks whole tubes down in one, blows them out onto the table. He doesn't care to correct her. He picks at his food and he strokes at his heart; he chews slowly, trying not to drift too far away. He especially tries not to think of the office, of what he'll have to face tomorrow, Monday.

They've been back in the house exactly twelve days. Twelve days within these pink walls. Tomorrow is day thirteen. When he thinks of the office nothing comes. He can't conjure up faces, 'to do' lists, Mrs Cyrus his secretary of ten years, anything. Where is it all, that part of him? He was doing so well, the CEO of a good-sized company; it feels like years ago. His head is light and there's a churning in the pit of his stomach.

Daddy, can I get down now?

Yes, pumpkin.

Will you watch TV with me?

Of course.

He dumps the dishes into the already dish-crammed sink and burps. The dog sits against the kitchen wall. He bends and strokes her behind the ears and she tilts her head for more. *Scratch, scratch*, good girl. Her bull terrier's nose is long and Roman, a pink patch at the end like a piece of a ballet shoe, worn satin; the tip of her nose is black and cold, reassuring to touch. He fights the urge to sit down on the floor and hug the dog close.

Come on then, Suzy. Let's watch TV, he says.

The dog gets up and he pats her side. She trots after him, tail up, and they both climb on to the kingsize bed with the little girl on it. The three of them form themselves into a kind of nest; the sheets around them are damp and smell of dog and feet. The Discovery Channel shows images of crocodiles in a place called Kakadu in Australia. Océan is transfixed. She is lying across his barrel chest and the dog is slumped across her legs. Immediately, as he tries to focus on the TV, his eyes feel heavy. Crocodiles, a creek somewhere, yellow eyes bulging from the water. Sleep arrives quickly and he doesn't try to fight it off; it's usual for him to end his days like this, with his daughter clinging to him, with the feeling, deep down, that it's the other way around.

*

In the office on Monday his staff float around him. How much longer can they trust him? How much longer would *he* trust him if he were them? When will the Board of Directors call him in, Steve or Mr Grant, the owner of the company; how much longer before they give him unrealistic targets, start to discuss his benefits? He is No. 3 in the company, the one hired to run everything; they can always replace a No. 3. At first there was time off. Curiosity, sympathy, cards, flowers. He didn't discuss any of it. It was a relief to finally get back to work.

In his private office, he examines his hands. They are feathered with dead grey skin stained here and there with yellow where he's splashed antiseptic ointment on the slits. The skin is now paper-thin. He can type, but holding a steering wheel is difficult, tying his laces is painful. His feet are the same, skin peeling off in welts. Psoriasis. It set in a few months after the flood. He's tried everything now, all the steroid creams, the pills, hard drugs packed full of chemicals which made his hair fall out, his pubes wither. He's started seeing an alternative doctor who can read his 'vibrations' on a little machine. He doesn't know or care exactly what this means. *You register a four,* the doctor says. Now he's been prescribed a glass of water every morning, with a squeeze of lime and a teaspoon of bicarbonate of soda to alkalise his body.

At 11 a.m. he walks to the coffee machine for his fourth cup. It's the coffee. If he could give up coffee, his one vice, all his other problems would come good. He knows this is an underlying truth, that he cannot give up this black toxic liquid. If he could put this one little thing right, he could put everything right.

He smiles at Petula at reception and her eyes fill with

love when she sees him; she's like a nun, so openly concerned. Only she has understood.

Hi Petula, he says and she beams. Petula, who is also so fertile – five kids. So fertile she can make her glasses fog up just sitting there all day. Petula who, like the dog, has come to run his life.

Doughnut today, Mr Weald?

No thanks.

Potato pie?

Oh God, no.

What I can get fer you?

Nothing. Thank you.

He is still full of last night's macaroni cheese. He waddles to the men's room and stands in the cubicle, counting to ten. When his eyes are open he can see tiny filmy black snakes in the air in front of him; floaters, the optician calls them. It's weird watching them; they look like bacteria breeding in a Petri dish. He closes his eyes and puts his fingers to his temples. He tries to steady himself but that rising panicking butterfly feeling threatens to get the better of him. He holds his head in his hands and counts.

When he hears the bathroom door open he unzips his flies and lets a steady torrent of saffron yellow urine cascade from him.

Pissing, *ahhh*, it's like a strange dull orgasm. Maybe he could move in with Petula and her kids. Each one of them has a different father. All good-for-nothing layabouts. Maybe they could form a pod, a kind of double family. Or – better still, maybe they could all live together in his pink house. Petula appears to him, through a haze, her glasses sparkling, her smile beatific. *Potato pie*? Maybe she could still work on reception here, but also be a kind of flatmate. Could that work?

Mr Weald?

Uh – yes?

Mr Weald, is that you?

He panics, looking at his watch. Oh, *God*. A piercing realisation, no . . . no, please no. He has fallen asleep again, standing on his feet. His flies are still open, his dick hanging limp against his trousers. Petula. He was thinking of her and then . . .

Mr Weald?

Yes, I'm here. It sounds like Elston from the warehouse, a good man. He won't mention this to a soul.

You okay, Mr Weald?

He zips himself back up and opens the cubicle door.

Elston, I'm fine. Was I snoring?

Yes, Mr Weald.

Well, I'm fine. I just got a little lost in there; you know what it's like.

Elston's face is huge and incredulous.

Never mind, Gavin says quickly and leaves the men's. He goes back to his office and tells Mrs Cyrus not to bother him. He has piles of paperwork; he tells her to put no one through unless it's a dire emergency.

In his office he sits very still at his desk until his sense of humiliation quells and his heart slows again. He says some kind of prayer and in that moment an image of his old boat shimmers before him. *Romany*. His 28-foot sloop, his old mistress, his great friend. He thinks of her sitting in the olive green water, her wooden deck, her upturned bow; he knows he's clutching at straws.

Gavin hides in his office all day. Hours of hot itchy hands and a racing heart and a mind slipping all over the place: images of *Romany*, the boat from his bachelor days, appear and disappear like a ghost boat in a haze. His old boat has been sitting moored at the yacht club for over a year now; they'd decided to sell her, finally. No time for boats any more, for sailing down the islands, for racing, nights gazing at the stars. His wife had never enjoyed sailing much. Then the flood came. By now, she is probably covered in pelican shit, full of rainwater.

He plays Solitaire online and then he plays Bridge. He checks Facebook seventeen times, checks for hurricanes, for sightings of UFOs, for information about Kakadu; then he finds all this checking makes his head spin even more. At 5 p.m., on the dot, he logs out and leaves the office without looking Mrs Cyrus in the eye.

*

At home Gavin stands on the lawn and scrutinises the pink garden walls. Seven feet high now, with buttresses, steel-enforced. Nothing will knock over these pink walls. What colour were they before? He can't remember;

mostly they were covered with orange trumpety flowers, a climbing plant of some sort, other shrubs. Now the walls are candy pink, princess-pink, to make his daughter happy. She chose these walls. He looks up and sniffs, he can smell the rain arriving anytime soon. The sky is heavy with thunderheads about to burst; the rainy season is a month from being over.

Daddy? Océan comes to him and holds onto his legs.

Yes, dou dou.

Can we have meatballs for dinner?

Yes, we can have meatballs.

Can Suzy have meatballs too?

Of course. How was school?

Okay.

He sits down on the step of the porch and hoists her onto his lap. The dog appears from round the corner; she trots over to them, mumbles something, and then flumps over onto her side.

We made butter today at school.

Really?

I have it in my school bag.

Show me.

She jumps off him, fetches her school bag and digs around in it, producing a small plastic yoghurt pot with, yes, a creamy pool at the bottom.

It has to go in the fridge, she explains.

He's impressed. Butter? Anchovies? This is what a private education is buying.

Go and put it in the fridge and we can have some

tonight on toast, then come back here and tell me all about how you made it.

She skips off.

A peal of thunder from the sky.

The dog replies with a low growl. He gets up and walks out onto the lawn again and shivers. He's done some-thing wrong, but he doesn't know what. The world is tetchy with him, but why? How did he end up like this; when, at what moment, did he make the wrong choice, end up here, gazing at these pink walls?

A fat spot of rain hits him hard on the centre of his head. The clouds are low, troubled. Another rumble. *Stop*, he shouts. But the rain falls quickly down on him, as if unzipped from a valise. In seconds he's drenched, but he doesn't bother to get under cover. The rain falls down on him in a low consistent thrum; it's only just begun. November rain in Trinidad. Then it picks up, falling louder from the clouds, long fluid ropes of tropical rain. He clenches his fists, seized by a rage for this rain, for its spite, its ridicule of him. How could rain make him feel so – weak? From inside the house he can hear another sound, louder than the rain, the screaming of his little girl.

*

In the morning he wakes with the dog and the child snor-ing lightly next to him. Each has found a space on the bed. Océan is spread like a starfish, on her stomach; the dog is close to falling off the edge. His sheets have knotted up and wound themselves around his legs. The radio clock says 5.30 a.m. A ceiling fan whirs overhead, stirring up the air. There's that sullen brooding feeling beyond the louvres, like the rain never went away.

He needs help. He realises this, has been coming to the conclusion for months. He needs his own private team. Not just Josephine once a week to mop and dust and change the sheets, not just Petula. He needs a chef, a dietician, a psychotherapist, a specialist dermatologist, a hypnotherapist to get him off the coffee, a masseur; and he needs to pay someone, a woman, for a hug every now and then, maybe even more. He is a man and he isn't coping. His wife made him healthy, stable. Now he is half-himself, not himself. Pathetic.

Only mornings can be innocent, just before light. This is the quiet time before it all happens, before anything starts, this half an hour before he has to rise and begin over again. These are his quiet moments, the only time he has to himself, and it's not enough for him to regroup, to think straight. He cannot figure out another plan in this tiny space of half an hour every morning before the merry-go-round starts again.

All he can do is admire his little girl; how on earth did he produce such an exquisite creature? Him so dark and curly-haired, olive-skinned. When they stand together it looks like he stole her from another family; she's like a fairy girl, her hair like silver seaweed and her mother's grey-blue eyes, her mother's pale skin. It was his idea to name her Océan, after the sea.

The dog snuffles and rolls over and falls in slow motion off the bed, landing on her sturdy feet. She farts and stretches and yawns, then climbs back onto the bed and curls herself back into her dreams. Outside, he can hear the patter of light rain and he feels himself freeze: will it wake her up? Dear God, no, please, and with these thoughts he sees his daughter's eyelids flicker, as if she now has some internal radar for rain. Her eyes shoot open wide. Her mouth opens and she screams and screams for her mother, *where is my mummy*, she wails. And it's not fair, because he cannot be her mother, not that.

She's screaming now, so bad, he sometimes fears what the neighbours might think, even though they know; they were there, too, in the flood.

Dou dou, shhhh, he tries, but it's useless. She is scream-ing herself awake, into consciousness. The dog barks and jumps from the bed and trots outside to bark at the rain and it's then, in the chaos of her screams, that he knows what to do, how to save them.

CHAPTER TWO

THE GREAT DANE

Océan sits in the front seat of the 4x4, mute. Baseball cap, tracksuit top zipped to the chin, pink ballet skirt, pink party sandals, frilly socks; that's all she'd wear at such short notice. The dog is in the back. They are in Hi-Lo car park in Maraval.

Daddy, where are we going?

Shopping, we're going shopping.

Now?

Yes.

But what about school?

School?

He hasn't formed an answer to this. Not to anything, yet. He needs to shop for a trip of two or three days, maybe longer.

School is closed today, sweetie-pie.

Closed?

The teachers rang us all up. School is closed for a few

days. Rained off. Come, quick. He stands outside the passenger door and motions for her to climb down.

I thought we'd go on a trip.

Where?

To fairyland, that's where. He winds down the back window two inches for the dog and says: stay here. The dog nods through the glass and leans against the back seat.

He takes Océan by the hand and hurries across the warm concrete. Tinned food, and dried food, rice, pasta, lots of it, that's what they need. He wheels the trolley into the cool air-conditioned supermarket, across the lull of the vegetable aisle.

He picks up a bag of onions, a bag of tomatoes, some potatoes and a lettuce, some apples and limes, some oranges. Then, like a swarm of locusts, he makes for the other aisles. He pulls armfuls of tins from the shelves: corned beef, spaghetti hoops, baked beans, chilli dogs, chicken Vienna sausages, tuna fish, Bachelors tomato soup, sweetcorn and peas and packets of Super Noodles and boxes of macaroni; Froot Loops, cornflakes, bags of bread rolls, Cheddar cheese, Crix crackers, mayonnaise and Matouk's pepper jelly. And then several five-litre bottles of water, bottles of Pepsi and coconut water; also toilet paper and dog chow. Tins of meatballs too, for the kid and the dog. Soon the trolley is heaving. Océan carries three large bags of Doritos and all of a sudden she seems to be enjoying herself. No school is always an easy bribe.

At the checkout point two young men come forward to

help bag things up. He daren't look up or around for fear of bumping into someone he knows. It is mid-morning. Anything could happen; his *boss* could walk in, or Mr Grant, the big man himself, or worse, Jackie, his mother-in-law. Anyone could stop this; what then? It's hard escaping from a small place. You can trip over yourself on your way out. *Head down, head down.* He doesn't even look at the checkout girl as he hands over his credit card. She slices it through the machine and a white slip putters out. With the heavy trolley, they head back into the squashed heat of the car park. He opens the car door for the dog.

Sorry, he says.

She yawns and scratches her ear. It wasn't so bad.

After unloading the bags of food, he gets back into the driver's seat and looks at himself in the mirror, checking he's really there. He sees a bloated forty-six-year-old version of himself. Green-yellow skin, bags under his eyes, his past handsomeness now vague. He sees flecks of grey in his beard, a large and distended belly, like that of a blowfish yanked from the sea. Breasts like a carnival whore, all this way and that, and he feels ashamed of himself and how he got like this. He revs the engine, reverses and drives the Jeep out onto the bumpy tarmac road; he turns on the radio. It's playing Madonna's *Holiday*.

We're going on a holiday, he says to his daughter.

But he can tell she isn't entirely happy. She's doing the quiet thing, watching out of the front window, trying to decide how to be.

In the back, the dog pants heavily. He half-turns in his

seat to run his hand down her long bony nose. Good girl, he says.

Soon they are slipping through the outskirts of Port of Spain, west, towards the sea and the marinas. The road tracks the coast and he gazes out across the smooth metal-grey Gulf of Paria; many large vessels are out there, abandoned workboats, tankers, container ships, harbouring from the global recession. The sea is settled for now after the early-morning rain. Besides, he knows these waters, and he knows his boat; they'll be hugging the coast of Venezuela for half the trip, this won't be a stupid thing to do. For now, the clouds are high and white, the sun burning itself up behind them. They are saying, *quickly, go now.*

At a petrol station, on the way, he stops and fills three large jerry cans with diesel. Further along, when they reach the marinas, he stops at Peake's, the chandlery. This is more serious shopping, mostly done over the counter. Océan stands quietly while he speaks to the assistant. He buys a spare engine impeller, fan belts, flares, life vests, harnesses with lifelines, two jack lines for the deck, a good torch, two foul-weather jackets, a new fishing rod, two sleeping bags, a pair of deck shoes and a pair of gloves, spare batteries for the GPS. He also buys fins and a snorkel, a first-aid kit, a new pump for the dinghy, and a logbook, also charts for Margarita and the Dutch islands, a cruising guide.

Back at the house he'd packed clothes for them both: two canvas duffel bags, plus their passports, papers, a lead for the dog, the hand-held GPS, the hand-held VHF. It took him thirty-five minutes to vacate the pink house. He left a message for Josephine on the kitchen counter, plus a small bundle of blue notes in the usual place to tide her over until she finds another job. She will clean the place, then lock up. He switched off his mobile phone; it was that easy.

As he's leaving Peake's, it happens. He runs straight into the friendliest man he knows, Alphonse, from the bakery.

Ayyyy, Gavin, how yuh goin? says Alphonse.

He remembers Alphonse also owns a boat, *Jouvay*, a 37-foot beauty, automatic pilot, auto-furling sails, water desalinator, a fridge, GPS, AVS, solar panels, a wind generator, everything. It's the kind of deluxe boat that would sail itself while Alphonse sleeps for hours on his way to Grenada or entertains lady friends in a comfy berth below. Gavin has seen him on it many times. Alphonse owns the bakery; he's a No. 1 of his own company. He can be anywhere he likes on a Tuesday morning.

I'm good, man. Gavin tries to fake his cheer. Taking a small trip, across to Margarita.

Plenty rain comin, Alphonse says. Venezuela rainin all now. Floods over der. You sure you leaving today?

Yeah.

Rather you than me. Ayyy. He looks down at the little girl. She get real pretty.

Océan goes shy around big men. She hides behind Gavin's legs.

Océan, say hello.

She says nothing, just hides.

Lookin just like she mudder.

I know.

Then Alphonse checks himself and a careful smile spreads across his face, as if suddenly he understands. The whole frigging island knows what happened to him.

You takin a break, den?

Yeah.

You take care of yourself, you hear?

I will.

What boat you goin on?

Romany.

Dat ol ting? Alphonse smiles, teasing.

My boat solid as a rock, man. Solid and stable and, Gavin laughs . . . slow. Slow as a pig.

Where you goin after Margarita?

West. Gavin jerks his thumbs behind him.

North much easier, man. It's a bitch to come back if you go west.

I been north plenty times, never west.

Allah dem Dutch islands, nah. You speak Dutch?

Nah, Gavin laughs. They speak other languages there, man. Papiamento, Dutch, English, American.

Pappy-what? What kind fancy language is dat?

Some ol slave language, nuh. Something creole.

Alphonse raises his eyebrows and steupses. Nah, I doh like dem Dutch Pappy . . . whatever fellers, dey too Dutchy – you know what ah mean?

Dutch-like.

Yeah. Dutch arses. Pardon my French, Miss Océan.

We're going to see the reefs, and the fish.

Well say hello to them for me. You take care, eh?

Yeah. I will.

Alphonse walks away. Gavin's throat dries – shit. Almost sprung. He looks down at his daughter. *Venezuela rainin all now. Floods over der*. The word alone makes his bowels start to squirm. Floods everywhere these days. Never mind about that. He's a proper sailor, a wrango-tango, hardass, learnt-from-experience man of the sea – at least he was. And besides, Caracas is miles away. For now, the clouds in Chaguaramas, Trinidad, are high and white and saying *go now*.

Come on, dou dou, he says to his little mermaid girl, let's get going.

*

Paco, the tender man, helps load up the taxi craft, a tall upright feller, black-brown and bald and sculpted from hardwood. His eyes are speculative, as always.

You going fer *days*, he says.

Alphonse, Paco, others on their boats have spotted him. So, it won't be a clean getaway.

Yeah, man. A short break.

Goin Venezuela?

Nah. Bonaire. Across so.

Margarita too?

Figure so, one night maybe. Not long. Pirates there, man.

Paco juts his chin, like he's heard the same. My wife shops in Margarita, he says.

So does mine. *Does,* that small word. He can't bring himself to use the past tense.

Bonaire meant to be a nice place. Nice reefs.

Yeah, man, I learnt to dive there years ago.

The taxi boat sits low in the water with all their loot. Paco takes them slowly out, threading through the moored yachts. Suzy rides the bow, patient and quietly expectant; she's been aboard *Romany* many times. She has a nose for salt air and likes to watch the waves and snap at the sea birds, likes to swim too. In fact, Suzy enjoys being on *Romany* almost as much as he does. It's been a while since they were aboard the old boat, how long? Years? At least two, maybe longer. Suzy is a deck dog, a hardass too. She will be his crew.

As they approach, he is amazed to see that the pelicans have left *Romany* alone. No pelican colony has taken ownership; in fact, the boat doesn't look so bad at all. She was on the hard for a year, in the water the last fifteen months; the sails and cockpit are well tarped up, the teak, from a distance, not so bleached. He wonders who came out to wrap up the boat so well.

Paco, you seen anyone out on this boat in the last few months?

Yeah.

Really? Who?

Mr Holder.

When?

Now and den.

Well, he never told me.

Clive Holder, his best friend and ex co-owner of *Romany*, never said anything about this. They haven't talked about *Romany* in recent months. In fact, he and Clive haven't talked much about anything, not since the flood. Did he stop speaking to Clive or was it the other way around? Either way, Clive, the wonderful bastard, has been taking care of his boat. Clive owns a bigger boat now; he's here, at TTSA, a lot.

Romany sits in the back of the bay, quiet and self-assured. She's small and slim and old-fashioned with her teak washboards, hatches and locker tops, like one of those Nordic Folkboats with her nose and tail lifted up from the sea. A Danish boat, she was sailed by the last owner to Trinidad across the Atlantic. A Great Dane is what she's called, a GD28, only two hundred and fifty ever made. Her long leaden keel gives her a low centre of gravity. She is a stable boat, designed by a sailor, an Olympic medallist. *Romany*'s hull is navy blue and her sails are white. The word ROMANY is stencilled on her in pale blue curly capitals. She looks shy on the water, but ready: easy to underestimate this small sailboat. His heart thrills just gazing at her.

Daddy, when can we go *home*?

He ignores this. Paco, dat is *boat*, he says to the old man.

Daddy, I'm bored. Océan is sitting beside him, her hands tucked under her armpits.

You won't be bored in a moment, Starbuck.

Starbuck?

My chief mate, that's you. I'll tell you all about him later.

Can we have meatballs again, tonight?

Yes.

Look at that beautiful boat, eh, Paco? Gavin gazes in rapture.

The old man nods, a cigarette crushed to the side of the mouth. I remember you plenty times with Mr Holder in dat ting.

Yeah, man. Pack up on a Friday afternoon, take a bottle of rum and a telescope, watch the stars. Spend the weekend cruising, fishing, girls on board. Plenty racing too in that slow ting. Sailing up the Grenadines.

Yes, man. Das a good boat. How old is she?

Oh God . . . he calculates . . . thirty, maybe thirty-five years old.

Still lookin good, man.

Boy, dat is boat.

They pull up alongside *Romany*. The dog is now more alive, her tail stiff as a mast. He can tell she wants to be first on board. He stands up in the tender and this is enough to make it rock. He steadies it back and they throw fenders out. He makes a pass at the steel lifelines with one leg, but he cannot throw it so high, his big fat leg won't reach any more.

Ah get fat, he says, making light of it. But it isn't funny, just one small thing he overlooked. His fatness. Fat men don't sail. Fat men don't go near the sea because fat men don't float too well, contrary to popular thought; they don't surf either, or windsurf, kite surf, boogie board, scuba dive or snorkel much. When did he get fat? He has some other image of himself, a long-ago younger man image, the one that had a gift for the sea.

He heaves and tugs and makes a giant effort and then, one and two – and when Paco helps, he's up and on the boat, face flushed.

Pass me the dog, he says to Paco. Lookin like she gonna jump.

Paco passes the dog up.

Next, Océan in her pink ballet skirt. Her face is blank, like she is trying to be patient, but just for now.

Sweetie, I want you to sit in the cockpit over there for about five minutes, he says.

Don't touch anything or move. Okay, Starbuck?

Okay, she says quietly.

Then Paco passes up the rest, armfuls of booty: equipment, food, fuel.

Yuh forget de rum, Paco quips.

Boy, plenty rum where ah goin.

But this isn't true. The Dutch don't make rum; they make a vile liqueur called Blue Curaçao. He has left rum out of the equation. A little girl, the sea and rum. Not a wise combination.

When all the bags are on board he reaches down to Paco and stuffs twenty bucks into his hand.

Listen, nuh, he says to Paco. If you see Mr Holder tell him *ah gone*.

Yes, man.

Tell him ah headin west. Tell him I'm going west and then west again, he will understand. We talk about it plenty times when we were young.

Yes, man, and then the ancient skipper turns his boat and revs the engine. He roars off, without looking back, making a small wake in the placid green sea, abandoning Gavin to his small boat with his child and his dog and plenty of things to do.

*

Like many boats, *Romany* has a legend. Gavin runs it through his head, or what he can remember. She was found adrift; that is a fact. It was twenty-odd years ago. Some fishermen from Mayaro spotted her, empty, her sails flapping, the VHF radio babbling in Spanish, a mile out in the choppy Atlantic sea, east of Trinidad. The fishermen were a canny lot; they had the idea to sail her north, halfway round the island, to the marinas in Chaguaramas, or that was the story he got from Clive. They were hoping to collect a reward. But no one knew of the boat, or the owner, and she wasn't registered in local waters; nobody in Trinidad had offered money to bring her in. By law, the fishermen weren't allowed to keep her;

they went back home by bus. The coastguard merely thanked them for doing their job. *Romany* was flying a Danish ensign, and, in due course, a 'missing persons' file was opened, a 'lost boat' file too. *Romany* was eventually hauled into the yard at TTSA, Trinidad's yacht club, and kept dry in the hope that she'd be claimed by family, or someone close to the owner. Months passed, but no one came forward. Only Clive had noticed this small, neat, orphaned boat. Only Clive Holder, then aged twenty-five, was keeping an eye on her.

Gavin knows only too well these things happen at sea. Lone sailors can trip, get knocked off balance by the boom, swept overboard by a wave. In a few cases, they jump off into the sea, dazzled with all the blue, hallucinating, leaving cryptic notes behind, things like *it is the mercy*. Thousands of men take to the sea every year, just like he's about to, alone. Some to escape, others to race, accomplish goals, others are making deliveries. Every year, a handful is lost: drowned, swamped by freak waves, capsized in storms, mown down by bigger boats. They snare upon fish pots, or forgotten nets. Nothing is fair or easy about sailing the high seas; even experienced sailors can make mistakes. Even Joshua Slocum disappeared on his boat *Spray*, run down by a steamer or struck by a whale on his way to the Caribbean. Other fine sailors have been mowed down – anything could have happened to the owner of *Romany*.

A year passed. *Romany* began to disintegrate. But Clive was smart. Being a distant relative of the yacht club's president, he made a modest offer of thirty thousand TT dollars. *My friend Gavin Weald will go halves with me*, he said. Clive had already told him about *Romany*, had wooed him with tales of the adventures they'd have with her. Clive was the one who'd sweet-talked Gavin into his affair with *Romany*. Of course he'd go halves.

Deal done. In Trinidad, no one was going to organise an auction; the boat would rot first. They kept her name, *Romany*, because it's bad luck to change the name of a boat. But all those years of fun, of racing in that slow stable yacht, of down the islands and up the islands, the fishing and stargazing and all they saw on *Romany*, they never once discussed how she was found. They never saw a ghost skipper on board and knew little about the boat. And so she went forward into the hands of her new owners, two young men, keen and brash and in love with her and the sea. All they ever talked about was how this boat liked to roam, and that must be the reason for her name.

*

It's two in the afternoon when *Romany* is ready to sail. In the course of unpacking, he has found many useful things stowed in the boat, including his old straw hat, a good omen. He'd wondered where it'd vanished. A cross between a stetson and a sombrero, it is the hat of his entire adult life, made of some kind of indestructible straw. He looks like a Mexican peasant in it, and it has been the object of much ridicule in the past, but it's huge and shady and sticks to his head like a claw.

Suzy has been in the saloon for most of this time, minding the little girl. Océan has organised all the tins for him, stowing them on the tiny shelves and in cupboards by label colour, then all the bottles, then her clothes, mostly tutus and pink dresses; she unpacked them all into lockers. They will be sleeping in the V-berth, the only proper sleeping space, in the bow, all three of them, or so she has decided. It will be their raft, and she has deposited her one toy, Grover, amongst the sleeping bags. They eat a small lunch of tuna sandwiches, and he tells her all about Captain Ahab and Starbuck, and the big white whale.

So, Mr Ahab only had one leg?

Yes, the white whale . . . He was hungry and well he . . . er . . . ate the other one off.

Owww. She makes a dramatic face. That must have hurt.

I think it upset him a lot.

That's why he's vexed with the whale?

Yeah.

I would be vexed with a whale that bit my leg off. He chased after it?

For a long time.

Will we see whales, Dad?

Not in the Caribbean Sea. But we'll see dolphins, flying fish, wait and see.

I hope we see a whale.

He's got things as ready as he could, set up the wind

vane on the self-steering, laid down the jack lines on the deck. The mainsail is good for hauling, the jib partially unfurled. Long time since he did anything like this alone. Long time, man. Suzy is on deck; he meshed the rails years ago so she wouldn't ever slip through. Even so, she is sitting there, steady as a bag of sweet potatoes.

Right, both of you, into the cockpit, he orders.

The dog jumps down but Océan looks at him blankly, like does he now think she's going to be bossed around with him in that stupid hat?

Suzy barks. She is stuck, outnumbered; it has been too long now fidgeting around, they need to get going while the afternoon is still young. The child is tired and will throw an almighty hissy fit if he doesn't get the boat off her mooring.

Okay, stay there then, he calls into the saloon.

He starts the engine and puts it in neutral. In moments, he casts off the stern line and then slips off the bow line, walks back to the cockpit and casts off the lazy line port side. He sits to the tiller and revs the engine. The loud chugging noise it makes sends Océan quickly up and out. She sits next to the dog.

Where are we going? she cries, half-excited.

Out to sea. He smiles.

They putter through the other boats moored in the marina and he is caught by a gust of *déjà vu*, a feeling from his long youth and something he once read about a time when youth must finally be left behind. He knows he's crossing that shadowline now and a dull notion of heroism surges in his veins; some whisper has come, *go now*. The salt in the air gets his blood up. He can hardly wait to do this. Slowly, they pass the other boats until they are all behind them and when it's all clear, he puts the engine in neutral and turns the boat windward. He puts on his gloves and makes his way to the foredeck and hoists the mainsail up. As he hoists, he feels a stinging in his palms; but as the sail rises so too do his spirits soar upwards.

In the cockpit, he steadies the tiller and looks out to sea. *Romany*'s sail catches the easterly wind and the boat tilts to starboard. She bristles, also eager to be out, no longer waiting around. *Come on then*, she is saying. They pass Five Islands, then Carrera, the prison island, then Gaspare with its banks of colourful island homes. They have the wind up and behind them and the boat sinks into the sea. In front of them is a wide-open ocean, more green than blue, more Orinoco than seawater for now. Boats everywhere, tankers and liners and a huge oil rig far out. The dog barks with joy. He sits down and smiles at the child.

See that? He points far out to a broken-off piece of rock which looks just like a tooth. It juts out from the sea.

We're going out there, and then round the corner.

Océan nods.

She is somehow fooled, that or she is getting it now. No more school. She puts her blue Snoopy mirrored sunglasses down onto her nose and acts as though she knows what is happening, like she knew of this plan all along. She hasn't sailed much, his mermaid child. She has been on one or two day cruises, they took her down the islands a few times; she will be fine, he reassures himself. Fine as this day. *Must get some sun block on her nose,* he thinks, and with that he takes his mobile phone out from his back pocket and tosses it over his shoulder, into the sea.

CHAPTER THREE

THE DRAGON'S MOUTH

They pass very close to the tooth of rock. As they do so, three dolphins appear off the starboard bow, one of them all piebald with pink-and-grey skin. Three dolphins swim to meet them.

Look at *that*. He points. Can you see them?

Océan is transfixed. What are they, Daddy?

Dolphins, can you see?

She nods.

Three dolphins, their sleek bodies and dorsal fins arch through the water in innate synchronicity. They fan out and upwards from the white caps like three movie stars appearing on a stage, like three acrobats, glamorous in spangles and tights.

Woo *hoo*, he shouts at them in appreciation. Océan claps and laughs.

It's exactly then that the seas start to pitch. The water is grey around the tooth, grey and all of a sudden disconsolate. How did he miss that? The high snowy clouds of only two hours ago have evaporated. In front of him, not far off, the clouds are heavy with rain, low and sullen and waiting. A squall.

The boat begins to buck and nosedive into the waves, as if the sea is trying to scratch itself. Forward and then backwards; up and then down; restless, unpredictable rollercoaster movements. Océan's face grows bigger as the boat begins to throw her around. Her eyes are wide; her mouth is shut tight.

Don't move; just hang in there, he says.

He lashes the tiller to the vane and goes down into the saloon and comes back up with a child's life vest and harness and a long lifeline. He gets the vest on her and ties it secure with knots. Then he clips on the harness and attaches the lifeline to the jack line. Her face is grave.

What's this, Dad?

It's to keep you safe.

Her face is turning a shade of algae before his eyes. The one thing he forgot to buy, seasickness tablets.

Sit tight for now, he says, pulling her closer.

He's also forgotten how quickly the sea can change. One moment it can be flat, quiet, agreeable, then of another mood entirely, wicked and vexed. The sea can be a bitch. She can hurl you from your bunk, have you vomiting out your guts, lash you with stray halyards. She never wants to be taken for granted. Take your eyes from her and she'll make sure you know about it.

Are they too close to the tooth? Has he lost his sense of

judgement; when was the last time he was this far out? The dolphins appear again, jumping and flipping and somersaulting, criss-crossing the bow. One slaps its tail fin on the water as it dives into the grey waves, slap, slap, *hello, ha-ha*.

It is giving them a show all right, having fun as they chop and mow along in dismal disharmony with the swells. The creatures are not here to entertain – but to tease them for being galumphing halfwits that travel the seas in boats.

Océan's cheeks have filled. He lashes the tiller again and grabs her in time to turn her towards the sea.

Her little body goes into a rigid spasm as she pukes. Out comes her lunch in a liquid spurt. Her torso racks and he holds her. *I'm so sorry*, he wants to say, sorry, my little mermaid girl.

She pukes again. This time her body stiffens slowly, the liquid shooting out in a projectile stream over the hull; then there's stillness again and her body goes soft.

He turns her around and holds her until she's calm. Her eyes are oysters in her head, dripping and fluid, spittle drools from her mouth. He dries her lips with the end of his T-shirt. Her eyes are vacant with confusion. He goes for a bottle of water in the saloon.

Here, sweetheart, drink some of this. He manages to pour her a cup amidst the wild pitching. He is so heavy it would take a raging beast of a sea to unsteady his feet.

Drink some of this, dou dou.

She sips and looks into the cup as if into a small world.

He pours some water over her head, over her face. He wipes her cheeks. Her Snoopy sunglasses have fallen off and lie on the floor in the corner of the cockpit.

You will feel a little better now you've puked.

She nods, but looks very far away. She leans against the bench seat; she has that horror-struck quietness of the seasick, her life vest is puffed up around her face.

He sits back at the tiller, in a different mood. The bitch sea is at him now. The dolphins have vanished off into the murk. *Romany* is taking it as best she can, her heavy keel planted in the water, nothing to worry about there. She is slow and careful, but even so, they're rolling all over the place, enough to make them all sick. He looks at the dog; she is lying on the cockpit floor with her nose in her paws, eyes closed.

Suzy, he says, to check on her. She doesn't respond.

Suzy, come on, not you too.

The dog opens her mouth as if to yawn and half-coughs a stream of viscous liquid. Océan stares in disbelief at the dogpuke and begins to cry. Not her usual attention-getting wail, not the one she uses to make him do anything. She sobs quietly, from her chest, a guttural sound, like an old woman grief-stricken, sobs followed by hiccups.

Océan clutches the plastic cup to her chest like a drunk, barely able to stand. Rain starts to fall down out of the clouds, a light whipping rain. He stares at his child, waiting for her response. But she is too sick to notice or care; she is holding onto herself. The rainwater douses her in moments, turning her hair to silvery reeds around her chin.

Drink some more water, for now, dou dou. This will be the worst of it, you'll see. It won't last long. But the child is sick again; this time only water spills out, onto the floor.

They plough along for an hour or so, in the rain, till the Dragon's Mouth is well behind them. Further out, the sea settles into giant grey-green swells. The dog and the child are quiet, in mutual and morbid sorrow. Ahead is only open sea, a sight he hasn't seen in a decade, at least, maybe not since the last time he headed out to Grenada in *Romany*, with Clive. What was he *thinking*, this time? To port side, there's a curious vessel trying to make it in, its red tattered sails are like a Chinese junk's. Pirates? It certainly looks like a pirate ship. Again, so soon? But the ship seems to be making its way behind them, heading into Port of Spain.

He is jumpy with trying to get things right; all his sea senses are asleep on him. He shakes himself physically, as if to stir them up. You can't forget this stuff, you don't just stop knowing what to do, he chastises himself. It's like riding a bike, surely?

He gazes to starboard, spots the massive Tobago cat bearing down on him with its cruel wave-cutter pincers. Its hull is forked and serrated and it looks like it can snip the water open. The cat replaced the old *Gelting*, the big iron ferry he knew as a younger man which trudged towards Tobago, taking hours to get there. Now there's an aggressive hydrofoil which zooms between the islands. It shouldn't worry him, sailboats have right of way, but it does. The hydrofoil cat is fast as a train, heading straight for him, barrelling forward. Inside him, everything freezes, all his knowledge, all his reason and understanding of why he is here; he could cry, and the thought comes that he should radio for help. Then he should turn round; head back in. Only Paco and Alphonse would know anything. He could tell everyone at the office that he was struck down with dengue. Things weren't *so* bad, surely. Surely? He could let the cat pass them, turn round and then sail home. Or let the cat run them down.

He does nothing. The cat sees them and alters its course, heading in a straight line behind them. He feels his chest to check how his heart is doing. It is thumping away like a bastard inside him. We'll be okay, he whispers. This will be the worst of it.

*

He is right. The sea calms once Trinidad is left behind. The child and the dog are still mute and inert, lolling about in the saloon. He boils water for Pot Noodles for himself and Océan. They are hot and salty and hit the spot. The dog laps water from her bowl. Neither wants to talk, both fall quickly into a half-slumber, Océan in her sleeping bag, in the saloon, Suzy at her feet. The day is coming to a close, the skies ahead are turning shell pink and the surface of the sea has the look of a fluid fabric, something unending and shifting, another surface, and he has the sense that the boat is sailing in a vast field of mercury. Or maybe *Romany* has even taken flight, landed on a different planet, where the ground is blue and ripples. Behind them are dark hills, not of Trinidad, a lush green island, but of another place, dull, volcanic, and lifeless.

The wind vane auto-steering system came with *Romany*; she'd already crossed the Atlantic when they bought her and it had been an essential part of such a seagoing craft. He rigs it so it will hold them on course, sailing with the easterly winds towards the north coast of Margarita. In the saloon he consults his charts and cruising guide and spots a bay in which to moor. At six to eight knots, if the wind keeps up, he calculates they should arrive early the next morning. It's been years since he sailed at night. In that time he's had his eyes tested several times; now, when he scans the horizon, he's aware that even his eyeballs are older, his sight weaker. And yet even so soon, he begins to feel a loosening, a swell in his veins, his body's way of aligning with the vast sea around him.

All night, he watches. First he watches the sky turn from pink to grey-pink then to grey and then into a purple ink-black night. Then it becomes hard to tell what is what: what is low cloud, what is sky, what is sea, where they join, how low the clouds are. Shapes, dark indefinable shapes, twist and lift from the sea. Can he see more dolphins? Is that the humped back of an island? He puts on an old Bob Marley CD, switches it on low so as not to wake the child. *Exodus* floats over the speakers. It is only then that he removes his straw hat, pulls on a jersey with long sleeves. He peels off his gloves and checks his hands. They're not bleeding.

The boat squeaks, her joints dry and crotchety. There are sounds all around him, the sawing of the ropes, the ruffle of the sails as they fill and flap, the gentle conversation of the sea. And there is Bob Marley too; Marley, the great bard, will keep him company as he watches the sea, as he meditates long into the night.

He gets out his logbook, makes columns to keep track of their journey: time, current, course, weather. He bites his pen as he makes notes, carefully recording lines of numbers. Then he goes back to watching, and then to contemplating how things were just over a year ago. Since the flood, one of his recurring fantasies is to track back to the days before it, remembering what they'd been eating, talking about, who had visited them, what were their plans for Christmas. The flood hit a week before Christmas Day. Memories haunt him, of the tree they'd put up, choked with lights, the presents under it. Claire had always loved Christmas lights; she bought more every year. He and Océan had decorated the tree. Claire had made soupies. His favourite thing is to let himself be in that time just before his old life ended.

*

On the horizon, lights have appeared. He's had his eyes on the boat for a while, is aware that it's been advancing closer and closer. Some kind of tanker, most likely. He goes to the saloon and retrieves the VHF radio and decides to wait. The tanker is port side, far off, well spotted, nothing to think about for now. He peeks inside the cabin; the dog has climbed up onto the saloon berth to be with the child and Océan has moved round to give the dog space. They're both snoring lightly. When he looks back at the lights, he realises something isn't right. He squints into the night. *Shit.* It's hard to tell, but then, it dawns on him . . . the boat is much closer than he thought, maybe just one mile off their bow.

He switches on the VHF. He speaks into it, impressed that his voice sounds authoritative.

Hello out there, this is the vessel *Romany*.

A crackle.

He waits.

Hello, this is the vessel *Romany*. You are a mile off our bow. Over.

Nothing. The sea is black and so is the sky. All of a sudden he is seized by a hallucination, the tanker lurching through the dark.

Nothing. *Shit.*

Hello, he says again.

Hello, comes a voice. This is the vessel *Santa Clara B*.

Good evening, Gavin replies. His heart is beating faster but his voice is calm. Just checking you've seen us.

Affirmative, comes a male voice which could be Spanish or Russian.

Thank you, he says. Goodnight. Over.

Over, replies the voice.

He is not alone on this rippling carpet. There are thousands of boats out there, other skippers, other captains, Spanish, Russian, German, Trinidadian. Most have radars, radios. The boats are not marauding about at sea, unmanned. All he needs to do is keep himself sharp as cut crystal. Crystal sharp for another ten hours.

*

The sun rises in the east. The clouds behind him are pink again; pink at sunset and pink at sunrise. The sun's appearance and demise always pinkens the skies, as though melting its orange blood all around itself. The sea is silver-blue, white caps are scattered here and there. There's not a thing in sight, just acres of lazily undulating blue, acres of midnight sea, a waterscape, a *champs de l'eau*, and it offers infinite possibilities for life or death. Already the sea is working her charms, tampering with his judgement. Throw yourself overboard, she whispers – why not? Or, take good care of yourself, and I will show you my best dress. The sea makes him feel lonely and yet so very much himself; she makes him gather himself up, a self which has vanished some time ago into the element of air. Overnight, the fluid in his veins is catching up with the fluid and the rhythms of the sea; he feels like the sea appears, placid, powerful.

It is morning, a new day. They have successfully

escaped. They are surrounded by an expanse of ocean and the blue feels huge and it is moving gently up and down in a way that looks like it's breathing. Instantly, the sight is sobering, offering him the perspective he so craved; all this sea, *thank God*, he whispers. Thank God he came out here. He senses movement in the cabin and Océan appears, still half in her sleeping bag.

Good morning, mermaid, he says.

She is sleep-eyed and her hair is stiff and messed up around her head. Can I be up there with you?

Of course.

She comes up and arranges herself in her sleeping bag on the bench. Her head rests on her life vest which she has brought with her. She snoozes and he says a silent prayer to his wife that he will take care of her, that she will come to no harm. They are slipping away; they are going for a sail, enjoying the mystical vibrations of a moon bath, that's all.

He yawns. He's tired, but not as tired as he expected. He managed two short naps in the night, half an hour each time. Only one other boat appeared, another tanker, far off. The GPS showed up lines of explosives, deep down on the sea floor, more of a worry to fishermen with nets. Music, coffee, an e-book on his iPod helped him through. Anything to keep awake. He thinks of the adventures he could allow himself, now he's fled, the great oceans which lie ahead, the Pacific? Oh God – and there's a dream, there, an old one, which he's never acted upon. The dream emerges now and then, in the office, in the bath; it has visited him in the small hours since he was a younger man: that he will sail west out of Port of Spain, and then west again, and then south, take his time, voyage towards a small famous archipelago in the middle of nowhere. But how? How? Now that he's fat and older with bad hands. He knows it's all too soon to think about it. For now, he can manage one night alone.

CHAPTER FOUR

THE BAY OF SMALL APPLES

As Gavin heads towards land, he spots the trees along the coastline and notes that he'll have to watch both the child and the dog with the small apple fruit. Manzanillo Bay is a narrow cove on the north coast of Margarita. Sandy beach, turquoise waters, and a small fleet of fishermen's pirogues moored together. '*Manzana*', he knows enough Spanish to translate this word: apple. The bay must be named after the tree with small apples; its green fruit full of a toxic lethal acid which can dissolve the gullet. Trinidadians know them well and call the trees by a more creole name, *machineel*.

It's 6 a.m. when they arrive. The bay feels active, lived-in, a safe home to the fishermen's boats. Perfect spot for a day or two. Margarita, a woman's name. On a map it is La Isla Margarita, an island which belongs to Venezuela. It is famous for pirates and pearls, for mangrove swamps and windsurfing and duty free shopping, also for the Virgin de Valle, a particular type of Virgin Mary who performs miracles and to whom locals bring gold.

Océan and the dog sit in the cockpit, much recovered. He feels a sense of pride and relief; he's brought what's left of his family safely over the sea. He knew he could do it, had faith he could and yet also, he didn't know. They'll drop anchor and go for a dip. Then they'll eat a fine breakfast to celebrate. Mooring single-handedly isn't easy. There's a routine to be practised as he checks the depth sounder and sees that yes, the bay is deep enough for *Romany*'s keel.

He furls the jib and drops the mainsail, quickly tying it with bungees. From the hatch he pulls out the anchor, prepares it on deck. He motors slowly to a space between the pirogues, then throws it off the boat. The anchor snags nicely as he reverses; then he switches the engine off.

He hugs his daughter tight. Right, Starbuck, he says. Time to lower the plank.

Plank?

Time for a swim.

Now?

Why not? A swim, then breakfast.

He opens the bench locker and removes the ramp he built years ago for Suzy, an ingenious device. She loves to swim, but hoisting her up and down the stern ladder became inconvenient and tiring. She is a heavy dog, elderly now. So he built her a ramp, from which she could easily trot into and out of the water.

This is Suzy's ramp, he says, holding it for Océan to

see. It's a long plank with ridges and a hinged wooden ledge at one end to hook onto the boat.

The dog barks and wags her tail.

We're going for a swim, he says to the dog.

He realises it's Wednesday morning. He hasn't showered since Monday. Briefly, he remembers what morning is supposed to mean, the office, Petula, his secretary. But this is only a flash, a small twinge of dread, *what have I done*? For now, he won't think of it. His phone is at the bottom of the sea. No one will be getting in touch. He latches the ramp to the stern and before he can turn round to beckon the dog, she is already there, at the top.

Good girl. He strokes her nose.

Océan is thrilled. Can I use it too?

Of course. Grab a noodle.

She goes down to the saloon and comes up with the long pink piece of floaty foam.

The dog trots down the ramp and leaps, landing square, like a coffee table, all four legs straight. She makes a noisy splash.

Océan runs down the ramp with her noodle. She is wearing a puke-stained vest and frilly underpants. She jumps into the sea with a shriek and lands near the dog. Suzy paddles round her in circles. Gavin hooks the stern ladder over the side, peels off his T-shirt and steps over the rails; he covers his face with his hands as he falls backwards into the sea.

When he comes up for air, the child and dog are paddling towards him, both smiling.

Come on then, he says, let's make a reconnaissance. He swims slowly so they can keep up and imagines they must make a curious party to anyone passing by. They paddle in and around the small wooden boats, pirogues, the same as in Trinidad. They are called names like *Don Philippe* and *Don Genaro* and *Santa Maria*, and he knows that any moment now the fishermen will be here to take their boats out. They paddle to the shore and sit in a line on the sand and watch the waves slide in and out. Océan throws the noodle for the dog and Suzy swims after it; she barks and gargles seawater as she tries to hold it in her mouth but it escapes. And then, by accident, she has it wedged under her elbows, and a queer look of satisfaction appears in her dark eyes as she floats, all of a sudden buoyant. Océan laughs.

Daddy?

Yes, dou dou?

Will it be Christmas soon?

Yes.

How long?

In about four weeks.

Will we still be on holiday then?

Yes, I expect so.

Can we have a Christmas tree?

I'll try to find a small one.

Last year we had the flood, not Christmas, didn't we?

Yes.

She stares at the sea and bunches up her lips in a look which betrays both consternation and resignation.

Okay, then, she says.

For weeks after the flood she screamed. The psychotherapist said she was suffering from post-traumatic stress. *What?* he'd said, isn't that something only suffered by men? You know, men coming back from *war*, or something like that? No, said the psychotherapist, it can happen to anyone who has been shocked to the core. Oh, he'd replied. Océan saw the psychotherapist once a week for months; gradually she improved. She became less 'hyper-vigilant'. For a while, she was fine, in the dry season. But it all came back when the rains returned. He doesn't know how she is any more, his little girl. He winks at her and she winks back.

Come on, mermaid; let's go back to the boat. What would you like for breakfast?

Froot Loops.

Me too, come on.

He piggybacks Océan as he swims and the dog paddles with them, chasing and snapping at the noodle. When they get back to the boat the child and the dog scoot up the ramp. He hoists himself from the water, up the ladder, conscious of the struggle to get back on board.

*

Around midday, he inflates the dinghy and lowers it into the water. Some of the fishermen arrived soon after they ate breakfast and left to go fishing, each giving him a cursory nod. Many of the pirogues are still empty. He rows towards the shore and ties the dinghy to a jetty, then realises that he has no way of knowing if it will be there on his return. He considers leaving Suzy there to keep watch but decides she will be more useful with them.

On shore, Océan holds Suzy by the lead. They are a well-matched team. The child is wide-eyed, she skips about, the dog is patient and astute. He keeps an eye on them both as they walk along the pavement in the heat. Clouds in the sky, grey and smoky.

They come to a spot just along from the bay called Playa del Agua, a long strip of sandy beach fringed with palms and restaurants, a place for tourists; it reminds him of Maracas Bay in Trinidad. In one of the nicer bars they stop and sit at a table. He has promised Océan lunch and then they will rent a car and drive about to see the mangrove swamps and the Virgin. There is a plasma screen behind the bar, on loud, and impossible to ignore. The barman is watching and seems entirely absorbed. Gavin watches the screen too, realising it's a scene of chaos, people living rough, in some kind of makeshift shelter. And then he sees Señor Hugo Rafael Chávez Frias, the President of Venezuela, arriving in their midst, sporting green army fatigues, a burly man, built like the South Americans, red-skinned, short and tough-looking.

Gavin becomes entranced, just like the barman, trans-lating the headlines and voiceover report. There have been floods in Venezuela, in fact heavy rain for weeks. Now people's homes have come tumbling down the hills, thirty-one are either dead or missing. Señor Chávez has pledged his private home and presidential palace to those displaced, vowed to build more houses. The people in the shelter throng around him, they press babies into his arms for him to kiss. He begins to sing happy birthday to a child which has been thrust towards him.

Cumpleaños feliz, cumpleaños feliz. He holds a microphone to his lips and croons. It is mesmerising to watch. Gavin feels loath to interrupt the barman, but he coughs, and asks if he speaks English.

A little, says the barman.

What's going on?

Bad rain, he explains. Chávez says he will help, but instead he sings. I am very worried for my family in Venezuela.

Oh, that's awful, says Gavin, feeling a clawing in his stomach. He really is concerned, and yet he doesn't want to talk about floods.

My family are stuck, in a village, on a hill, either side two rivers, now very full. They cannot get out. They have no water, no electricity, and now no telephone. I am scared.

I'm so sorry; Gavin manages to squeeze the words out of his throat. The barman is about twenty-five, toothsome, with long eyelashes.

Would you like to order a drink?

Oh, yes, please, he says. Two Cokes.

Sorry, we don't serve Coke.

Oh.

Imperialist.

Really? Gavin is so taken aback, he laughs.

Coca Cola, very bad. American, says the barman. How about Pepsi?

But, Pepsi, that's American too!

Not as bad as Coke, says the barman.

Okay, two Pepsis.

And to eat?

Fish, catch of the day.

Wahoo?

Yes, and fries. And a bottle of water. Can I have a bowl for my dog?

The barman nods, writes down the order and hands him a bowl from the shelf behind. He goes back to watching Chávez, who is now speechmaking and waving his fist. The people in the shelter are nodding, rapt.

He hands the Pepsi to Océan who drinks half of it down in one go through a straw.

Daddy, what's on TV?

Frank Sinatra.

Who's he?

A singer. And some kind of communist. Now don't drink your Pepsi all at once, comrade.

Comrade? What's that?

A friend.

A special friend?

Sort of.

When can we go see the Virgin, Dad?

He'd told her all about the famous Virgin de Valle over breakfast, the one who protects sailors from harm.

Soon.

Is she a comrade?

No.

What is she then?

A holy woman, the mother of Jesus.

Comrade Jesus?

No. Just Jesus.

What's a virgin, Dad?

I'm not going to answer that now. He flashes her a look which says *really, not now*.

She rolls her eyes.

He pours water for the dog and sits down. He finds he actually feels queasy, gripped by an overwhelming sense of guilt. The sight of those houses, falling down the cliff. Brown water all churned up; it stirs his stomach up, makes him feel a little blind with heat. He remembers Alphonse, wonders what it would be like to be a man who owns his own business.

*

Along the beach there are shops selling day trips and excursions and shops renting cars and there's a man standing outside Wonder Tours who stops them in their tracks.

Hi, he smiles. Can I give you some *information*? He says the last word with a smirk, like he has some kind of secret to share.

The man is wearing a Hawaiian shirt and shades and

his hair is greased into an American D.A. He is in his late fifties, tanned to the colour of molasses. A wart next to his nose dances as he talks.

Maybe, Gavin says, fascinated.

You want to go on a tour?

I was thinking of hiring a car.

You don't wanna go on a Jeep safari?

No.

You sure? Jeep safari is good, lots of fun, open top, loud music. Nice girls.

I'm too old. And I have my child and my dog.

How long you staying?

Not long.

What hotel?

I'm on my boat.

What about snorkelling? Try a snorkelling tour.

I can snorkel off my boat.

Where are you moored?

Manzanillo Bay.

You gotta watch it there.

I will. And then, he doesn't know why, but he tells him. I ran away. I'm on the run. I sailed here from Trinidad. I left my job.

The tour guide lifts his shades up onto his head. He grins at Gavin in genuine appreciation, half conman, half good man. His accent and manner are Las Vegas meets Caracas meets the New Age.

Wow, man. My name is Sonny, he says, extending his hand. Where you going next?

Bonaire.

Not Los Roques?

Where's that?

Paradise, man, on the way. You gotta stop there. Make a good investment in your soul, be in nature, you know what I mean?

I think so.

What happened to you, man? He smiles down at Océan, who's gone silent. The only reason why he's talking to this Sonny is because Suzy seems to be grinning up at him, liking him.

I had to leave town, 'be in nature', something like that.

Nice kid.

Thanks.

Listen; go to Los Roques, man. I am a feminist, you know. I believe in the feminine, in Mother Earth.

He laughs at his joke, but Gavin doesn't.

Go to Los Roques and you will replenish your spirits. They are islands, between here and Bonaire. Beautiful. An archipelago.

Really? Vaguely, yes, he's heard of Los Roques, a tiny world, just north of Caracas. He can remember sailors in Trinidad mentioning these islands, but didn't think of them when fleeing his old life. OK, he nods, maybe I'll go.

See the world, man, says Sonny, and with that his mobile sings a Beyoncé song. Gavin steps away and into the car rental shop with Océan and the dog.

*

They drive along the north coast of the island, heading west. They find Restinga Bay, miles of deserted beach; the ocean that meets the shore is rough. They stop when they reach the swamp and board a tiny colourful wooden boat and speed out into the maze of green water. In the swamp there are waterways and passages fashioned into the tangled mangrove roots well known to the boat driver; signs are nailed to the mangrove trees, with phrases like *TUNEL DE AMORE* and *CANAL DEL BESO* and *CANAL MI DULCE AMOR*. These are clearly canals for lovers, and briefly he is visited by a swell of nostalgia, a swirl in his heart, for Claire, for his lost lover, his mate. *I'm not single*, he wants to shout.

They see gnarled red mangrove trees; they see blue crabs swimming sideways in the water, herons and even pink ibis flying overhead. There are swamps in Trinidad too, just like this; but in Trinidad he rarely stops to be in nature; those green hills all around his home. Nature is always around him and yet he doesn't use his eyes to see her. *Make an investment*, he hears Sonny say.

They drive to the church where the Virgin de Valle is guarded. It is a vanilla-yellow church, a mini cathedral, with tiered spires pointing to the sky. In the church there are pews and high windows and the scent of sandalwood.

Océan stops dead and points.

Is that *her*?

Ahead, to the right of the altar, there is a woman wearing floor length white robes, a white veil. She is standing in a glass box.

I guess that must be her.

Océan's face lights up with reverence. Her eyes are wide and she clutches her hands to her heart, as if she might faint.

He looks at the woman in the box. She is some kind of mannequin, a plaster of Paris statue. She resembles a huge Barbie-doll bride, which must be the cause of his daughter's fervour.

Shall we go take a look?

Océan nods.

They go towards the doll in the glass box.

Now don't touch the glass, he advises.

Océan is enchanted. He wishes she wasn't; it's embarrassing. The Virgin is wearing a bulbous golden crown; her face is pale, her eyes blue, her expression earnest. The Virgin's hands are pressed together in prayer, or even in Namaste, like in India. She is Our Lady of This Valley, the patron saint of eastern Venezuela, patron saint of sailors.

Is she alive? asks Océan.

Of course not!

You sure?

Sweetie, she isn't . . . real, you know. Like a human.

She's so pretty.

Yes.

Suzy isn't the least bit interested. Gavin fears she may cock her leg in the church. He holds her close and pats her.

Sit, he says.

Daddy, can you lift me up?

He picks her up and balances her on his hip so she can get close to the statue of the Immaculate Virgin, the Mother of Christ.

Océan puts her face an inch from the glass and stares at the statue. She jams her thumb in her mouth. He feels a flush of awkwardness, as if he should say something. But Océan doesn't ask the questions he fears. She just peers long and hard and sadly at the pretty young mother trapped behind the glass.

He guides her towards another room, a small shrine or museum. In it are glass cabinets with trinkets on display. According to legend, a sailor lost his leg in an accident diving for pearls. His wife prayed to the Virgin de Valle for his swift recovery and it worked; he did recover well enough and quickly. He promised that he'd donate the next pearl he found to the Virgin, and, when he returned to sea, the first oyster he opened contained a pearl, in the shape of a leg. Ever since, people from far and wide have come to lay trinkets at her feet, in gratitude for her miracles.

They gaze at hundreds of tiny gold objects: cars, hearts, cats, dogs, soldiers, boats, feet, heads. Océan stops at the tiny houses.

We should put something here too, Dad.

Why?

The Virgin gave us back our house, didn't she?

Uh, well . . .

Can we bring her a house to say thank you?

I'd rather not.

She looks crestfallen and he tries to ignore her.

In the gift shop next to the church there are gold houses for sale, fifteen Bolivars each, nine carat. But he cannot bear his daughter's stoic face; her eyes have turned glassy and vacant. And so he buys a gold house for the Virgin and gives it to his daughter and she lays it in the cabinet too, amongst the others.

*

At five, they return the car and walk back to the bay of small apples: he realises that they haven't yet cleared immigration. Not good: he makes a mental note to do this first thing tomorrow. The dinghy is still tied to the jetty and he wonders if the Virgin has been looking after it. He unhooks Suzy from her lead and she noses him under the elbow and mumbles.

What do you want, eh? He strokes her long nose and she puts the black wet tip in his hands and snorts. They row out towards the boat. The skies are gathering to pink again. It didn't rain. It was a long hot day in Margarita. Tomorrow he will check over the boat more thoroughly.

As they draw closer to *Romany*, his heart goes cold. A pirogue is tied up alongside his boat.

Shit, he whispers.

He pulls harder on the oars for a few strokes and the dinghy glides towards the stern of his yacht. He loops the rope around the stern cleat. The pirogue is battered, its paintwork corroded and scarred. It is empty. He turns to

Océan and says in a low voice, just sit right here and be very quiet.

She nods.

He picks Suzy up and lifts her onto the stern, lashing the lead to the rails. The stern ladder is lying by the rail side and he quietly hooks it on, climbing up. He unleashes the dog and stands on the edge of the cockpit and his stomach plummets. The hatch is open, the lock broken. In the saloon he can make out the shadow of a man. But the man either hasn't heard him or isn't bothered he's returned.

He can feel the dog tense and keeps her held tight.

Ayyyyyy, he shouts, in warning. He stands with his feet planted either side of the tiller; the cockpit isn't big, maybe four feet between himself and the hatch. He will give the man a chance, let him go.

But the man doesn't respond.

Hello, he shouts in a gruff voice.

Suzy growls.

This brings the man to the entrance of the hatch. He is young, with bleached yellow dreads; he is wearing only a pair of red Adidas shorts and there is a weapon thrust into the waistband, a cutlass. The man is calm and unperturbed by their presence; he looks at the dog but doesn't register concern, not even with this old dog that could still bite his face off.

What de *frig* you doin on my mih boat, Gavin says. He is surprised at himself, at his show of aggression.

The man stares.

It's then he notices that one eye is missing. The left eye

is clouded and blurred, just a smudge remaining. The feller is a badjohn, a bad fuckin one-eyed tief.

Get off mih friggin boat, man, Gavin warns again.

The man is four feet away. He smiles and goes for his cutlass and that's when Gavin lets go of Suzy's collar and the dog leaps. All of a sudden she is a ferocious white blizzard of teeth and bestial sounds. The badjohn yelps as she crunches her jaws around his forearm, the cutlass clatters to the floor.

The badjohn begins to bawl something in Spanish and shakes his arm, trying to beat the dog off, but she is clamped to him and will bite through his arm before letting go. Suzy must weigh over forty pounds, hanging off his arm like a small devil. He begins to smack the dog against the frame of the hatch to get her off.

Nooo, Gavin shouts.

The young man is wiry and strong, not scared of the dog and it's then, watching him fight Suzy off, that Gavin realises, with a mixture of despair and fear for his life – for his daughter's life – that he won't be so easily removed. The man is a pirate, come to take what he likes. This is a fair fight. Badjohn versus bad dog. He should be calling the dog off, instead he orders her to fight.

Get him down, he shouts and Suzy's growls become hideous. There's blood all over her long nose. She's like a shark, her white fur now pink and frothy and she will bite off the hand of this man unless he stops with his shaking.

The man is shouting at the dog, and beating her. He bends and goes for the cutlass on the floor. He grabs it and lifts his free hand as if to strike the dog with the knife and it's only then that Gavin freaks. He hurls all his weight at the man, seizing him by the other forearm so the cutlass falls again and now the badjohn has a fierce dog and a crazy fat man on him. Sheer bloodlust surges and even though he too could kill he shouts an order to Suzy, *drop it*.

She obeys, unclamping her jaws. She sits, heaving and slavering blood, at any moment ready for more. The man's arm is badly lacerated. Gavin lets him go. The younger man is injured, heaving with excitement.

Get off mih friggin boat, man, Gavin says, steel in his voice.

But the man doesn't understand English. He only focuses a malevolent glare on him with his one good eye. The man isn't going nowhere. The man lookin at him like he's a fool and not dangerous either.

Jesus Christ, Gavin whispers, half to himself, incredulous at this man: younger, half his age, twice his resilience.

Gavin pulls back his right arm, balls his fist and punches the man hard in the face, *smack*. It's like hitting a breezeblock and it hurts his hand.

The badjohn doesn't go down or crumple. He stands there, utterly dumb, as though the punch has only stunned him. It will take a lot more to get him down, this island man, made from rum and oil.

The badjohn scowls. Gavin hits him again, an artless motherfucker of a punch, a wallop. *Smack.* This punch splits open his top lip. Only then does the man concede defeat.

Coño de tu madre, he snarls, holding his head in his hands and clambering for the rails of the yacht, falling into his pirogue.

The dog growls and barks and Gavin watches the man's every movement as he fumbles for the key in the engine and starts the motor, still holding his face. The injured man throws off the lines and roars away towards the next bay. But from the look in his eyes, the badjohn doesn't seem the least bit hurt or frightened or sorry. One of these frigging pirates he's heard so much about.

Océan has been sitting quietly in the dinghy all the while. She has heard everything, seen nothing. He clambers down to her, shaking, his fist throbbing. He sits down in the dinghy and she gives him a look he cannot dodge, a child's bewildered look. He wraps her in his arms and says, it was nothing, my mermaid, just a man, just a man who came to visit while we were out.

CHAPTER FIVE

FISH THAT CAN FLY

The sea is calm but his mind is busy, busy with it all. He can't stop thinking of the singing communist. Chávez. The dictator has been on his mind all morning. And those people with their houses bobbing in brown water. *Venezuela rainin all now*. Chávez soothing his citizens, like a father would soothe his children, these father-leaders so common in the Caribbean. Good man or bad man? Just like Sonny from Wonder Tours, hard to tell entirely. Chávez rose from poverty, educated himself in leftist revolutionary politics. He hated George 'Dubya' Bush. He is a man opposed to Republican America, is outspoken in his hatred of capitalism. He has set up a system of co-ops in Venezuela, free health care. Once, when a reporter thrust a mike into his face, Chávez asked whom he worked for.

Fox News, the reporter replied.

Ha, those stupid people at Fox News, Chávez laughed

in his face. The reporter withered. It was funny at the time. He even seemed to outtalk the cool Stephen Sackur on a BBC HARDTalk interview, mostly because he knew the history and politics of the north of the world as well as the south.

Thirty-one now dead or missing in a flood in Venezuela. When *his* home was flooded a year ago in Trinidad, scores of people lost their homes; it didn't even make a line of international news because the north doesn't care about floods in the southern hemisphere. But Chávez cares about the south with his Bank of the South and his commitment to South America – and yet he also silences his citizens, doesn't tolerate opposition. Hard to know who to care about; hard to know if anyone ever gets it right. Good man, bad man, who cares?

His hand throbs. It's bruised black and purple around the knuckles and he has split open more welts in his hands. He has bound it in a J cloth under one of his gloves. No fun washing blood off the dog's nose in front of Océan. She didn't ask questions, she simply went to sleep with Grover. Now it's dark again and he worries if he should have set sail so quickly. He panicked, like he did in Trinidad; he sailed off. Easy to do. Easy to vanish like that when you own a boat. Remove yourself. But she disappeared first, his wife. Escape is a selfish act, but sometimes necessary, to hide oneself in order to survive.

*

Night watch. Handfuls of Patsy's channa for dinner, mugs of black coffee to keep awake. This time his eyelids are heavy and the immense sea lies around him, so soft. How nice it would be to fall asleep into it, into the calm loving arms of the sea, now so hushed. *Jump,* she whispers; you'll find yourself. *Jump* and meet yourself, come lie in my bed. How he loved the sea as a younger man; the sea was his first mistress, his first woman. She kept him from marrying for a long time. He would rather have the sea, this canny boat, than human love, the love of a real woman. The sea loved him, kept him for herself. The sea offered him her adventures, and her surprises. His body is covered with small scars, wounds from his love affair with the sea: where a man o' war lashed its tentacles around his legs, where a kingfish rib bone pierced his hand, where fire coral burnt his chest, where a tarpon almost took his finger off.

Now her curves undulate; she makes muffled intimate sounds. How simple it would be to shut his eyes and fall into a profound sleep, oh, *how he needs to sleep*, but what a mistake that would be. His boat is like a pod, or a small womb. His child and dog are curled up asleep in this womb-ship, around them a protective fluid, an aqueous solution. In this boat they are safe – and yet he is awed, on edge. The sea is black, massive; there are creatures living in it; winds which can spring up at any time.

What of the man who owned *Romany* before him? Was he so easily lulled? Did the boat pitch – did he fall over the rails, into the bewitching sea? The sea which is all-absorbing; it will take everything. Did he die in the arms of his beloved? Or, like him, did he have good reason to flee, leave town? Perhaps *Romany*'s previous owner had some kind of death wish, maybe he went to sea to jump. Or perhaps he lost himself, got all confused, *it is the mercy*. Like Donald Crowhurst, did he leap or trip and be done with it? And is this skipper still up there, by the port side of the bow; has he always been there?

*

In the morning, the sun is huge behind them. It hovers above the horizon like a fierce eye. Océan wakes up and sits with him, gazing at it through her Snoopy sunglasses.

You okay? he asks.

She nods but he can see there's something already on her mind. She's been turning something over in her sleep. The pirate?

That man, she says.

Yes.

He wasn't a comrade, was he?

No.

What was he, then, Dad?

A pirate.

Like Captain Ahab?

No. Ahab was a whaler. He didn't steal. He just killed whales.

The bad man didn't have one leg, then?

No. But he did have only one eye.

She scrunches up her nose. She shuts one eye.

Pirates have parrots sometimes, don't they, Dad?

Yes, that too, or a monkey.

She laughs.

Pirates are the opposite of friends, he says.

She nods.

Suzy will protect us, won't she, Dad?

Yup.

She could bite off a leg or an arm, just like the white whale.

Maybe she could.

Daddy. She looks out at blue earth-sea all around. Are we going to be okay?

Yes, we're going to be fine.

It's weird out here.

I know.

The land has turned blue, Dad. Everything is blue.

We'll be on an island again tomorrow. You'll see green then too.

She nods carefully. Still, she's not sure of it all, her own kidnapping.

Are you hungry?

Yes.

Sit here, then, with the tiller, keep an eye out for pirate ships. I'll make breakfast.

She puts her tiny hand on the tiller, which is still rigged up for auto-steering, and sits like a small blind man behind her mirror shades.

Can you see anything in those things? he asks.

She nods. She looks different already. Suntanned and dirty, her hair is all stringy.

In the saloon, he puts the kettle on. The small space smells of dog and is covered in white hairs, already a chaos of clothes and charts and sleeping bags. Suzy looks sheepish and friendly.

Good morning, he says to her. She yawns and wags her tail. The pirate seems long forgotten.

He makes scrambled eggs and fried bread and finds some ham in the fridge cooler, all the while rocking around with the boat. When the gas rings are on, it's even hotter down there; sweat drips as he cooks.

Keep an eye out for dolphins, he calls up to Océan.

He puts a bowl of water on the floor for Suzy with some dog chow and she climbs from the berth and wolfs it down.

They eat breakfast in the cockpit, balancing plates on the benches. Orange juice, tea, ham, scrambled eggs on toast. Flying fish speed over the tops of the waves, like silver bullets.

Wowee, says Océan.

The fish zoom past in twos or threes and then a whole shoal of flying fish, like someone has shot a quiver of arrows up from the seabed into the sky. Forty or so fisharrows rise and arc through the air. Two land on deck. *Bap*. They flip and beat about. Océan squeals. Suzy barks.

Nobody panic, he says.

He puts down his plate and climbs up onto the foredeck. He picks the small fish up carefully with his fingers, spreading them across his open palm. They're like silver angels, their gauze wings fanned out. Their gills rise in and out quickly; they look like they've fallen from a Christmas tree. He takes them back to show his daughter.

You can touch them, he says. Océan touches the scaly skin of one and pulls her finger away fast. Suzy gets in close too and he allows her to sniff one carefully.

They are fish that can fly, he says. *See*, they have wings.

She nods. But isn't that crazy, Dad. To make wings on a fish?

That's nature, dou dou. Nature makes some birds which can't fly at all, and some beasts which can fly and swim easily. Nature makes odd creatures, some which can seem quite *un*natural.

Like a white whale?

Yes.

Suzy whines in a motherly way, seeing the fish are in some kind of distress. Okay, okay, he says. He throws them back into the sea.

They go back to their breakfast. All around them is glittering sea, and crazy speeding fish and the sun like a golden planet behind them. They don't speak as they chew. It's a slow breakfast; they both help themselves to more eggs, more ham. The sea has given them an appetite and he is catching up with himself after their hasty exit from Margarita. Quickly, he has come to feel restored and okay. *Romany* is handling well, her mainsail is full; they are skimming along at six knots. He remembers again what to do, how to be on a boat. There are no other vessels about, nothing else heading west, on these following seas. They have the whole Caribbean Sea to themselves.

Right then, he says, when they are finished. You stink. Time for a bath.

Nooo, she wails.

Yes.

He brings up two large Pepsi bottles of fresh water, some soap and shampoo. All of them are dirty; they've been wearing the same clothes for days. He clips Océan into the safety harness and stands her up above the tiller. She closes her eyes as he pours water over her head; it covers her in a transparent cloak and runs to the cockpit floor. A tenderness washes over him as he sees her there, eyes closed, trusting him entirely. His little girl.

He squirts shampoo and lathers her hair, soaps her up until she's like a poodle, all froth and foam.

Now close your eyes again, he says, as he pours water over her and the foam and soap runs away. He rinses her down again and then wraps her in a towel and she sits on the bench, her back against the cabin, much cleaner.

Suzy looks a little forlorn and he grabs her by the collar, hoisting her onto the stern. He's trained her so she doesn't crap on her own, not unless it's an emergency; she needs to let him know. In a routine they've performed many times before, she squats and defecates in a neat brown castle onto the aft deck. A small private emotion passes between them; she is allowing him to watch. She is a polite old woman of a dog and would rather he didn't. He picks the turd off the deck with a scrap of newspaper and tosses it into the sea. Sorry, he says to her and laughs. Well done.

He washes himself too. He washes his matted hair, scratches his scalp and in doing so feels like he's scratching his soul. He removes his T-shirt, finds another one in the duffel bag which he still hasn't unpacked. He rubs cream into his stiff sore hands and wishes for a magic cure. The flood flipped a switch inside him, issued a freak command to his body to attack itself. He was also shocked to the core by the giant brown wave which swept through his home, and now he cannot flip the switch back. His hands are peeling themselves, his skin moulting. His body is sloughing himself from himself.

When they arrange themselves in the cockpit again, they are clean and fed and have the wind behind them. Suzy's black nose glistens and twitches with the salt air. Océan gazes towards the horizon like some eccentric magus from behind her Snoopy sunglasses.

*

The morning's sail is a quiet affair. The wind drops and he shakes out the reef in the mainsail. A small concern if the wind dropped some more; to be flapping about in acres of open water would be unnerving for sure.

More dolphins appear, a small pod. They play chicken with the bow as it ploughs the water, diving under the nose of the boat, reappearing on the other side, keeping pace; they're welcome companions. Like with the Virgin,

Océan goes dreamy watching them. And so does he. They bring a feeling that all will be well. The mere sight of them plumps the skin and enlivens the senses. It's their lines, their shape, their smooth skin; the dolphins are like young naked women.

He bends over the lifeline with a bucket and lets it drag in the sea. Even this feels like a risk; one jolt and over he could go. But he doesn't go over; everything about him is remembering how to exist on this boat. He is heavy as an ox and yet he is, somewhere, the young man that sailed *Romany* single-handed many times.

In the cockpit, he washes up the breakfast things in the bucket and Océan helps. In his logbook he writes down a row of numbers which keep track of their progress. In the column for remarks he writes down a fragment of a poem he has committed to memory.

> *So let us rather not be sure of anything,*
> *Beside ourselves and only that, so*
> *Miraculous beings come running to help.*
> 'Zero Circle', Rumi

He's not sure of anything. Right now, he'd like to be led. Helped. He has escaped to the only place of wisdom he knows, the sea. Last night they sailed past the island of La Blanquilla, a green hump in the dark water port side. The sea is flat this morning, though he spots some rain dancing from low grey clouds far ahead and worries for the child. The GPS is working, thank God. Océan and the dog are no longer seasick but that could change at any time. They are heading for an archipelago of islands he barely knew existed, Los Roques. The rocks. Hours of peace out here in the Caribbean Sea, no office, no pink house. Tiny fish with wings, miraculous beings.

Clouds gather around them after lunch. The small boat sails beneath the curtain of rain. A wind picks up and a colder rain begins to fall. Océan stares upwards, but doesn't react at first. He climbs into the saloon for foul-weather jackets. He zips her into a cagoule and fixes her harness back on. The sea gets choppy again, though not like the chaotic pitching in the Dragon's Mouth. He reefs down the main. Rain and grey sea and more to come. Wind from behind, eighteen to twenty knots and *Romany* moves along as best she can. The dog lies down in the cockpit and bends her head against the onslaught.

Océan opens her mouth and wails. The blue hood of her cagoule has come down over her eyes. But he isn't frightened of her crying out here, let her cry. The boat is moving with sure intent, the wind is pushing them along and the sea is so up and down; the rain is pelting them. Now is a good time to cry.

She wails from under her blue jacket, sits rigid on the cockpit bench.

Mummmmyyyy, she wails. I want my *mummmmy*.

But his heart doesn't break for her this time. She'll be okay.

For some reason he feels he is sailing towards his wife,

not away from her. He can see her clearly, see them all, in a new time. This is a squall, not a storm.

He lets Océan bawl out her lungs.

We are on our way to find your mother, he says.

But she only wails and spittle drools from her mouth. A whole year without her mother and she's had enough.

Romany sits in the sea like a battleship, solid as iron, and yet she is alert to what she is doing, pushing through the waves, her sail like a wing. Who designed this boat? Some old sailor who knew what he was doing. Old and seawise, she rides and surfs the swells with a steady grace. The sea must be met, on her terms.

They sail out of one squall and into another and then it's quiet again. The sun shines down and dries them off. He puts on his straw hat and it offers the shade of a palm tree.

He laughs at Océan. She's fallen asleep in her cagoule, her cheeks pink from all the emotion. He covers her face to keep it from the sun. Suzy gets up onto the bench seat too and together they snooze in the shade of the mainsail; the sun is hammering down.

So, he says to the sea. You're happy again.

The sea flattens out into a desert of blue. The wind drops almost completely – this is more worrying. Flat sea, dead calm. Up ahead, there is an island showing up on GPS, an island called Isla Orchilla, well-known for its pink sand, an island protected by Venezuela. There's a military base on the island used only by Chávez and some top-ranking officials, though people can visit these days, once they have a permit. Already he didn't clear in or out of Margarita. He imagines lots of cruising sailors do this, now and then; certainly it is common in the Grenadines for Trinidadian sailors not to bother with all the paperwork, to island hop up the chain. Never mind about the old customs and immigration; he will sail straight past lsla Orchilla.

A tanker appears far off port side, travelling in the opposite direction. A tern dive-bombs for fish.

A large package appears, starboard off the bow. It is wrapped in white plastic and trussed up with twine. It is tangled up in the branches of a felled tree. As it passes, he sees that the package looks very suspicious indeed; in fact, if he's not mistaken, it looks exactly like a stray bundle of cocaine. Very possible it *is* a stray bundle of cocaine; they are out here in the Caribbean Sea. Could someone have dropped it from the back of a pirogue? It is so evidently illegal that he laughs at it and considers, for a split second, hauling it aboard. If it *is* cocaine gone astray, he will let several million US dollars float past. He keeps an eye on it, so that the tree doesn't get caught up around his rudder.

The package floats closer. It's only a few feet away from him.

Before he knows what he's doing, he has the boat hook in his hands. He makes a stab at the package and the hook snatches up the string. He yanks hard and the package comes up from the sea bleeding water; the tree branches come too but he knocks them away. The heavy white package dangles from the pole.

Jesus, he whispers.

Océan is suddenly awake and excited; the dog barks.

What is it, Daddy?

Gavin dumps the large white package on the cockpit floor.

I don't know, he says. The parcel is pudgy, like a bundle of clothes.

Suzy whines at it.

In the saloon he finds his Swiss Army knife and extracts the sturdiest blade.

Only one way to find out, he says.

He cuts the strings, then slices through the white outer casing. Underneath is thinner black plastic, the type of bag used for garbage. He slices through this to find thick wads of sodden newspaper, printed in Spanish. He cuts through the damp paper to discover a layer of silver foil. Ahhhh. He pokes at the foil and draws a line down it with the tip of the blade. White powder falls out.

Oh dear, he mutters. His heart whacks against his ribs.

Daddy, what is it?

It's white powder, sweetie. Like Mummy's. Talcum powder.

So much?

Yes.

In the sea?

He took cocaine once in his life, during his university days, in Canada. It was at a party. His roommates were cutting out lines on the kitchen counter top and asked him if he wanted one. He'd snorted the white powder up his nose with a ten-dollar note. Minutes later, he found himself charged up and talking, talking, talking a lot of rubbish to some girl who was also high. His dick shrunk to nothing; an acid flavour ran from his nose into his mouth. That was twenty-five years ago.

Yes, dou dou.

He licks his index finger, stabs it into the powder and puts his white-tipped finger to his lips.

Océan stares.

He sticks his tongue out and tastes the powder.

He grimaces. It is bitter, numbing his tongue instantly. Strong and bitter and chemical.

Help me, Jesus, he mutters. Several kilos of cocaine – as he'd imagined. Millions of US dollars on board his boat. He stabs his finger into the powder again and tastes a bit more. Holy Christ in heaven. Holy Virgin, help me now. Pure fucking cocaine, probably the purest, the whitest, the baddest, probably from Colombia.

Oh no, he says. He looks at his child, dumbstruck.

Océan sticks her tiny index finger in the powder.

NO! he shouts and grabs her finger. He slaps her wrist and wipes the cocaine from her fingertip.

Océan, you must NOT put this powder in your mouth.

Tears spring in her eyes. *Why?*

Because it's horrible. And dangerous.

She starts to cry.

Suzy comes forward and buries her wet black nose in the package and snoofs up the powder so that it sprays up into the air like sea spray.

No! he shouts again.

Suzy barks, happy, her nose dusted white.

NO, he says.

But in a fit of clownishness, she disobeys and dives down for more and stuffs her nose in the snug dent she has already made in the powder.

You *stupid* dog! He picks up the package whole. It's heavy; enough here to build himself a new life, enough for a business of his own, another home, a bigger boat, a private helicopter.

Neither of you are to come *near* this stuff. DO YOU UNDERSTAND?

Suzy barks and starts to make snuffling sounds, shaking her head and pawing at her nose.

Océan's eyes are huge and blue and lost; a surge of emotion visibly rushes up from her chest, engulfing her. She wails in the way he hasn't heard since they left Trinidad.

That crying will not help, he says. He stands there, clinging to his prize. What should he do with it? Sell it? Hand it in to the nearest port authority? Are there pirates nearby, looking for it; might there be some kind of black market reward, corrupt cops somewhere prepared to give him a cut? All these possibilities fly through his head, including the idea that he could get his arse shot, he could get killed by more pirates, worse pirates than the one he left behind in Margarita. He could leave his daughter orphaned, an only child, no family, Christ in heaven. He must get rid of this stuff. Hard drugs on his old boat.

He stands on the stern and balances the package on the rails and as he tears open the densely packed foil he makes a silent prayer and says sorry to God and all the fish that might die from the cocaine he now pours into the sea. I'm sorry, fish, he says. Sorry, fish.

The cocaine makes a white puff, like a tablet fizzing in a glass of water, then dissolves into the salty ocean.

He turns and looks at his child and dog. Océan is bloody with tears, angry with him. Why did he taste the powder when she wasn't allowed to? Suzy is coughing and waving her head.

*

Romany ploughs on, westwards. Things are happening to him that shouldn't be happening. Is he some kind of fool? Is he doing it all wrong? From nowhere, a terror clutches him: *this was very, very stupid*. He could get them all hurt. He was swept up in some kind of fantasy: dreams, islands ahead of him, worlds to explore. He overreacted. It was a bad Monday, that's all. They should go home, fly back when they reach the next port. His tiny boat in all this big sea. Badjohns, cocaine, what else is out there? His testicles have gone cold and shrivelled; he could sob now, bellow like a bull for his own foolishness. He has been desperate. *Do not panic*, he tells himself.

He will keep his head down from now on, obey the rules. Check in to immigration at every port, moor carefully, in less secluded spots. Only marinas from now on, wide bays with other yachts. He will not hoist suspicious-looking packages from the sea. Isla Orchilla is now not far off to port side. He imagines Hugo Chávez there, discussing the missing cocaine. He feels like an arse. He wonders if he should make one single call home when they get to Los Roques.

No. He will wait until he is far enough away, until everything is different, for this now seems to be the reason why he left. To be here, in this position, to be somewhere else; not the place he'd been before. He is fat. He is middle-aged and stupid, but that's all. He has left his hometown and gone off. He isn't going to go nuts. He isn't one of these madmen who take to the sea, who enter a race and never return, sail off forever, like that French man. He will not lose his reason aboard this old boat. There's wind in his hair, Caribbean sun on his face and this feels good. He will make some strong coffee and sit still with it all.

CHAPTER SIX

THE ROCKS

To the south, Los Roques is encircled by a wide skinny arc, an atoll of pale yellow sand which, on the chart, resembles a crooked smile. To the east it is guarded by a long running scar of a barrier reef. There's only one way to enter this small world, through a narrow mouth between land and reef, the Boca de Sebastopol. The small world behind the reef and the atoll is a tattoo of islands and sandbanks, cays and reefs. Los Roques is naturally protected and hidden, lying in the middle of the Caribbean Sea, exactly north of Caracas. It's a dot on the map, a speck on the sea, disguising itself from the world with its smile of sand.

He drops the mainsail, switches on the engine and motors through the mouth into a green and turquoise leopard print sea. From the deck the sea squirms. It is jumping with fish, long silvery shadows, and there is a flock of pelicans, a *flock*; fifty or so, swirling around overhead, diving altogether, turning on a sixpence mid-air to execute a group dive, rising up with their gullets full.

Suzy barks at them. She is up at the bow.

Where have we come to, Daddy? asks Océan.

This is an archipelago. He enunciates the word.

She registers no response. A long word, Greek. It means *chief sea*. It was the word the Greeks once used for the Aegean.

Even he is rather caught off-guard. The strait is long and slender and the sea below is so clear it seems shallow. When he looks down, he can see a vivid forest of reef. If he sticks to the middle, he'll be safe; but all of a sudden he is on edge. He's studied the charts, read the cruising guide, but this is like entering a maze.

It's like a secret place, he says. With many small islands inside. You'll see, you'll like it.

Does it have a Movie Town?

No, sweetie, this is more like a garden, not a town.

Mid-afternoon. The skies are reflecting sea reflecting sky reflecting sea; this world is so electric in its shades of blue that when he lowers his sunglasses, he has to squint deeply. He decides to head straight for the main island, Gran Roque, where there's food and fuel and other yachts. Customs.

On the northernmost island of Gran Roque there's a small town with sand streets and colourful cube-like houses, places for visitors to stay called posadas, and a square with two pizzerias and a bank and a few shops. Boutiques and a bakery and even a church with walls which open like wings to let in the turquoise world, and one of those overdressed Virgins surrounded by cut lilies. Pirogues are pulled up to the shore and there is a jetty crammed with small powerboats and an airstrip overrun with friendly pot hounds.

They roam the soft streets until they find the small air-conditioned office and he presents himself, for the first time in days, to a person who will account for their presence in the world. He hands over *Romany*'s papers, his passport, Océan's passport, papers to say Suzy has had her rabies shots; papers to say who he is, that he owns his yacht. The man behind the counter is young-ish and handsome and has the rheumy eyes of an alcoholic.

You left Trinidad? he says, matter-of fact.

Yes.

On Tuesday?

That's correct.

You sailed straight here, two days non stop.

We did. He shoots Océan a stare to say *shut up*.

You're sailing with your daughter, eh?

Yes, just the two of us

And your dog?

Yes, and the dog. Suzy is sitting attentive and tidy by his side, like a ship's mate. She is on the lead.

Keep the dog on a lead on the islands, he says. They are not allowed to run free.

Okay.

Got any other pets? No cats on board?

No. Just us.

Just you three, eh? He pouts and gives Océan a look which says, quite blatantly, *no mother*?

Océan makes a sour face and eclipses herself behind Gavin's legs.

Fuck off, he wants to say.

How old is your daughter? the official asks, and he can see the man is suspicious.

She's six. Turned six in June.

Océan comes out from behind his legs and seems to understand what is going on. She gives the young man a cut eye.

You can stay forty-eight hours, the man says. 'Barco in Transit'. You have to clear in through the mainland to stay longer, Caracas or even Margarita. This is a National Park. You will have to pay for a permit and park fees.

The little shit. Gavin pays the fees, takes his passport and papers and pushes his daughter out through the door, into the hot sun and sandy street.

Let's get a pizza, he says, seeing that tables and chairs have now been placed in the square outside the pizzeria with yellow walls. You like pizza, he says. With anchovies, remember?

He buys a Polar beer and a Sprite for Océan and orders two pizzas, one with pepperoni and one with anchovies, which Océan decides she hates and feeds to Suzy. Suzy tries to chew the oily little fish but can't and spits the anchovies onto the sand. There's a youngish white man with an American accent, who also speaks perfect Spanish; he is taking orders but seems to be the owner too. A tan-coloured sausage dog follows him around. Suzy is generally patient with other dogs. They sniff each other, the sausage dog fits under her.

He realises he hasn't had a conversation with an adult in days. The sausage dog decides to loll all over Suzy; it is younger, more playful. Suzy mumbles something and rolls over onto her side in a gesture of acceptance rather than play.

That your dog? Gavin says, when the American man comes out and stands for a moment, surveying his tables.

Jesse? Yeah, he's mine. You have to be careful where you sit around here, he likes to sit on the chairs at these tables.

He likes sitting on my dog, too.

The American man laughs and smiles at Océan who suddenly goes coy and glows at him.

Hello, he says to Océan.

Océan lowers her eyes and stares into her half-eaten pizza.

We just arrived, says Gavin. We're here for a couple of days. Can you recommend a spot to anchor?

Ahhh, he says, and comes close to the table. For the first time, Gavin notices there's a map of the archipelago on the table. He clears away their plates, so they can see it.

Eighty per cent of the islands are protected, he says. I'm Ricardo, by the way. So you can't anchor in certain places, and the reefs are hard to navigate without a guide. Best not anchor where you don't see other yachts.

Okay.

But this is a nice place to stop. He points at a group of cays on the outer edge of the group.

Cayo de Agua. Very peaceful.

Where I can be in nature?

Yes.

I came out here by chance. Someone told me about Los Roques in Margarita.

Oh, I came here by chance too. Fifteen years ago. It was a small hippie community back then. Water delivered by truck once a week. We never knew when a big storm was about to hit. It's changed.

How?

Oh, this place is going like the Galapagos.

Gavin goes funny inside, at the word.

What do you mean?

People. They bring their dogs and cats, goats. Rats and mice arrive with their boats. It all destroys the wildlife.

Gavin looks at Suzy.

Don't worry. Cats are the worst. Expert hunters. Kill everything on islands like these. All the birds and reptiles suffer when there are too many cats.

But you say a lot of the reef is well-protected.

You can still find big species of fish here. Tarpon, barracuda. And sleeping sharks.

Wow.

Sharks, Daddy? says Océan.

Don't worry, he says. We won't be looking for them.

Are there any whales here? she asks Ricardo.

No. But lots of bonefish.

Bonefish?

Yeah, long silver fish, they can grow huge. Up to six feet. Lots here and fly fishermen love to come and catch them. But they're not good to eat.

I think we saw some bonefish on our way in, Gavin replies.

Very likely.

I come from Trinidad. Tobago was peaceful too, fifteen years ago. He wants to blurt everything out again, tell Ricardo about his hands, that he can no longer work; that's how different things have become. But the man seems to understand. He's a runaway too. A mutually awkward moment passes between them.

Jesse, come here, boy, Ricardo calls his dog off.

The dog leaves Suzy in the sand, grinning and half-asleep.

Anyway, enjoy your stay.

Cayo de Agua, eh?

Yes. You can anchor there, no problem.

Thanks. I'm Gavin, by the way. My daughter, Océan.

Ricardo nods. It's a nice place for a day or so, and overnight. But beware of poori poori.

What's that?

Sand flies.

At the crack of dawn, they motor out of Gran Roque and sail through aquamarine sea, a scattering of white islands and sand bars with single palms, and through some darker sea, until they get to Cayo de Agua. They find no other boats there, and the cay is long and curved, the sand looks like snow and the sea is clear as tequila. Suzy is so excited at the sight of the seabath that he fears she'll leap.

Once he's dropped anchor he takes the ramp from the bench locker and latches it to the stern.

Come on, then, he says to the child and the dog.

In seconds they're in the sea.

Océan and Suzy use the ramp as a diving board and make many sorties up the plank, running down it and bombing the sea. No one else around and it's as if they've arrived in a lost place, in a stretch of unchartered world. Gavin swims back to the boat and fetches Suzy's lead and they go out of the sea and up onto the sand to find the island crawling with black lizards, about eight inches long. Suzy goes nuts and tries to chase after them, scattering them into the green foliage which looks a bit like samphire and a bit like the succulents he has in pots at home.

Suzy, *no*, he says, restraining her on the lead. Now he sees what Ricardo and the customs man meant.

No, he says again, but she is hell bent on chasing them.

Lizards. Small black lizards *everywhere*, not the least bit wary of their presence at seven in the morning. In fact they seem to be running out from the shrubs, as if to greet them. The sand is latticed with lizard tail tracks.

Suzy woofs in a challenging way, like she's about to get heavy again, like she did with the pirate.

Calm down, he says. But her ears are pricked and she's desperate to go off, chasing lizards.

This won't do, he says. Océan, we'll have a look around after breakfast. The sandy cay is deserted. It's like a long empty street of white velvet, some green tufts higher up, a few wind-twisted trees. It's like a psyche-delic film has been placed over his eyes, like he's taken an acid-based drug and can only see two colours, turquoise and white.

They paddle back to the boat. He unclips Suzy from the lead and she tries to swim back to the lizards.

No, he says, pulling her towards the boat by the collar. No lizards.

She mumbles and whines.

When they are back on board he pulls up the ramp and cooks up a feast: chilli dogs and fried bread and scrambled eggs and orange juice and coffee, and Suzy gets some chilli dogs and eggs too.

He eats thinking about Chávez and all his oil. This place is a small miracle, secluded from the world, a National Park, an area set aside for conservation of marine life, yet oil destroys nature. Oil has killed more creatures in the sea and on land over the last two or three decades than any other single substance. Oil and sea don't mix; oil does not dissolve as easily as cocaine.

Daddy, can we go back onto the island?

Okay. But we'll leave Suzy on the boat.

Why?

Because the lizards are scared of her.

Because she might eat them?

Yes.

What if the lizards were bigger?

Then she might be scared of *them*.

What if the lizards were like monsters?

Well, they sort of are monsters.

What if they were bigger than Suzy? Would she be scared of them?

Yes. But that's not the case here. They are tiny and Suzy is bigger.

Okay.

Come on, then, let's go explore.

He puts the dirty plates in the sink, and this time he and Océan climb into the sea from the small ladder off the stern, leaving Suzy whining on board.

Stay here, he says in a commanding voice and she sort of gets it, but she is annoyed to be left out.

On the shore, he and Océan beach-comb, picking through the line of driftwood. It's not good. In amongst the brown-grey flakes of seaweed and sticks there is much bleached and broken coral, the likes of which is common throughout the Caribbean. Coral destroyed by anchors, by drops in temperature. There are many plastic things too: toothpaste caps and shampoo bottle caps and plastic bottles and quite of bit of it all mixed in with the seaweed. The scientists call it 'marine debris'.

Daddy, what's *that*?

She's pointing at a pink inhaler, the kind used by people who suffer from asthma. Weird amongst all of this, like finding an amputated limb. He was asthmatic as a child and knows that an inhaler is a private thing; he was

ashamed of his inhaler growing up, now he feels a similar shame to see it so public.

It's an inhaler, sweetie.

What's *that?*

Some people use them to help them breathe.

It is pink, so she likes it. Can I keep it?

And take it on board the boat?

Yeah.

No. It's junk. Somebody threw it away. In fact, we
shouldn't take anything from this beach. We should leave
everything as we found it. That's the law here.

There's a buzzing sound. They look seaward, to see a
powerboat approaching, full of people. Quickly, the boat
is upon them, not far up the beach. A man hops out and
pulls the boat up onto the shore. The people in the boat
begin to clamber out, eight or so. Big white coolers are
unloaded and then the captain begins to put out what
look like beach umbrellas and chairs on the bow. There
seem to be couples; each couple looks for their patch of
space on the long white street of sand. The man from the
boat is fast, scurrying ahead of them, digging a hole in
the sand, throwing the pole in and hoisting the umbrella
up. He manages to erect four umbrellas in a very short
space of time, all at intervals up the beach. White plastic
beach chairs come too; each umbrella gets a couple, a
cooler and two chairs. Then the man hops in the boat and
the boat speeds off.

Océan stares.

Daddy, what happened?

I don't know.

Where did they all come from?

I think they've come from hotels.

Are they nice people?

I'm sure.

But we were here first. I thought this was *our* place. Our island.

So did I.

I'm vexed, man.

He laughs, so am I.

The black lizards peek out from the green shrubs and run about, even across their feet. They seem to find their presence interesting.

The lizards now have more people to go and see, Gavin says.

Yes, replies Océan, but she doesn't like the look of their new neighbours, the beach is all of a sudden a different place. Once quiet, now busy. There are women here, tanned and lithe and wearing bikinis, and already she is studying them. She will soon, again, think of Mummy and he will too. From nowhere he is already feeling sad and lonely and single. The world is full of frigging couples. They ruin everything. They all look so fucking tidy.

Come on, mermaid; let's go back to the boat.

Suzy is pleased to have them back. He washes up the plates in seawater and within the next hour three other powerboats arrive. They watch exactly the same performance, the coolers, the couples and the umbrellas and chairs, until there are about forty people now on their remote piece of the world. Forty is not a big number of people on a beach, but out here, it feels like four hundred.

They observe these people for quite a while; even Suzy finds them perplexing. The couples play and splash in the sea. Some of them shout things in Spanish; they must be Venezuelan. One or two of the women are topless. He hasn't seen so many young couples for ages, not since he was young. What are they all doing here and are they all as joyful as they seem?

Daddy, says Océan.

Yes, dou dou.

Can we go somewhere else?

*

They motor back into the centre of the archipelago. There, they drop anchor at an island called Crasqui, bang in the middle of all the other cays and sandbars. There are two other yachts there, but no couples, no umbrellas on the beach, just a café. It's then that he begins to feel it. Really, are they mad? It is Friday. It was raining in Trinidad on Monday. Now they are hundreds of miles away but the rain has followed them. The world is full of happy people, fulfilled, in love, on holiday for real. Can he keep sailing? If you get to be as *un*happy as he is, maybe you should stay put.

Everything they bought at Hi-Lo is pretty much eaten up. They will need fresh water too before they go anywhere else. The saloon looks like a hurricane has swept through it. It smells of Suzy and fried breakfast. They aren't at all ship-shape. They got here on an old boat by luck more than skill. They're now anchored in the centre of a secret spot, a place nature tried to protect, but which is already half-destroyed by man. He is another man, who sailed here looking, escaping. His dog could happily kill all the lizards.

I'm sorry, he says to Océan who is staring at him, guessing that he's confused.

It's okay, Dad, she says rather quietly.

I guess you miss school, eh?

No, not really.

You must miss your friends.

Yes.

You will see them again, I promise.

I just want everything to be the same again. Like it was . . .

I know.

He feels stupid and ashamed. He looks at his daughter. She hasn't complained. She's still on his side. She fixes him with a solemn face.

My brother died, didn't he, Dad?

Yes. He did.

It was in the flood.

Yes.

And that's why we're here.

Yes.

Her face is huge and pink and she is too sad to look at him or even cry. She is as lost as he is.

She looks down at her feet.

Come here, mermaid.

She climbs onto him and they sit wrapped together for a while, in *Romany*, moored in the bay. Tears come and they fall silently down her cheeks.

*

Later, they leave the boat. They swim ashore and clip Suzy on the lead. The café is a hippy beach bar with faded buoys hanging like a mobile at the door and colourful glass bottles and pieces of driftwood decorating the low wooden tables. There are hammocks strung up, and a sand floor and low-lying furniture covered in faded sheets and cloth. A macramé lamp dangles and there are lizard tracks all over the place. A black cat appears silently on the soft sand and hops onto one of the tables. Suzy doesn't react.

It's nice here, he says to Océan.

They sit down at one of the tables and a man comes out and takes their order. Fresh coconut water and fried chicken and rice. There are other people in the bar, a family, and the adults look at them with curiosity. It is unusual to be a man alone with a child, a pretty little girl. Over the last year he has gradually become used to the glances from others. They eat silently. All the while he is thinking: never mind. Tomorrow, we will tidy up, de-fumigate the saloon. Clear the decks. Scrub Suzy. Go shopping in Gran Roque. Buy pasta, milk, bread, water. Tomorrow we will regroup.

They pay and leave and walk up the beach. Suzy is straining less on the lead and he lets Océan hold her. Funny how quickly it can happen, the process of becoming a beach bum. Flip flops, straw hats, bleached hair, salty skin.

Océan stops ahead on the beach.

Daddy, *look*!

He stares too, and goes a little dumb.

A PINK house, she squeals, in delight.

He cannot reply. There, only a few feet from the sea, is a beach house, painted fuchsia pink. They walk towards it, as if towards an art exhibit. The house is made of wood. It has an A-roof and a jutting-out piece of galvanised tin roofing which sticks out like a cap. Long sun-bleached palm fronds have been arranged over the galvanise which gives the house a fringe. There's a front door, made of wood, closed; two windows are bolted shut with wooden shutters. A low white shelf sits beside the door with pots on it breeding lime-green vines. To one side, hanging from the galvanise, there are fishing lines threaded with chunks of bleached coral. The chunks of coral make up a curtain, a wall of white sea bones. Océan touches them, in awe.

Daddy, she whispers. Can we live here?

He stoops and fingers the coral bones.

No. This is not our house, sweetie.

But nobody's *here*.

Maybe they're on holiday, like us.

Or the person who lives here will not come *back*. Maybe

they had a flood or they went sailing, like us. Maybe they left the house for us.

We have our *own* pink house, remember?

But this one is nicer.

He laughs. She's right.

I want to live here, Dad.

That's not possible.

Why? It's empty. No one's home. We came all this way. I love this house, Dad. We could buy it.

No we can't.

Of all the colours in the world the owner could have chosen.

Suzy sits in front of the door and it's then that he remembers her being washed away. She was outside in the yard when the garden walls went down in the flood, it all happened so fast. All the dogs in the neighbourhood were washed away that night, washed a mile down the road. When the big brown wave swept through the house, it took everything with it, including his good faithful dog.

Suzy yawns, she doesn't care for the house. She looks tired and fed up. She must be thirsty. He can see that Océan is not about to throw a fit. The pink house, here in the small secluded world, metres from the sea, isn't safe, either. He will have to think things through, hope ideas come. Sail some more west.

Come on, he says, pulling Océan away from this pink house which looks very nice indeed, very homely, and yes they could live there but not today or tomorrow.

Let's go back to the boat. The boat is our home, for now.

A. B. C

CHAPTER SEVEN

BLUE TANGS

White mountains glimmer into view. A Trinity of cones –
snow or sugar – but he knows they're neither. They are
peaks of harvested solar salt, dazzling and miraculous,
rising up like unicorn horns, or hills of a distant moon.
They are at odds with everything he knows in the
Caribbean and they strike an unlikely picture on his eye.
They could be the Swiss Alps deposited in a mixed-up
dream. The mineral is found in great quantities here. In
the south, Bonaire is more or less one large salt-infused
wetland. When the seawater evaporates in the searing
sun, piles of salt are left behind. You can pick up clumps
of salt in your hands.

He's visited this island before. Bonaire is where he
learnt to dive as a younger man; it is an island of many
natural wonders he'd like to show his little girl. But Océan
is asleep as they sail along the south west coast of Bonaire.
ABC, that's what these islands are called, *abcabc* he muses,

watching the snowy cones on the shore. He thinks of Claire, paler than ever, gone so quiet in her self-wonder, in her crack-up – if that's what it could be called. A falling inwards, poor wife. He sends her his love.

In Bonaire yachts don't drop anchor. That's forbidden; this whole island is a conservation park, and just like in Los Roques, you have to pay a fee just to put your toe in the water. There are moorings in the harbour at Kralendijk, buoys you tie your boat to, and the sea is so transparent that as he enters the harbour he notices there are people snorkelling. He spots a queue of taxis and maxi taxis waiting on the quayside. To the right, there is some kind of mega-jetty and a cruise liner, the *Sea Empress,* is moored there.

He curses the ship under his breath. The *Sea Empress* rises two or three storeys upwards from the sea. Rows of portholes for crew, a row of lifeboats and then several decks for cabins, hundreds of minuscule windows looking out at the sea, at the islands of the Caribbean, high, high up. Americans, mostly, behind the windows. He's seen people emerge from these boats, huge waddling middle-aged middle-income people with surgical scars on both knees; many of these people will be addicted to cruises, one every year. Some will have saved hard for the trip, and believe they're on the adventure of a lifetime; these boats chew up the Caribbean, eight ports in twelve days. These cruise liners invade Port of Spain and Scarborough too. They carry thousands of white people, spreading dollars in their wake which are seized greedily by the contemptuous Trinidadian and Tobagonians. Cruise-liner tourists are often the butt of calypsos, the subject of scorn. This is because tourists can't dance, they blister in the sun, cannot handle their rum.

When his daughter wakes, he is making breakfast. The first thing she notices is the giant cruise ship.

Daddy. She points.

Good morning.

They gaze at the humongous ship.

Is that a *boat*? she asks.

Gavin frowns. Yes, it is.

Along the quayside the cab drivers are still waiting patiently in the sun. Three days a week these floating cities arrive and no local can flag down a taxi or expect things to run smoothly on the island. Three days a week, the working people return to saying *yessuh* and to whoring for the Yankee dollar. These ships are full of voyeurs, not travellers, who stare and point their cameras and take back dolls made of recycled plastic Coke bottles filled with sand, earrings in the shape of tiny flip-flops, calabash husks crafted into ashtrays or pots for the flip-flop earrings.

Can we go on it? Océan asks.

No.

Why? I like it.

Really? Why do you like it?

It's BIG, she says with loving awe.

So?

It's bigger than our boat.

So?

Our boat is *old*, she says with regret.

Well, I'm sorry about that.

It looks beautiful, Dad, she says wistfully.

She is somehow right about that. The *Sea Empress* is one of the wonders of the Caribbean. A grotesque and a spectacle in its own right.

After breakfast, they climb into the dinghy and he rows them ashore in order to get to immigration. The taxis have mostly departed, but there are still people milling around, selling tours. They bump into a woman with long black hair and brown skin. Her smile is wide and bright. Her eyes are clear, green and clear. Océan goes quiet.

Hi, the woman says. I'm Lulu.

He can feel himself become awkward. He suppresses the urge to make an old-fashioned gesture, to take off his straw hat.

You just arrived?

Yes.

She hands him a leaflet. On it is a picture of a catamaran, some underwater shots of yellow-purple coral reefs, children snorkelling, and turtles flapping their fins as though they're flying.

We have a boat, she says. We go out six days a week. We're leaving in an hour if you'd like to do some snorkelling, see the reef.

I've dived here before, he says. And yes, I want to show my daughter the reef.

Where are you from?

Trinidad, he says.

Her face breaks into a knowing grin. Me too.

Really? This news makes him feel glad. Whereabouts?

From the south, way down by Icacos.

And you live here now?

Yes, I married a sailor. We sailed here.

So did we.

She looks down at Océan who is wearing her Snoopy sunglasses and a floppy hat pulled low over her tangled silver hair. She sometimes tries out an attitude like Rizzo from the film *Grease* that she's watched so many times.

Océan, say hello. This lady is from Trinidad.

Hello.

You're going in an hour? he says.

Yes.

Would you allow my dog? She's very obedient.

The woman looks down at Suzy. Sure, why not?

Do you have fins, for both of us?

Of course. We have fins and masks and wetsuits for every age, shape and size.

In an hour?

Yes. That will be enough time to register and clear in.

Where are you moored?

A five-minute walk up that way. She points along the harbour wall. We're moored just past the big casino. You can't miss us; the boat's called the *Windtree*.

Okay then, he says. See you in an hour.

Lulu smiles and turns, heading back towards her boat.

Océan, he can tell, has gone sour.

What? he says.

I don't want to go snorkelling.

Why not?

I don't like it.

But you've never even *tried* snorkelling.

I don't want to go.

Well, too bad, we're going.

I don't want to.

Well, Suzy and me do. We're going. You can stay behind.

That got her.

Anyway, Snoopy, that lady is nice, she's from Trinidad.

Is that why we're going?

Yes.

Is that why you like her?

He laughs. Yes.

Will it be all *old* people?

You mean like me?

She nods.

Probably. And with this he feels a surge of something he registers as shame.

*

An hour later they're on board the cat. There are around twenty people in the party, some clearly just off the *Sea Empress*, and he tries to make peace with the part of himself which already hates them.

The crew is all young and deeply suntanned. The man behind the steering wheel is about forty with a pin-up's body. His forearms and chest are covered in tattoos. He wears white plastic mirror shades and his hair is shaved into a sun-bleached Mohawk. Océan stares openly at his haircut and tattoos, growing a crush which Gavin suspects will be altogether different to the one she has on Rizzo. He can't help stealing glances at the man's taut torso too, folding his arms across his hippo swells. Lulu and her team are all gorgeous. They serve the passengers drinks and squeeze themselves into wetsuits and make a fuss of Océan, who is now pleased to be going snorkelling.

They sail out to Klein Bonaire, the small island opposite the harbour. Here, one of the crew throws out a yellow line from the stern and sizes people up for masks and snorkels. They split the passengers up into three groups, one for beginners led by Lulu; he and Océan choose to go in this team. Mohawk man agrees to look after Suzy – there's something about him which is a bit like Suzy or vice versa. Suzy seems to like him too.

Océan is given a life vest, a small pair of fins, a junior mask and snorkel. When all kitted up she is half-frog, half-lunatic. Océan could swim before she could walk and when Lulu gives her a lesson on how to breathe through the snorkel, she takes to it easily.

The first two groups leap off the back of the cat. Many hit the sea fins first, slapping the water and falling over them. Lulu jumps in backwards, neatly, and the six beginners follow her. Their group consists of the weaker swimmers, one or two who say they can't even float. They all wear life vests; one man looks scared. But Lulu seems confident to take almost anyone to see the reef.

Right then, mermaid. I'm going in first, then I want you to jump in, towards me.

Okay.

He jumps.

Océan leaps in after him, landing almost on top of him. He takes hold of her hand and says, let's take a look underwater.

She plunges her head in and he can feel her body going stiff.

He plunges his head under the water too, unprepared for what he sees and how it makes him feel, for the sight and the emotion don't match. Under the water there are long violet finger anemones and wide orange fans of lace and snubby yellow brains and fields of lush red waving hair and shoals of yellow and silver striped sergeant majors. And, right below him, snuggled together, he spots a crowd of neon fish, blue tangs, together against the red waving hair. They are slim oval-shaped fish with indigo bodies, but their dorsal and tail fins are iridescent blue. Together, they look like a section of a carnival band as they move together in a harmonious water-dance, part of something, but uniquely startling to the eye. A feeling close to grief washes over him. He is humbled and sad, full of joy; he could sob into his goggles.

He looks across at Océan. She has seen the blue tangs too and is enraptured. Her skin has turned jellyfish white and her arms hang downwards, limp in the turquoise water; her legs are spread, her yellow fins are wild and angle-poised. Her face is spilt by the mask; her eyes are far apart. He has never seen his daughter like this. Suspended in salt sea, hypnotised, breathing like a fish. She has gone somewhere else; she is like a creature of the sea, a juvenile porpoise or a radiant sunfish. This is what he came all this way for, to show her this fairyland. He laughs and bubbles erupt from his mouthpiece. She is oblivious to him, she isn't scared; she's out of herself.

He takes her hand again and together they swim after Lulu, who free-dives and points things out, then comes up for air and tells them what she is pointing to. They encounter a parallel universe of creatures going about their business, liming, gossiping, shopping; there are the pack fish, the shy loners who lurk behind the coral fans, the party animals, and the show-offs, the wriggly striped coral peckers, the pantomime clowns, all there; all have names fit for a life of cabaret. Lulu names them all and when she does it makes for a vast poetry: tiger groupers, honeycomb cowfish, French angelfish, midnight parrot-fish, white spotted filefish, Spanish hogfish, trumpetfish, sand divers, West Indian sea eggs, Christmas tree worms, sea cucumbers. And then Lulu dives deep, comes up for air and says, an octopus!

They look down and see nothing. Lulu dives deep again, so she is inches from the sea floor; she points at a patch of sand and it blossoms into a slow and rippling H-bomb cloud. The octopus emerges reluctantly from the sand, clambering off on rubber legs. Océan squeals with delight.

Octopus, she gasps.

Did you see it?

She nods vigorously and plunges her head back in.

A small spotted carpet sails past them, several feet below. It has a very long point for a tail.

An eagle ray, Lulu shouts.

The ray doesn't seem perturbed by its spectators. Océan points and he nods at her and together they track its slow, graceful progress. It is like being happy again.

They snorkel for about forty minutes. For that time he is lost. He is happysad and not quite himself; he feels *back*. Back in a world where he's been many times in his youth, back in the sea which he loves, which he left for another woman. He is at home in this other world; he can feel its great sympathy and a telepathy with its sensitive nature, how everything moves as one. Now it all makes sense.

Lulu takes the group back to the boat. They go snorkelling in two other spots. Both times they see wonders. Between snorkels, back on the boat, they drink rum punch and fresh guava juice and devour a late lunch of local stew. Océan is quietened, sodden and drunk with it all. She is pink in the cheeks again. Both she and Suzy have fallen for the man with the sun bleached Mohawk. Suzy has stationed herself next to him, on the deck, by the wheel; deck dog, second mate. He is not jealous. He is happy. Free at last. Free at fucking last.

Later, when they head back to shore, he gets talking to the young female underwater photographer on board.

Some job you have, he says.

Yeah. I'm very lucky.

Bonaire's reefs have been protected for how long?

Sixty years. It takes a total ban on everything to keep reefs intact. There's nothing like these reefs now. 'Protected' means protecting nature from man.

When I was young, says Gavin, we had conch studding the beaches in Tobago, Buccoo reef was just like this. Now it's dead. Bleached and broken by anchors and tourists.

Well, we have the lionfish here now.

No!

Yes. Not many, but they are here. There are local retired people, Bonaireans, who have committed the rest of their lives to spearing them.

Lionfish: in the Caribbean, anyone who dives knows the tragic story. These fish originate miles away – in the Pacific Ocean. They are flamboyant to look at, tiger-striped with tendril fins which look like spikes. They are a warrior fish, dangerous predators that eat everything in their sight, especially juveniles. Six of these fish escaped from a broken tank in Florida during Hurricane Andrew, in 1992. Since then, the fish have propagated and moved south down the Antilles chain, an unstoppable invasion.

Jesus.

Tell me about it. We can't get rid of them. Locals here talk seriously of opening a lionfish sushi restaurant to help.

It's like hearing the news of a far-away grand-scale

death; like how he felt when he heard of the Twin Towers, when he heard about Srebrenica, an unfathomable genocide in another world. Caribbean fish do not register lionfish as predators. In the Bahamas there are only twenty-four species of fish left, so he's heard.

The girl shows him photos she's snapped of Océan swimming, looking like a sea turtle.

I'll buy some of those, he says.

Océan is out cold next to him, wrapped up in her towel. Her skin has goose bumps. When they arrive at the jetty he carries her ashore. The Mohawk man hands him Suzy's lead.

Nice dog, he says.

Yeah, you look good together, Gavin jokes.

I know, he says. I had a dog like this some time ago, called him Mumps. Best dog I ever had.

Really?

Yeah. I got a cat now. She lives with me on board my boat.

He carries Océan all the way back to where the dinghy is moored. He rows them back as the sun is dropping into the sea and the sky is pink and orange and the sea is silver-grey. He and Suzy drink a two-litre bottle of water between them and then both fall into slumber in the saloon, no dinner, no change of clothes.

The sea has leeched the water from his body. He is tired like he's never been before. He can hear himself starting to snore. A decade of fatigue descends on him but his sleep isn't peaceful. Lionfish, dastardly Samurai, zebra-striped and grim-faced, glide across his dreams, reminding him of someone or something. A hurricane hit a man-made aquarium in Florida. It spilled deadly lionfish from the Pacific into the Caribbean Sea. A wave knocked down his home in Trinidad; they had a fish tank too. The wave swiped it – leaving dead goldfish in the mud. He remembers Claire, so peaceful that night, before the wave hit, so sure nothing bad would happen. Rain like that comes every year in Trinidad. Heavy rain she knew, grew up with. Claire is a creole woman; white as paper, part Scottish, the daughter of cocoa planters long ago. She grew up with threats of hurricane, the bombing lashing rains, a lifetime of rainy seasons. She was quiet that night, quiet ever since. Sleep comes to him. But his head throbs and his heart struggles in his chest with trying to understand that night – his part in it all.

CHAPTER EIGHT

WHITE MOUNTAINS

Everything seems to have slowed down. In the morning, Gavin feels lighter. He knows what he's doing now aboard *Romany* and that makes a difference. He's no longer winging it. He remembers her. She remembers him. They've arrived safely in the ABC islands. Really, they should be called the ACB islands, for that is how they lie across the sea, in that order; from the west there is Aruba, then Curaçao, then Bonaire. They will moor here in Kralendjik for a week, at least. The sea has thrown him about; one minute he is unsure, then he's sure of himself. The islands have the same effect. Los Roques made him sad, but Bonaire makes him happy. Today, they'll go ashore and drive about. Océan will like the flamingos.

He rents a car and drives across the island and when he hits the coastal main road, he drives south. On Bonaire's east coast, the sea isn't flat and gentle and full of beckoning sea forests. This coast is rough, so swimming can be dangerous, sailors cannot moor, divers will encounter predatory sharks. There's very little here, as a result. They track the coast and drive through well-watered desert, tall candle cactus, prickly pear cactus and wild donkeys, brought by the Spanish five hundred years ago, wild goats, too, and lizards, more lizards. These ones are grey and wattled, the males almost five feet long. They lounge in the green bushes by the side of the road like concrete statues, basking in the sun. They are like conquistadors with their spiked helmets and pewter body armour which catches and reflects the colours of the rainbow. He stops the car to gaze at one.

Dad, what is that? asks Océan.

A very big lizard.

Scary, boy.

Yeah. These are called iguanas.

Like the one that falls out of the tree at Granny Audrey's house?

He laughs. At his mother's home in Trinidad a green iguana frequently falls asleep in the sun and falls out of the coconut tree in her garden.

Yes, more or less the same.

These big lizards can climb trees too?

Yes.

And fall on our heads?

If they fall asleep, sometimes.

Boy, not that on MY head, she says, putting her hands over her hat.

They come from South America, sweetie. They float

here on currents, they can swim for days, sometimes they hitch a ride across the sea on a floating tree.

Like the white powder, Dad?

Yes, he grins. Exactly like that.

White powder and lizards float around on trees?

Yes they do.

In the Caribbean Sea?

Especially in the Caribbean. And worse.

Like what?

Like asthma puffers.

He drives further south, until the land flattens out and turns ash grey. Rain here too. The silver land is tiger-striped with silver-blue. Closer inland a vast expanse of low-lying fresh water has collected and formed a wetland, one of the five on the island. The last time he came this way, he saw only arid plains. Now there are tufts of green, pools of placid water. But flamingos like to feed in brackish water, where they can dig for brine shrimp and grubs. This water is fresh rainwater and newly fallen; it hasn't yet attracted the flamingos. They drive on, into the haze, past more pale shimmering wetlands, until they start to see windmills here and there, and then the salt pans expose themselves, vast flat pools, only inches deep, where the water is sucked in from the sea. Sure enough, he slows the car right down. Flamingos, six of them, each standing on one leg, bobbing their heads into the salty shallows. He stops the car and points.

See, he says.

Pink birds, she says.

Yup.

Pink squiggly birds, Dad.

Yes. Flamingos.

Can we go and see them?

They're shy birds, but we can try.

He winds the back window down two inches for Suzy and they jump out, leaving her in the car. Holding hands, they walk across the long empty road, towards the flamingos. The birds can see them advancing but don't seem at all concerned. When they're about twenty feet away they stop.

Dad, they're not scared?

Not yet.

How can they fly with those legs?

They take a good long run, then they flap up into the sky.

If we go closer, will they fly off?

Well, we can see. Come on, he says to Océan; holding her hand, they inch a little closer to the birds. Océan has gone into a kind of spaced-out walk, like Armstrong on the moon. They go closer.

Dad, they don't seem to mind us.

No.

They are almost as tall as Océan. They stand over three feet high, each balancing on a single pink stick. They are a salmony carotene pink, like moussianda petals.

They are funny birds, says Océan.

He stoops down so he is bird-and-child-height. This seems to give them the signal. The birds turn away as one, wading in the opposite direction, in a grazing crowd, their heads and necks bobbing up and down as they fleece the water for crustaceans and juicy crabs. They are a bit like robots, awkward in their strut, though graceful in the looping neck. All of a sudden the birds flap their wings and turn into a fluffy cloud. They begin to run, a loping run, more akin to the way a giraffe might run across the savannahs of Africa.

Océan's mouth falls open. All six run off, like pilots of their own crafts, each hoisting up the undercarriage of its legs.

They are both stooping now, close to the brackish blue pool; their ankles are in the water. They watch the birds fly away, towards the south. When the pink birds have disappeared, they both stare down into the water. Océan puts her face close, as though to a mirror, and then plunges her head into the shallows.

Océan! he cries. His daughter is upside down, her backside in the air, her head, hat and Snoopy sunglasses in the water.

What are you *doing,* he exclaims, yanking her head out.

But she blinks and says nothing. She puts her hands on her head, as if to protect it. Ouch, Dad.

Ouch?

I just wanted to try it.

Try what?

Being a bird.

You one mad-arse chile.

If fish can fly, maybe I could too, one day. If those birds can fly with those legs, why can't I?

Because children are supposed to *walk*.

But I can snorkel now. Breathe under the sea.

Well that's different. He looks at her, meeting her eyes. He can get so mixed up with her line of questioning; he wants to say, *stop asking*, stop asking when I am also mixed up. Océan puts her hands on her head, making a shelter, and looks at him like the world might fall on top of her.

They continue further south. He daydreams again of life before the flood, of his old naïve self, of a time before the walls broke. He remembers listening to Neil Young while Claire was out, cooking curry crab, being the man about his house in an old T-shirt, baggy shorts. Barefoot in his kitchen, married, a father of two; not so long ago, everything was how he'd hoped. Family life had suited him; he was at the centre of it all.

He hits the brakes, screeching to a halt. He knew the houses were here, somewhere, but had also forgotten all about them. Now, he thinks *oh God, oh God, not these, not now. Why didn't I think this through?* Now they are in them, surrounded by them on either side of the road.

Océan is stupefied.

Pink houses, lots of them. They are abandoned, a small colony, an evacuated community. The houses were once roofed with mangrove bush, but now have slate. Some are graffitied with words he cannot decipher, Papiamento or Dutch; some have plaster falling off in clumps. They are built from coral stone and they are the same pink as

the flamingos, as though they've been washed in carotene or cochineal. They are starkly empty and all lined up
in neat rows, some only feet away from the sea. Tufts of
grass grow between them, making them look homely,
like pretty seaside cottages. Each has a small single
window front and back, and through some of them you
can see turquoise sea.

Daaaaddyy.

Yes, I know.

The huts are so small, it's like they've arrived at a
deserted playground. He feels loath to take a closer look.
These are the infamous slave huts of Bonaire. They get
out of the car and take Suzy too.

Océan walks around them slowly, peering into the
windows. She even goes inside one of the huts. He follows
her and kneels, peering in. There's a thin puddle of rainwater in the hut and he wonders how it got there. He
imagines a man sleeping in the small space, his feet
poking out of the door. His daughter leaps up, trying to
touch the ceiling, jumping up and down. She twirls and
then steadies herself, as though checking out this new
living space for herself.

Who lived here, Dad? Lots of children?

No.

Then who?

Tall men, like me.

She stares.

But you are too big to be in here.

Well, the people who lived here were not as choonksy

as me, you see. But many were as tall, so they couldn't really fit, even when they lay down. They couldn't stand up inside like you can.

Did they have to hunch over?

Yes.

Who *were* these people?

Enslaved people. Slaves, people called them.

What are *slaves*?

Black people from Africa. They were forced to work here against their will. For free. They searched the wetlands for the salt which came from the sea.

Black people lived here?

Yes.

Like Josephine?

Josephine doesn't work for free.

But Josephine wouldn't fit in here.

No, she wouldn't.

Josephine is huge.

He nods.

It feels funny in here, Dad.

Like how?

Funny. You know, funny. Like . . . Mummy.

He winces. Something like that.

And yes, he can feel it too. It doesn't take someone with a particular sensitivity to pick up on the melancholy here in this spot at the edge of the island. The place is haunted no ass by the ghosts of these enslaved people, the sorrow here is evident. This is a place of trauma. There are many such places like this in the Caribbean, spots where someone massacred someone else, or where slaves were housed, where the horror still resides in stones, in walls.

And they lived right here, Dad, by the sea?

Yes. Right on the edge of the island.

But they could have swum away, sailed away on the trees, like the lizards.

I suspect some of them thought of it, some may even have tried. But many of them had families, you see, in the north. Once a week they would walk north, to see them, to a small town called Rincón.

I wouldn't like to live here, Dad. She says this decisively, as though it has clearly crossed her mind.

Good.

It feels sad.

I agree.

It feels sad like Mummy.

She comes out of the hut and they sit with Suzy, with their backs against the pink wall of the slave hut, looking out at the calm sea. They sit there for some time, all three of them, letting the sun get quiet and the wind brush their cheeks. Océan, he can tell, is trying to work it all out: how could their home be knocked down by a giant wave which came down the mountain from nowhere? Where is Mummy? How could big men be expected to live in these tiny homes? And how do lizards float on trees? And he can see she is sitting there on the edge of things, trying to understand her life. And it's okay, only just okay for them both.

*

They drive north again, back towards Kralendijk, and this time Océan sees the huge white mountains of salt. He slows and says, don't they look like the moon? She nods and says, yeah.

This is what the enslaved people used to do, he says.

Make white mountains?

Yes, but not quite so big. They made mountains of salt by the sea. Then sailing ships took the white mountains away; they came and moored their boats and the slaves ran along narrow planks from the beach to the boats with baskets of salt on their heads.

Where did the boats go, Dad?

They took the salt back to Holland, mostly. These people here are Dutch and the Dutch liked to salt their herring.

Dutch?

Yes.

Dutch *arses*.

What? He slows right down. *What* did you say?

Dutch arses.

Océan, *where* did you get that from?

Alphonse. He said it.

Alphonse? And then dimly . . . he remembers their brief conversation in Chaguaramas and that, yes, he'd said something rude, but he can't quite recall what because he was so keen to get away.

What did Alphonse say?

He said the Dutch were arses.

Well, they are NOT, and please don't say that. It's rude.

Dutch arses.

Océan. You cannot say that here, not here in Bonaire or at all. Ever. It is ignorant and rude. Alphonse was very mistaken. In fact, it is Alphonse who is the arse. Okay?

No.

YES. Do not argue with me now.

She goes sullen.

He feels sullen too.

The white mountains now don't seem at all important or interesting. He is vexed and so is she and they drive along each looking out of the opposite window and they see more flamingos, wondrous silver-pink squiggles all over the place, churning up shrimps in the fields of water, but neither of them say anything and he is beginning to wonder if he is the arse; if he will ever see Alphonse again.

When they get closer to Kralendijk he parks near the casino. Océan has dropped off to sleep, but now she wakes up and they notice the *Windtree* down on the jetty. It is 5 p.m. and they can see Lulu and the Mohawk man down there.

Come on, let's go and say hello, he says.

They unclip Suzy from the lead and she trots down towards the boat, spotting Mohawk man. She woofs at him and they greet each other like old friends. Océan goes a little shy again, at the sight of Lulu. They wander towards her holding hands.

Hi, Lulu says. How are you?

Good, thanks. Kinda sleepy, but good. Thanks for yesterday. We loved it.

Océan nods.

Wanna come for a sail?

Now?

Yes, we do it now and then, an evening sail. My brother is here from Trinidad; I'm taking him out to the reef. It's just us. Wanna come too? A Trini lime, nuh.

He looks at the catamaran; it's huge and empty.

Just us?

Yes, and Charles. She nods at the tattooed skipper.

Charles? He grins, amused at his formal name. Why the hell not?

Okay, then. He steps across the jetty onto the cat, carrying Océan, who is also pleased to see the skipper. Charles brings Suzy too.

This is a pleasant surprise, Gavin says. We were just going back to our boat, for dinner.

Well, we have dinner, and rum punch. Make yourself at home.

Ten minutes later, they're sailing towards the small island of Klein Bonaire, talking on deck, Lulu, her brother, his wife and the two of them. Charles is quiet behind the wheel, behind his shades; a brief envy flares, but mostly it is a relief to be with people who come from home. They talk about carnival, about whether to play mas next year, about Christmas, about living in Bonaire, about the whole island being protected, land and sea. How Ivana Trump once wanted to buy the island of Klein Bonaire and turn it into a casino, how it is now owned by the people and will be left alone for eternity. The rum punch flows and he can feel himself getting drowsy and relaxed and happy again; it seems to be happening all of its own accord, this invasion of happiness, or at least it happens every time he is around Lulu and her boat.

Océan has placed herself between him and Lulu and is watching her closely. Lulu is pretty and young and has luminous skin. When there's a lull in the conversation, Océan chips in.

Do you have a husband?

Oh, God. Océan, *no*. He squirms inside.

Lulu smiles. It's okay. Yes, I do.

Do you have children?

Yes, three. Two boys and a little girl about your age.

Gavin rolls his eyes to apologise. The rum punch makes him feel fuzzy. He doesn't try to rein her in.

I have a *mother*, she says.

Lulu nods.

This time she has a captive audience. He notices that Charles, behind his mirror shades, has tuned in; so has Lulu's brother and his wife.

Océan is rosy in the cheeks, the colour suddenly risen.

My mother got lost in our flood, she begins. Finally, she's worked it out, this story, and she wants to tell it out loud. Gavin's eyes prickle. Can he bear to hear it?

My mother has become a mermaid. Now she lives with my other granny, Granny Jackie, the granny who is my mummy's mummy. It happened when my brother died. She is waiting for him to come back. She is waiting for us in Trinidad. She is making socks for my brother and she sings a lot and in the day she swims in Granny's pool and turns into a mermaid. We have gone sailing to find her.

Océan, he whispers. That's enough. He looks at Lulu and mouths the word *sorry*.

Lulu shakes her head.

Charles flips his mirror shades up onto his forehead.

They all look at Charles.

I lost my brother too, he says particularly to Océan. It was a diving accident, many years ago. He became a mermaid too.

Really?

Yes. I still know when he's around, you know, in the sea.

Me too. Océan brightens. My brother is always with me; he swims in the sea with me.

Yeah, says Charles. I know what you mean.

Come on, dou dou, Gavin says, pulling her close.

She goes to him but stares at Charles, glad, like she has said the right thing, what has been on her mind, and it is the right thing because an adult has even agreed with her. And Gavin's sure that Claire, her mother, would've loved this story too, her version of events.

They arrive at a spot just off the shore of the tiny island.

Who wants to see the turtles, says Lulu.

I do, says Océan.

Me too, says Gavin.

Minutes later, they are kitted up and in the sea. It is now early evening and the reef fish are not so abundant, the sea feels more spacious. Lulu dives deep and points; at first it is hard to see, and then it becomes clear; a small brown-shelled turtle is lurking, hidden in the coral. Its head has a kind of yellow and brown cobblestone effect. It dislodges itself from its hidey-hole and then begins to flap away. It looks like a flying saucer. Over the next hour or so they swim with turtles. Maybe twenty or thirty appear from the floor of the reef, so many at this hour, flying about in space. Again, the sea turns things upside down. On his boat it looks like a rippling earth. From underneath, the sea could be sky, with these gentle reptiles in flight with their dark eyes, with their silent wings.

CHAPTER NINE

BOOTY WALK

They stay two weeks in Bonaire, *Bonnay,* the low country. By day, they snorkel up and down the west coast, taking the rental car, parking high up on the cliffs where there are yellow-painted stones every now and then, in the bushes by the roadside, marking out the sites. They don't have to swim very far out into the sea, and they leave Suzy on the beach. They witness whole cities beneath the sea, ornate and of the old order of things, gingerbread castles and fret-work which dangles from balconies; cupola windows and turrets and spires and all kind of fancy tra-la-la you would even find today in West Indian homes: baroque, rococo, *ancien régime.* All these buildings are fashioned from coral, all causing the eyes to fizz, for the coral preys on the optic nerve with its neon ochres and magentas.

Dad? Océan says, when they are driving home one night.

Yes.

My life feels better.

He laughs. I'm glad.

Does yours?

Yes.

I like fish, she says.

So do I.

They are like people.

How?

They are busy. And pretty.

And what else?

And they live in water.

And?

So they will never drown in it.

I hadn't thought of that.

She looks out of the window, pleased with this. She's slowly making sense of the flood, this trip. But this only makes him feel uneasy. She is so small, so, so small, and the wave was so big.

They drive to the north and come to the old slave village of Rincón where a street market is happening. They eat a Venezuelan pastelle made of polenta, just like they have in Trinidad, and they see a black Dutch bike for sale. In the north they marvel at the way the island has been thrust upwards in great chunks which cause terraces, the rock face full of bat caves. And everywhere they see great tridents of candle cactus and kapata plants, the seeds of which make castor oil, growing wild in throngs by the roadside, and herds of goats and now and then the tail of a papa iguana disappears into the undergrowth.

Why is the ground so uneven? Océan asks, staring up at the hunks of earth moved upwards, as if in one jolt.

Sometimes the earth shifts about, he explains. He doesn't want to go further and explain about earthquakes.

It looks like one of Mummy's broken cakes, she says.

Yes, it does.

Did an earthquake cause it?

He slows the car, looks over at her.

Sometimes the earth laughs, he says.

Laughs? she replies.

Or it can roll around in its bed.

I don't believe you, she says.

Well, you don't have to.

The earth doesn't laugh, she says.

Maybe you just haven't heard it, yet.

Ha, ha, ha, she says without laughing. Like that?

So when did you become sarcastic?

What does sarcastic mean?

Never mind. Anyway, the earth laughs, you just haven't been aware of it.

Well, I'm only six, she says.

Precisely.

When I'm older will I hear the earth laugh?

Only if you listen very closely.

That's weird, says Océan.

They drive even further north and find a flat wide lake, Lake Goto, and here the landscape could be that of a temperate country, like Ireland or Canada on a summer's day. At the tip of the island, right there, at this final point, they meet with giant iron vats which store the refined oil that Hugo Chávez sells to the rest of the world.

By night they eat burgers or wahoo in Kralendijk. He cannot cook on the boat; it is too hot. In Kralendijk there are flamingos made of pebbles in the sidewalks and at night there are gangs of boys in the street, teaching each other how to dance salsa and tambu. And everywhere there is this creole language he's never heard before, Papiamento, a callaloo of Portuguese and African and Dutch. It is impossible to understand, a language spoken only on these three islands, a language which could have expired overnight in modern times of YouTube and inter-net-speak or been killed off by the Dutch. Instead, it has flourished, for it was born in self-defence, a self-taught mix-up thing, just like all other nation languages in the Caribbean. It is supposed to be difficult for the white man to understand, who in turn learnt to speak it in self-defence.

It feels like he and Océan have blended. They have softened in themselves and with each other; the sea has dissolved them, and they are suppler in their skin. They have been disappeared for weeks now, and they are sun-henna brown and covered in mosquito bites and their hair is shades lighter and they have both become a little dreamy. His daughter seems to have fallen in completely. And he? He didn't expect to feel so lost in his own escape; a new space has opened up, an ocean. Clive, Petula, Jackie, his own mother Audrey, they feel far away. We should head west, one day, Clive used to say to him aboard *Romany* in their youth. *Le'we go west, nuh,* but they never did. Sailing west was no problem; it was getting *back*, against the winds. That was enough to stop them from leaving Trinidad.

And now he is here and there are all these islands to explore which are so very different to the island he knows and at the same time very much part of the longer chain, the grander archipelago.

*

They set sail for Curaçao at dawn. It is mid-December 2010. They arrive in Spanish Water mid-morning, motoring past the enormous Hyatt port side, a hotel with three hundred rooms which can accommodate entire companies. They arrive into a golf-course-sized expanse of water shaped like a heart and indeed it is the heart of this island, Curaçao, which some say comes from the Spanish word *corazón*. Though they don't plan to stay long, they find a little spot for *Romany*, a mooring which costs ten dollars for six months while all around him are super-yachts and homes by the water's edge which belong to millionaires. When people speak of the Caribbean being a rich man's playground, they mean a place like Spanish Water, Curaçao, where rich people can hide together.

He is struck by the low-key atmosphere. Super-yachts, sure, but the waterfront homes are quite modest in size, low on the water; some are actually on the water with wooden clapboard fronts. They have skinny jetties and grassy gardens and look like homes, like this is a place where people live, not just entertain. No sign of American-style condos and New Money. This is an exclusive secluded world, also open to the common sailor. Behind this vast inland water, visible to the west, loom the towers of an oil refinery miles away in Willemstad. From the towers, already there are streams of dark trailing smoke. Hugo Chávez rents this refinery from the Dutch; it is here that he turns his black crude into oil. Gavin has heard the talk already, that one day Chávez will simply snatch these islands for himself. *Boy*, then war in the Caribbean.

With Suzy at the bow, he rows the dinghy to the nearest marina jetty. There are things to do: customs in Punda, a supermarket and a chandlery in the suburb of Saliña. On the jetty, a few people have gathered around a man and a boy gutting a large silver-blue barracuda on the wooden boards.

They join the group of onlookers. The man is red-skinned and lithe with a long wiry ponytail sticking out under his baseball cap. The boy is about eleven; they are talking to each other in Papiamento. Océan immediately gets in close and squats near the big fish with its belly sliced open.

Are you going to eat it? she asks the man and the boy.

Yes, darling, says the man in English.

She turns down her mouth.

Gavin watches, feeling a little uneasy. Pulling a fish out of the sea, gaffing it; there is often a fight, blood. In the past he's caught big fish too, tarpon, small reef sharks, barracuda. So far he hasn't put a line out over the stern of *Romany*, maybe too much action for him what with a dog and child on board. The man begins to tug the entrails and organs from the fish; the tender innards slip out in bags and loops, all pink and white and grey. Something about this sudden disclosure makes him want to weep. The glistening innards slide into the sea beneath the jetty. Océan turns white. The barracuda's deadeye watches them, and he feels the need to pull away.

Océan, come, he says.

I want to watch.

No, we're going.

He tugs her hand but she doesn't move.

Come, we're going shopping now.

She gets up slowly.

The man holds the long slim fish up by the gills and the boy pours water from a bucket over it. The barracuda now looks more like an empty suitcase, its black eye still shiny and fixed on those watching. The pair are matter-of-fact about their prize, like they have gutted fish many times before; they are very natural together and he notices the boy calls the man by his name, *Rafael*, not Papa, or Dad. The boy is a miniature version of the man, learning to be like him. He is his father's assistant. And it's then that Gavin feels a need to run or cry, only then that a slow feeling comes over him, which almost stuns him. He has lost the future with his son. He has lost his son. He will never show his son how to be in the world. That is gone now, no fishing trips, no gutting fish.

He pulls Océan away.

We're going, he says.

Oh, Dad. The fish is empty now.

Yes.

I'm so sorry for it.

Me too.

In the nearby suburb of Saliña they eat at Burger King, mostly because it is a drive-thru service and this is more fun. They eat triple-deckers in the rental car, feeding Suzy the extra layers of their burgers.

There are two or three big chandleries in Saliña. In one he buys a bigger chart of the ABC islands, a light bulb for the V-berth, patches for the dinghy which he suspects has a leak, a new hand-held VHF system, the one he's been using is giving out. They drive to Punda, the more touristy part of Willemstad, and clear through immigration and customs. Then they wander around the streets. There are shops selling diamonds and Calvin Klein underwear and tobacconists where you can buy a mojito over the counter. Everywhere they see bottles of the colourful Curaçao liqueur: orange, green, blue, red, all flavoured with oranges, though, even the blue one. *Blue Curaçao*, even the words make him feel liverish.

They walk to the water's edge, where the buildings are huge old trading warehouses painted in ice-cream colours; they are baroque in design with Dutch gables and swirly curlicues like fancy moustaches. There is a swinging bridge from Punda to Otrabunda, which means 'the other side', the more down-at-heel part of town. They watch the bridge swing slowly back and forth as a barge enters the harbour and chugs inland. A cruise ship called *The Millennium* is moored up at a super jetty, steel blue and tiered like a cake, easily two or three blocks long.

When the bridge swings back into place, they decide to walk across to the other side.

On the way, Océan talks to herself, saying *Mummy, we got here all by ourselves, on our boat, with Suzy*. It is baby talk, she still does this from time to time; it's her heart, mind and spirit chattering all at once. *I'm okay*, she says, *we are on a trip. Dad says the earth laughs and I don't believe him. I've seen dolphins. I have left school and Suzy is my best friend. We are sailors. I saw a pink house. I sailed here all by myself. I remember the flood. I remember it, Mum. You will be okay; we are in a strange city called Heart. It is shaped like a heart, Dad says.*

He squeezes her hand. His own inner chatter isn't too different. The sky is going pink again and he likes the way it is so familiar, this evening sky in the Caribbean.

In Otrabunda, the buildings are crumbling more and there is an atmosphere he recognises, that of neglect, the same as in parts of downtown Port of Spain. There is a wide square with a bandstand and young men are gathered, doing all kinds of tricks, handstands, back flips. Spinning on their heads, moonwalking, breaking and body popping and throwing themselves chest-first to the ground only to move along in spasms just like a caterpillar. Océan laughs out loud at this and claps. They walk closer to spectate.

American hip-hop pumps from iPod speakers plugged into a beat box on the ground. These boys are young men, all black and clad in trainers and beanie hats. Some wear kneepads and others have wrapped up their elbows. They take turns occupying the centre of the space. Again, he is surprised; he didn't expect to find break-dancers here in Curaçao. He expected to find Dutch people with clogs, white women with wimple-type hats baking rye bread. Not Harlem, not young men posturing like bucks in an urban rodeo. Behind them other young men zing past on skateboards.

Come on, dou dou.

They walk towards the opening of a long main street which is studded with neon Christmas decorations. Christmas, yes, in a few days. But this feels like an unde-fined time, a limbo space where they can wander for as long as they wish. They have bought themselves this time, this space to slow down and look. Skinny stray dogs patrol the streets and Suzy strains a little on her lead. Men hang out on the sidewalks; no pretty pebble-stone flamingos here. There are parlours and rum shops and high fashion boutiques; kiosks where you can buy lottery tickets and people sitting at cafés drinking Polar beer and liming; some men even have one leg cocked up against the wall, the casual standard pose of the Caribbean male of all races. And there are casinos too, here, in this other side. A doe-eyed bald man stands outside one and smiles at him in a way which is openly sexual.

Océan is bewitched, as he is. This is the familiar creole

mixture he knows, of the Old World which has smudged, become something else. Like Havana, Port of Spain, Georgetown, Willemstad's grand old buildings are collapsing into the streets, some are even buttressed with planks. Trees sprout from rooftops, baroque shop-front lettering from another age is encrusted with dirt and fading, replaced by neon words like *CRAZY* and *SEXY BABY*.

This is like home, eh, Dad? says Océan.

Yeah.

Except everyone is speaking that funny language.

Papiamento.

Dad, what do we speak in Trinidad?

English.

But not *everyone* speaks English.

Yes they do.

Not town people.

Yes, it's English.

Town English?

Something like that.

Did we ever speak Dutch in Trinidad?

No.

Since the *Dutch arses* conversation, she hasn't brought up the subject of the Dutch again.

Why not?

Because the Dutch never came to Trinidad.

Was Captain Ahab Dutch?

No.

What was he then?

He was American.

Was he fat?

No.

Did Ahab ever come to Trinidad?

No, sweetie. He stayed away from the Caribbean. He was chasing whales.

It is getting dark. The skies are now fading to petrol-blue. Small bats flit across the abandoned roofs.

Are you thirsty?

Yes.

They buy cold Cokes at a rum shop with a porch out front with umbrellas, a busy local place, full of men. And then he sees them, the man and the boy from the jetty, sitting directly opposite. When the man gets up to go to the bar, the boy is left alone at the table and Océan goes into her Rizzo stare, sending him a cut eye for the fish he killed and gutted.

The boy stares her back down.

Océan, be good, now, Gavin warns.

The boy gets up and comes over.

English, he says.

They nod.

Rafael speaks English, he says. He seems intrigued by Océan, as though she might be some kind of curious pet. He hangs around their table and the two children start making faces.

His father appears with a beer and a Coke. He recognises Gavin and Océan. Hey, sorry if my son is bothering you, he says.

He's not, Gavin replies. These two are falling in love.

Ha, this young man is always falling in love with little girls. You the same guys from the jetty this morning? The man speaks with an American twang.

Yeah. Nice big fish you got there. Gavin feels a twinge of something he cannot define. They are a pair, this man and boy. They are allies; the boy has a silent self-assured grace as he hangs around his father. The man seems amused by the tough-girl thing Océan is trying.

I'm Rafael, he says, offering his hand. This is my son, Jon.

I'm Gavin; this is Océan.

Ah, like the sea.

Yes.

Do you like the sea, little girl?

Océan nods.

What do you like about it most?

Fish.

Gavin smiles.

I like fish too, Rafael replies.

Océan shows him the face of an old nun.

Rafael laughs. What's going on with this one?

I don't know, says Gavin. She can be . . .

Like her mother?

Gavin freezes.

Océan scowls and pokes out her tongue.

She is funny, your little girl. Funny.

Again Gavin is struck by how much he longs for adult conversation, or maybe even for male adult company. Rafael and Jon sit down. They order more drinks and

Rafael insists they try the *stoba*, the local beef stew with rice and peas. They talk for an hour and he discovers that Rafael is Colombian-born, but was brought to Curaçao as a child. He went to university in the Netherlands only to drop out and get drafted into the Dutch army, where he learnt to shoot and drive a tank.

Wow, says Gavin, impressed. Rafael has the air of a free man. No running away for him, no ball-breaking office job, no No. 3; Rafael isn't checking his watch, wondering if his wife will call him home. And yet, he finds he wants to ask the same question everyone has been asking *him*: where is the mother? Where is the woman? What are you two doing out alone?

He doesn't ask. Instead, he allows himself to get drunk. Three beers, that's all it takes. Océan falls asleep in her chair, her head on the table; Suzy starts to witter and chase cats in her dreams underneath. Jon wanders off, content to wait for his father. Another hour slips by, more beers, more talk and then he vaguely realises he cannot drive back to the jetty at Spanish Water. He cannot remember where he left his car, let alone his boat.

*

When he wakes up, he's sitting in the passenger seat of Rafael's white transit van. Océan and Jon are asleep on the bench seats behind him. Suzy is snoring on the floor. They are in a large half-empty car park. It is eleven o'clock. He hasn't blanked out since the day he fell asleep in the men's cubicle, standing on his feet. Initially, he is alarmed, reminded of the office, of Petula, of Mrs Cyrus, of a time when he blanked out a lot. A surge of the old dread rises up, but quickly disappears; he is here, in Curaçao. But still, this isn't good.

His heart thuds. Where *are* we? he asks Rafael.

Campo Allegre. Happy Camp.

What's that?

A resort. *Man*, you were tired.

I feel better now. Gavin stretches and yawns.

You look better. Man, I won't ask questions.

No, don't.

Listen, there's someone here I have to see. I won't be long.

Okay. I'll stay here.

No, don't be silly. The kids will be fine. Jon has a cell phone; he can call me if he needs to. We won't be long.

Really?

Yeah. Look, this place is secure, security everywhere. This is a gated community. Trust me. I've been here many times. This is the safest parking lot on the island.

This place looks an army barracks.

It was.

And he's right; the place is crawling with men in uniform.

Nah, I can't leave the kid. Her mother would . . . look, just no. I'll stay put, you go.

Okay, okay. What if I call my cousin Leila to come out and look after her, just for an hour or so?

Your cousin?

Yeah, three of them. They're working here, at the moment; Leila, Tina and Marianne. Good women. They've come from Colombia. Leila is a mother, trust me. A good mother, just like your little girl's. I'll buy you a nightcap, c'mon.

A nightcap? When was the last time he enjoyed such a thing? Before he was married? He finds himself nodding to this suggestion. Nodding thoughtfully.

Rafael takes this as a yes. He makes a call and speaks quickly in Spanish. Minutes later Leila appears, buxom and wholesome, wrapped in a stonewashed denim jacket and skin-tight jeans. Her black-brown eyes are made up with glittery blue make-up, like scrapings from a blue morpho butterfly's wings, but they hold a quiet serious-ness. She nods at Gavin and seats herself in the front seat of the transit van, opening a *Hello!* magazine.

At the door there's a queue and they are thoroughly searched. It is only when they get past security that he fully understands where they are.

This place is a brothel?

Yes.

They are in a concrete courtyard of some sort. Everywhere there are groups of scantily clad women. They wear tiny strips of Lycra which cover their nipples and the slit between their legs. They model vests made of string and nothing else, or minute fringed garments, and high heels. They wear micro-skirts and some are wearing felt reindeer horns; others have got into the Christmas spirit and have bound themselves in tinsel. They are mostly black or dark-skinned and their hair seems luxuriously long; these women are buffed and shining and have long legs; some are very young. They look amazing, Amazonian and strong; alarming and endearing and graceful and terrifying.

There are picnic tables like you might see in a park and to one side a large dance floor. Women are dancing together in small groups. There are plasma screens above the dance floor. On one he can see a white-skinned woman with a shaved pudenda being fisted by a man. She is groaning with pleasure and begging for more. All of a sudden he feels different, sensitive in his prick, a stirring which he hasn't felt in months.

Wow, he says.

Yeah, says Rafael.

He's only ever encountered whores on stag nights, all-male affairs where two or three women are hired to lap dance and strip and rub foam all over the stag. He had whores at his own stag night ten years back; he couldn't stop his friends from getting the girls in. But he has never been with a whore or seen anywhere quite like this.

Prostitution is legal in these islands, says Rafael. This is a big place; the biggest in the Caribbean, a hundred and fifty girls work here. My cousins come all the time. It is very safe for them and they make good money. *Looots* of cash.

And sure enough, a girlwoman bounces over to them,

all freshly made up for the night; she is wearing a fluorescent yellow g-string and matching bra top and a silver Cleopatra wig. She is about eighteen and looks like she has come from a Brazilian beach.

This is my other cousin, he says proudly. Tina, this is Gary.

Gavin, he corrects.

Gavin is here from Trinidad. He may like to meet some of your friends.

Oh, no. Gavin panics.

Why not?

I'm not really . . . you know. I'm too fat.

Rafael laughs. No man is too fat for sex.

Rafael, are you married?

Oh yes, happily so. My wife is the Captain. She knows my cousins work here and that I come now and then to make sure they're okay.

Nice wife.

Yeah. You?

It's a long story.

They head for the bar and Rafael orders two beers with tequila chasers. Some of Tina's friends join them; one sits herself on his lap, a woman in a red thong and red tassels pasted to her breasts. They are fascinating; he asks her how she stuck them on but she doesn't understand him because she speaks only Spanish.

The beers flow and soon he is dancing with the woman in the red tassels and his dick is rock hard and has formed a tent in his pants. He is still wearing what he had on this morning when he left the jetty. He is a sailor, come straight from port to the whorehouse and he is having some kind of experience here – love. He is feeling a type of love for the woman in the red tassels. He wants to wave his dick about for her, dance it for her, like a magic wand, make her laugh, like he used to make his wife laugh. When he waggles his hips and waves his dick about the woman in the red tassels doesn't laugh. She smiles, politely.

You want to have sex with me? she asks.

Uh, well . . . yes. I would. But I guess I'm going to say no, for now. I'm married.

I make good sex with you, she says.

I'm sure you would.

She puts her hand on his cock and smiles like a wolf. In an instant he loses his erection.

See? he says. It's gone all soft again. I'm a married man. My wife is watching.

She laughs in mock horror and they dance back to the bar, but then Rafael says, come on, come with me. Tina has invited us to her room for a drink.

Okay, he says. He feels happy and safe. His cock belongs to his wife, after all.

They go to a long alley which has a name, Booty Walk. It seems to be a street of small apartments. There are girls sitting outside their apartments, the doors open. Inside the apartments he can see beds, other girls, some fat, some thin. Some are showering; others are lying about on each other's beds. Some of the doors are shut, a red light on above them. Rafael disappears into a room with his cousin and sits on a chair by her bed. He seems to be getting drunk and talking to her in Spanish. Gavin feels awkward, so he wanders up the avenue of apartments by himself, saying hello to the women sitting outside them on the chairs. Every one of them makes a gesture offering sex: one slowly licks her lips, another parts her legs, another slides her hand between her thighs and rubs herself. He smiles and nods a curt *no thanks* and seems to be easily getting past this sexual assault course when he arrives at one door where three women are standing.

They are all wearing fluffy wings. They are black women with white wings; one wears a gauzy negligee and he can see her perfect breasts, like dark figs, ripe and bursting underneath. He can see the curve of her stomach and the golden pin in her bellybutton. She lifts the thin veil of her negligee and swivels her sleek waist as the other two purr and giggle.

You want sex with me? says the goddess in the negligee. He cannot think of a true or adequate answer; he has never seen such an enchanting creature.

I'm fine, thank you.

Really? She parts the negligee and lifts it back to reveal a round ample breast, like a small mountain in her flesh. The nipple has been painted gold. She traces her finger around the tip and it stiffens to a point. This makes him stiff again, and lonely for his wife.

You want to buy me? she says. She laughs a little and does some kind of samba street dance for him and her friends.

Yes, he says. Yes, I would.

She turns and bends over and proffers her backside to him and before he knows what is happening he is on his knees, his face and tongue buried in her backside and holding her by the thighs, tasting that salt taste.

CHAPTER TEN

KADDISH

When he wakes, they are all in the V-berth of *Romany*. The sun is beating down on the glass of the hatch and his daughter and his dog are lying next to him, both snoring lightly. Suzy is dribbling and her breath stinks of bone marrow. The heat is stifling but it's hard to move and make his mind active, to try and understand anything. The pain is acute, like his brain has been squashed into a hole smaller than his skull. There's a thumping inside his head and nausea in his throat. He gets up and stumbles elephant-like through the saloon and retches violently into the head. He supports himself with his arms, heaving and quivering with the shock of it and then he heaves again and empties the rest of the tequila and beer and whatever else has been fermenting inside him for the last twelve hours.

He staggers to the cockpit where the sky is brilliant blue, an orchestra of joy, and he pours a large Pepsi bottle of fresh water over his head and into his mouth. As the water washes over him great pangs of loneliness do too and he sits down on one of the bench seats with the shivers, his skin crawling. He cannot work out how he feels. Tears fall from his eyes, down his cheeks, as though his body and his emotions are in a squall, pitching left and right; he cannot comprehend anything.

He can remember fragments from the night before. Those women. Jesus, all three of them. He remembers some kind of orgy in that small apartment room, saying yes to sex with all three, one against a wall, her leg up and wrapped around him, sexy jiggly sexy sex and himself in love and delirious at the same time, claiming her like an amorous half-drunk soldier returning from war. He even sang to her; he *sang*, like an arsehole drunk. He sang to a prostitute as he fucked her, oh God – how far away was he and how far away is he now from the woman he loves? He wants to be back. Back in his old bed, in his old life, in his wife's arms. Last night it was another Gavin who went elsewhere in that happy camp. He remembers lying flat on the bed, a woman sitting on his face, another on his cock. Who were they? He cannot remember their names, they all spoke in thick Spanish, mostly to each other. He remembers laughing and shouting and singing and making a lot of noise.

Rafael found him eventually, and that was how he was able to get away. He can't remember how long he spent with those three winged women. They'd kept their fluffy white wings on throughout. He remembers that he paid them two hundred guilders before Rafael dragged him off, back to the van, where his daughter and dog were still sleeping. He paid Leila too, for guarding his child. He remembers rowing back to the boat in the dark, a rash of stars above. Those women and their sex, their salt smell is still all over him.

Oh, *God*. He should return to Port of Spain immediately, go home. Beg for his old job. His old life was good enough.

Daddy? Océan appears in the doorway of the saloon.

Yes, dou dou.

Are you okay?

She looks rumpled and dozy; like him, she is a good sleeper, like him she is slow in the mornings. She comes over and tries to put her small arms all the way around him.

Yes, I'm fine, darling. He rests one hand on her silky head.

You smell bad.

I know.

You smell really bad, Dad.

Sorry.

What are we doing today?

Aha, he says, squeezing her gently. I am taking you to a magic place.

Where?

It's a secret.

He tries to work out what day it is. Sunday, yes, Sunday 19 December. Then he tries to retrace their steps of the day before, where they left the car. He remembers that he didn't drive all the way back with Rafael; they found the rental car. By then he was more sober and so he managed to drive himself and his child and dog back to Spanish Water in the end. *Jesus.* This is why men end up in offices and grow fat like he has, this is why they stay boxed in; because it is so easy for a man to become undone, to wind up in trouble.

And he has been in trouble for some time, way before the prostitutes, way before he threw his phone in the sea, sailed off to be in nature. He has been in trouble for years, living the wrong life. His hands, how fat he is, his shitty job, No. 3. The flood washed it all away, his house of cards. And what did he do? He *rebuilt* his home, built it right back the way it was. He went back to the same job and the world which had already made him ill. Acid in his stomach, pints of coffee every day, so much that his urine was a strange yellow, his breath stank. *Potato pie, Mr Weald? Doughnut?* How many doughnuts has he eaten for breakfast in his life, a million? God, those whores last night, the most fun, the freest he's been in a decade. His wife doesn't sit on his face, his wife will never wear fluffy wings or nipple tassels and fuck him so hard he wants to sing.

He didn't become the man he wanted to be. When he was younger he was more himself, when he and Clive first sailed in *Romany.* Now he is a fat man who married a nice girl and got a good job and had two kids and worked hard and then got his fucking house knocked down in a flood which poured down the hill.

Last night he was himself again.

He looks at his daughter and says, we are going to have some fun today, my mermaid.

*

Lulu had told him about the sea aquarium in Curaçao right by the sea. *You should go there, you can swim with the dolphins.* Now they are queuing at the Dolphin Academy.

Océan is wearing her Snoopy sunglasses and denim dungarees. She has grown a little, he thinks, since they left Trinidad. And he has shrunk a bit, yes; he is slowly getting thinner as she springs upwards.

Remember those dolphins we saw on the way here? he asks.

Yes.

The ones when we left Trinidad and the ones we saw coming across?

Yes.

Well, today we are going to swim with some dolphins.

In the sea?

Yes, sort of, in a large pool with seawater in it, right next to the sea.

The sea aquarium is huge, tracking the shoreline not far from Spanish Water; the ocean is very close. It is home to seals, sharks and stingrays you can feed and swim with, flamingos and turtles too, and there are large walls made of glass where you can see all sorts of reef fish. But it is the dolphins he wants Océan to see.

In a small room there are eight people including them:

two young women who seem to be friends, a couple, and a mother and daughter. The daughter is in her forties and has green hair and a nose ring; her mother is shaking a lot, as though from Parkinson's.

A young marine biologist from the Academy team gives them wrist tags and instructions on how to behave with the dolphins: she explains how they don't like to be touched around the face, or ridden on like a motorbike; that flapping around and splashing make them nervous; they don't like to be poked or scratched but they like long, loving strokes on their torsos. They will not swim close if they don't like your vibrations.

The group are kitted up with fins and life vests. Océan is now a tiny dolphin girl, aquatic in nature, just like him. She takes to all the gear, the vests, the fins, she is confident and buoyant in water.

They are led to a part of the aquarium which has large seawater pools with walls and behind the walls there is the sea. In one pool there is a low transom jetty and three trainers in wetsuits are standing on it. They climb down to the transom and see that there are six dolphins swimming around.

Cool, says Océan.

He can feel a flutter inside his chest.

With the others, in twos, they swim carefully out into the sea pool. He has Océan securely in his arms. The trainers each work closely with one of the dolphins; each uses a whistle and hand claps to give commands. When they give the signal, the dolphins swim out into the pond and very soon the dolphins are weaving between the people, grey-blue sleek creatures. One swims close to them – Océan reaches out and smoothes her tiny hand along its flanks. He puts his hand out too and strokes the fine sandpaper shagreen; the dolphin has white cuts and scars where it has been play-fighting. It arches up in the water close to them and moves so that its tail fin flips up into the air. He is struck by how supple and powerful these animals are. Up close they are a cross between a tuna and an anaconda, a shark and a goose. They are gentle but still wild and as clever as an eight-year-old child.

He likes being petted, doesn't he, Dad?

I think so.

He likes me, doesn't he?

Yes.

He's a big fish, eh, Dad?

Actually, he's a mammal. Like a whale. They have warm blood, like humans, that's why he likes you. It's like he knows you.

The dolphin swims round them and its eyes are clear, watching them. Its mouth is set in a contented smile and yet he can see the hundreds of sharp teeth in it. But the dolphin seems more curious about Océan than him and he feels safe around them, instinctively relaxing his grip. Soon she is swimming alone in her life vest and fins. The creature stays close to her; he trusts the dolphin with his child. The creature and Océan swim along for a while, side by side, and all the while Océan's face is as wide and luminous as the moon. When she turns around and swims back towards him the dolphin follows her, tracking her like Suzy might. And then it dives low and disappears and when it resurfaces it comes up under Océan, lifting her up out of the sea with its snout, keeping her in the air as if on a throne. Océan squeals. The dolphin bends its head down with the child on its nose and then lifts her up again out of the water.

It's okay, says the trainer. She's only playing. She likes children.

She?

Yes, she's ready to have her own.

They watch as the dolphin pushes Océan around like a ball, nudging her and whistling, blowing water up through her spout and splashing her with water and when the dolphin brings him back his child, Océan is phosphorescent, glowing like a lava lamp. He is awed and, like he was on the reef in Bonaire, a little sad. Mammals are the mothers of the natural world; they feed their young, nurturing them for a long time. Sometimes they will notice an orphan and even show empathy. Dolphins have radar and he wonders if this one scanned his little girl.

You okay, mermaid? he asks.

She nods.

They spend the next hour playing with the dolphins. They dance with them and are shown how to get the dolphin to do tricks like moving backwards through the water. With Océan holding onto his back, they are taken for a ride by two dolphins, hanging onto their dorsal fins.

The older woman manages not to get her hair wet through-out and when it's her turn for a dorsal ride, the dolphins rise up from the water, catching her swiftly and neatly by her outstretched hands, speeding her through the water, and depositing her on the transom, with her hair still dry.

When they leave, Happy Camp feels like another time. They fetch Suzy from the car and buy ice creams and wander around the indoor exhibits, the glass walls full of reef fish and an area where a small flock of flamingos all stand on one leg. Beneath them there is a shallow pool full of green and hawksbill turtles. He lifts Océan up so she can see them. It feels weird to be looking at turtles and flamingos held in captivity when they have seen them wild so recently.

There is one very big turtle, four or five feet across and Gavin wonders why they are keeping such a big animal in such a small tank and as he is looking down at the turtle it dawns on him that there is something wrong with it.

Where there should be front fins there is only twitch-ing flesh, two amputated stumps. For some reason the sight of the twitching brings him back on himself; the flesh looks so tender, so irredeemably hurt. Some thug must have cut them off, some badjohn with a cutlass or worse. He remembers seeing a massive creature once, a leatherback turtle, maybe a hundred years old, on its back, in the sand at Las Cuevas beach in Trinidad, all four of its fins sliced clean, just its large reptilian head remain-ing, its sad old head. The animal must have taken hours to die like that in the sun, on its back. The twitching stumps make him feel ashamed; the twitching suggests the use of radar, a sonar call, as though the severed flesh is searching for the lost parts of itself. His daughter notices the injuries too.

Oh *gosh*, Dad, she says and tears fall. The turtle has no legs.

No.

I'm so sorry for it.

Yes.

Dad, why does it have no legs?

I don't know.

Did something bite them off?

Maybe.

It must have hurt, Dad.

Yes. It must.

Is it like Captain Ahab?

A bit, yes.

*

They eat lunch in a square in Punda, hotdogs and croquettes. They wander the streets again and find themselves outside a large lemon-coloured building, Dutch gabled with high arched windows, a church of some kind. When they go inside they find that it's not a church but a Jewish synagogue.

There's a museum attached to the synagogue and a gift shop too, all very quiet, in a small square. When they peek into the place of worship he gasps and crosses himself.

The place is a temple standing in white sand. White columns and balconies made of dark polished mahogany, pews with red cushioned seats and an altar of some kind in the centre of the space; above it hangs a chandelier of glass lanterns.

By the open door there is a basket full of kippahs and he takes one and puts it on the back of his head, the little skullcap neat like a bonnet. He takes one for Océan too and places it on the back of her tangled straw head and says shush now, sweetie, this is a quiet place for prayer.

He ties Suzy to a post outside and takes his child by the hand and they wander round looking up. Sephardic Jews are part of the social mix here in Curaçao, along with the break-dancers, the descendants of enslaved people who were traded here like spices and rum, like sugar and salt in the big yard, the Kura Hulanda, on the other side. Like them, the Jews are part of things in the Dutch islands. But unlike those of African descent, they came of their own accord.

He sits down on a pew, Océan by his side.

Daddy, why are we wearing these little hats?

Out of respect, he says. All religious people wear hats. Muslims, Christians. The Pope wears one too. Even rastas wear a hat. It's to make sure the soul doesn't escape from out the back of the head.

The soul?

Yes, the part of a person which keeps them alive. Like

electricity. It works the same way. You can't see it, it's invisible.

Like a ghost?

Yes.

A hat keeps the soul inside us?

Yes. But only in places like this where they might like to float away. In general, the soul likes to stay in us.

I have a ghost inside me?

No, it's a soul. A ghost is the soul which doesn't make it to heaven; it gets separated from the body.

So when I have on a hat, then my soul is safe?

Very safe.

Like now?

Yes. These hats are like a reminder, that we have a soul, that there is a heaven.

Okay, she says.

They sit there for some time. There are no Virgins in glass boxes here, no overdressed Marys in layers of satin, nothing but a holy quiet place in this grand decaying city of the New World. He rubs his bare feet in the sand and allows himself to think of his son and that he should say a prayer of thanks that his soul went with him, up to heaven, that he entirely disappeared when he was drowned in his cot.

He remembers the small white coffin, the neat square in the ground in the cemetery, how he carried the coffin there himself, on the back seat of the 4x4. How he went up the hill to the church on the mount, the lone mourner. His wife couldn't come and they didn't invite anyone else to the funeral. It was just him and Father Andrew, a private service up there on the hill in Maraval.

Let's pray for your brother, he says. I know the Jews have a special prayer for the dead, but I don't know how to say it.

Okay, she says.

You want to say something?

What shall I say?

Anything you like.

She shuffles her feet in the sand, then straightens her kippah and looks at him.

Dear God, bless my brother and make him safe up there with you. He was only small when he died. I hope he is watching us and coming with us on the boat. I saw a turtle with no legs. My mother has a soul and it has gone to sleep. We had a flood and it took away our baby Alexander. Now we are wearing hats to keep our souls safe. I love my brother and wish he was still here, but if he can't be here it's best he is in heaven with you and Captain Ahab. Amen.

Amen, he says.

The sun is dropping from the sky as they drive back to the boat. On the road they pass more coral stone homes built by enslaved people for the white man, some abandoned long ago; and they drive past the still smoking towers of the Venezuelan state rented oil refinery. Everywhere there is evidence of rain, lush greenery and candle cactus and expanses of water by the side of the road. Everywhere Curaçao looks like its sister, Bonaire, volcanic and stark.

At a T-junction they stop to turn left. The road is busy. Cars are speeding from both sides and it's right there that a huge iguana pokes its armoured chest from the road-side foliage and decides to make its way across.

They both see the lizard.

No, they shout together.

But, just like the black lizards in Los Roques, the iguana doesn't seem to register alarm at the human race. For some reason, the speeding cars are not predators. The lizard lumbers, slow and careful, out into the centre of the highway.

No, he shouts.

Océan covers her eyes with her hands.

He thinks surely no one will run over such a creature and then *baf*, a car rides straight over the lizard, leaving it in the road, bleeding, its back broken. He drives quickly across the stream of traffic and pulls over by the side of the road. The lizard is about four feet long, still breathing. He holds his hands out to the oncoming traffic and goes to the centre of the road and looks at the dying reptile and says, for God's sakes, I'm sorry.

He picks the creature up by the scruff of its spiky neck and near its hind legs, and takes it to the side of the road, laying it to rest in the bush it just crawled from, feeling sick to his stomach, cursing the driver who didn't stop, cursing anyone who could run over this four-foot monster like it was theirs to crush.

CHAPTER ELEVEN

ONE HAPPY ISLAND

They leave for Aruba the night before Christmas Eve. Large swells greet them on the trip across, like the sea is taking deep breaths, its stomach rolling towards them, sweeping east. *Romany* enfolds them in her wide hull, hefting her way through the blue. They moor in Oranjestad on Christmas Eve morning, stern backwards to the jetty. Renaissance Marina is a meeting point of every type of boat: mint white super yachts, fishing boats with double decks and lookout posts, a towering cruise ship called *The Thompson Dream*, tiny pirogues with names like SEAFLY spray-painted on. Again he is struck by the level playing field of this marina; how ten bucks is all you need to moor next to millionaires, and how every vessel is worthy of note. Each has a name, carries an ensign, bears scars; some carry bicycles, others carry washing lines, even potted geraniums. There is homeliness here, a community afloat, the boats all treated as equals, and yet there is a helipad nearby which speaks of big money.

The sky is heavy with purple clouds and the jetty is sun-bleached and infested with iguanas. Aruba is the third island in the Dutch Antilles, the island nearest the USA. There are volcanic boulders all around the marina and the iguanas perch astride them like ghoulish mermen. The iguanas here look much more alert to humans, they seem to be throwing their weight about. They jut their heads in and out like cockerels and sunbathe, fat-bellied, across the planks, daring passers-by to walk around them. They are everywhere, like miniature alligators. Big blue crabs clamber along the rocks in the water beside the jetty; in fact the jetty is bristling with armoured creatures. Right across from his boat is a casino, open at this time of the morning, full of one-armed bandits and a red Toyota Yaris parked inside, as a prize. The licence plate has a number and under it a little insignia, *One Happy Island*.

They disembark and head straight for breakfast. In the marina arcade there is a Subway and a Dunkin Donuts and a Taco Bell. This Dutch island has the most casinos, the most high-rise hotels. Gavin finds himself locked in a battle: why does he accept the earlier invasion of the Dutch, the fancy buildings, the wild donkeys brought by the Spanish, and yet he minds the twentieth-century invaders, those who brought the casinos and Taco Bell? Because Americans are also New World – and they haven't built grand cities like the Spanish, the British or the Dutch. They haven't brought people, trees, plants, animals, languages. America is still young and has arrived in modern style, in recent decades. America has colonised invisibly, via cable and satellite TV.

They choose Starbucks and order orange smoothies and pastries. Iguanas rattle past on the grass and he keeps Suzy firmly tethered to his chair. Océan notices that the café is named after Ahab's first mate.

Daddy, was Starbuck a nice man?

Yes. He was very gentle and intelligent. He didn't agree that Ahab should go hunting for the white whale.

Why?

Because he thought the whale was an animal, a beast, that it didn't have the same reasoning humans have. The whale hurt Ahab but it didn't care or understand.

Ahab was trying to catch the whale, wasn't he?

Yes, and the whale was much bigger and bit him. Starbuck thought it was mad to chase an animal for revenge.

Ahab wanted to hurt the whale badly, didn't he?

Yes. But Starbuck felt it wasn't wise to fight nature. I think Moby Dick represented God, you know, or nature.

When we were flooded, Dad, was that nature?

Yes.

We were hurt too, then, weren't we?

We were.

Nature didn't know it hurt us.

How could it know? Nature is its own creature.

I'm scared, Dad.

Of what?

Nature.

Don't be silly. You are nature too, we all are.

An iguana appears not too far away, chest proud, horrifying and yet casual in its armour; it is after some crusts of bread thrown down by others at the table near the grass verge.

Suzy growls.

The iguana stops and bobs its head. If she were off the lead there'd be a bloody battle. He reaches down and holds Suzy by the collar.

If the iguana bit Suzy, she would bite it back?

Yes.

Did Ahab think he was a whale, Dad?

No, he was a man carrying a deep hurt, the hurt of all men. He'd been injured by a lot more than the whale. But he was taking it out on Moby Dick. Animals fight. But it's different. They don't hurt each other's feelings, not like the way humans can hurt each other. With Ahab it was all emotional.

Suzy has no emotions, then?

The pastries arrive. The waitress sets them down but Océan doesn't notice; she seems bent on pursuing this line of questioning.

Dad?

Look, Suzy is intelligent – and she has emotions, yes, just like the dolphins. Animals also feel pain, they also grieve and suffer, sometimes they even sulk. They can carry hurt from when they were babies; but they don't seek revenge.

Revenge?

Yes. Now eat your pastry.

He flashes her a look to say, really now, *eat*.

As he eats his warm Danish, he thinks of how much he's been hurt in his life, how once, with the woman before his wife, the only other woman he ever loved, he was dumped by telephone. He cried and was wretched for weeks afterwards. He might even have been dumped from his post as No. 3. He has been rejected in the past, and in response he built himself a small home, a family, and when that was knocked down, he built it back with a stronger wall around it. There's no such thing as keeping out of the way of hurt. There's no such thing as a safe job, a reliable world. Right now, he doesn't know how to get anything right, how to live well, how to keep out of the path of floods, of white whales, freaks of nature that can hurt or ruin his life.

After breakfast, they stroll around Oranjestad. Calypso booms from high street shops and there's lots more of the candy-coloured Dutch baroque buildings and shops selling white clothes alongside Duty Free signs and Hilfiger, Gucci and Victoria's Secret. Again he encounters the creole mix, a Dutch-built town on a Caribbean island which has melted into itself. Océan chooses a potted poinsettia as a Christmas tree for the boat and in the supermarket they buy a BBQ chicken and a Christmas pudding, some oranges and balloons, chocolate mousse. They head back to the boat, arms laden, Suzy leading them.

At the chandlery in the arcade near the marina they stop to look in the window and see a notice board with messages from skippers needing crew and crew looking for boats to travel on. Most of the notices, he sees, are out of date. He puts down the shopping bags and pulls at his now shaggy beard. This is something he's been preparing to do since they first arrived in the ABC islands, something he's been mulling over. The Aruba to Cartagena crossing is famously difficult. High winds smash each other mid-air on a latitude just north of the coast of Colombia. And Colombia? Even worse for pirates. Heading further west now means some proper sailing, a three-day passage in open sea. So far he's island-hopped, undertaken single night sails, when Océan was safely asleep below deck, travelled a following sea, skipped from safe port to safe port, bar Margarita.

One moment, dou dou, he says. From his pocket he takes his small notebook and from his wallet his trusty Fisher Space pen. Quickly he scribbles a note.

Skipper leaving for Cartegena in the next week or two. Single-handed sailor with child and dog on board. Need crew/night watch for three days' blue-water sail. My boat is Romany, opposite the casino.

He enters the shop and pins his note to the board.
What's that, Daddy?
It's a note.
Why?

Well, we are going to need help to keep on sailing west.

Help?

Another sailor, another man, like me.

On our boat?

Yes. He would be a guest. Just for three days or so. It would be fun.

I don't like guests.

We might need one.

If we have to have a guest I hope he is a small man.

Well, I'll try and find one.

They walk back through the arcade. A loud crack in the skies startles them, followed by a brutish groan. Suzy whines and he reaches down for Océan's hand.

Come, now, he says and they dash across the grass and along the jetty as the first raindrops bomb the planks. They reach *Romany* as the sky tears and yards of silver water unravel like bolts of cloth. He lifts Océan over the rails, then Suzy, then the bags, and hops over himself, noticing it is easier now for him to negotiate rails.

They cower below deck, in their home, now so pungent with child and dog and sea and maccy cheese that it is a carnival of stinks. He puts the kettle on and starts to unpack the bags and organise the galley. Suzy and Océan sit on the bench and watch him, both damp, both expectant. He wipes them down with a towel and both seem to wag their tail. Proper rain, rain like in Port of Spain. Rain like the rain that hurt them, gushing from the sky. Deafening rain, hurricane rain, so bad the boat rocks, so bad he has to shout over it. Océan sits, but says nothing. She doesn't cry, she doesn't fit.

He puts on a CD of Christmas carols, turns the volume up and starts to sing *Jingle Bells* loudly.

Océan laughs. Suzy barks.

Jingle bells, Batman smells, he sings.

Batman smells, sings Océan.

Robin's on his way.

The Batmobile . . . has lost one wheel.

They sing over the rain and Océan jumps up and down and dances to all the disco carols, and it rains on and off for the rest of the afternoon and early evening.

Christmas Eve and they've been gone a month. They've sailed over five hundred nautical miles, and this is the Point of No Return. To go back, east, would be a heavy slog across into the face of rough seas, wind straight in their sails. To go forward, west, is equally a leap, the biggest yet, more serious than leaving Port of Spain: high clashing winds, unknown open water. But then there is his old haunting dream. He dares not talk of it, has never spoken it aloud. When Océan falls into a sudden profound sleep in the V-berth, he writes down his dream under remarks in his logbook:

The Galapagos. That's where I want to sail. World's End, some call it, or 'the enchanted islands'. Even Melville himself visited them. I've wanted to visit these islands since I was a boy. Clive and I discussed them all the time, where would we go, if we took this old boat and roamed? I want to go there, to

*the end of the earth. To an island in the centre of the Sea of
Peace, an island called Indefatigable.*

On Christmas Day it is still raining. The boats in the
marina huddle against the onslaught. There's life on the
other boats, songs and carols, the tooting of horns; like
them, many other sailors are trapped on board. The jetty
is black and slimy with rain, no iguanas, no sea birds,
everything has retreated. Inside the cabin, he spreads a
sarong on the small table and carves the chicken, saying
a prayer for peace on earth and a prayer for Mummy.
They sit down to chicken and mashed potatoes and peas
and gravy and Christmas pudding. His palms, he
notices, are pink and baby-new and he recognises the
cycle; every now and then they heal over. Then they
split open again.

He's glad he threw his phone away. Good idea early
on. Best thing he did. No calls from the office, no one
dragging him backwards: this direct action worked well.
He left his laptop behind in the pink house. No emails
either. He has no idea who's tried to contact him or chas-
tise him, his mother-in-law, his boss, his friends. No idea
if Paco told Clive anything, if he even remembered his
message, *ah gone west*. He's used a logbook to track his
course, charts, the VHF, only what's been necessary to go
forward. It has bought him a month of freedom. Enough
to get him away, truly away from his past life, enough
time to feel into himself. What has he done? The question
has been on his mind for some time. Only now is he

remotely able to answer for himself. *I ran away.* I was dying on my feet, falling asleep in toilet cubicles. I was only just surviving.

His dreams have mostly been empty since he left Trinidad. Dumb as sand. The odd lionfish has appeared to him, windmilling past, its zebra stripes and grim mouth turned down. Lionfish and iguanas, fish and reptiles have peopled his dreams. It has surprised him how little he's been troubled with guilt, and how his love for his wife has expanded in this time at sea.

Dad?

Yes.

Will Mum be having Christmas too?

Yes. She'll be having Christmas with Granny Jackie.

Will she be awake by now?

What do you mean?

When we went to see her last time she was still asleep.

I really don't know, dou dou.

Why did she go to sleep, Dad?

To get better.

She's getting better, then?

Yes.

Can we call Granny?

And it feels like this might be possible, like if he called it would be okay. He is stronger in himself, less tired, clearer in his head. Yesterday, he noticed international phone booths on the other side of the marina. Maybe even then it'd crossed his mind to make a call.

When it stops raining, dou dou. We'll call then.

She eats her mashed potatoes with her mouth open to test him. Can we speak to Mummy too?

Maybe, if she can come to the phone.

And Granny?

Yes. Now close your mouth when you eat, please.

Suzy has also dined on chicken and mash. She mumbles, sitting on the floor, eager to be part of the gathering. She has also taken this trip in her stride; they both have, his child and dog. Neither has been sick since they left the Dragon's Mouth. He is proud of them and feels oddly proud to know them.

Anyway, he says, I bought you a Christmas present.

Océan's face ignites.

Here it is. It's something he bought in the tourist stalls near the marina. He managed to wrap it while she slept.

His daughter grabs the present and rips the paper open to reveal the stuffed iguana inside.

It's an *iguana*, she squeals.

Yes.

She stares at it not knowing what she thinks of it, if this is a good enough gift.

It's a *cuddly* iguana, he says, encouragingly.

She frowns and then smiles, then she nods, deciding that she likes it; she attacks Suzy with it. Raaaaaaow.

What will you call it?

I don't know.

It needs a name. How about Raaaaooooow?

What about Mr Ahab?

Mr Ahab the Iguana?

Yes.

I suppose he was a bit of an old lizard.

Later, the rain stops and the dense clouds stand still in the air, creating a gloomy assembly of ancient faces gathered over the marina. He zips Océan into her purple terry-towelling tracksuit and she fixes him with serious eyes.

Dad, will you speak to Mum?

Why do you ask?

Just in case you're scared.

I'm not scared, dou dou.

Her eyelids lower and she juts out her bottom lip.

Okay, he says. Maybe I am a little bit scared.

Of Mum?

Yes.

Why?

In case she's still sleepy. In case she can't come to the phone.

Is that scary?

Yes.

If she could talk, would we sail home?

Yes, we would. I promise you that.

They walk hand in hand to the telephone kiosk. It is especially for the sailors on the dock, it takes coins and credit cards.

He slips his card into the slot and punches in his mother-in-law's number. His stomach swims. He closes one eye as the connection is made, as the phone rings the other end in Trinidad: once, then twice, then three times. Océan holds his free hand with both of hers.

Hello?

Hello, Jackie.

Silence.

Jackie, it's me. Me and Océan. Happy Christmas.

Oh, Jesus Christ.

Jackie, this can be easy or difficult. I have your grand-child here; she'd like to speak to you.

Silence.

I'll put her on. Say hello to Granny, sweetie.

Océan manages to say hello, shyly, like she is very far away. She says something about iguanas and turtles and Dutch people and flying fish. She gabbles for what feels like ages, telling half-true mixed-up stories of coral reefs and giant cruise ships and a boy called Jon.

That's enough now, sweetie. He takes back the phone.

Silence again.

Jackie, how are you?

Me? She is cold, indignant. I'm surprised you care.

Of course I care. This is a lie; he's never liked Jackie much. Jackie has been a widow for so long it has turned her bitter; her breath smells of stale smoke and Nicorette gum.

Where the *hell* have you been, Gavin?

Away.

Yes, we all know that. Gavin, where are you?

In Aruba.

With my grandchild?

Yes.

Bring her straight back. *Now.*

Jackie, you can't speak to me like that.

Clive thinks you're heading to the Galapagos. You used to talk about going there together. Is that true?

Maybe.

You've caused a huge scandal here. Everyone is outraged. There's no job to come back to, Gavin. Have you any idea how much trouble you've caused? Everyone thought you were DEAD until Clive went down to TTSA and spoke to Paco and they found your car in the car park and your boat gone. You didn't turn up for work, your phone was off, the house locked up, we thought that . . . her voice wavers, then cracks . . . that you had *killed* yourself and my grandchild, my . . .

I'm not dead. We are both fine.

I'll never forgive you.

I understand, he says.

I can't believe you sailed off in that . . . that . . . *bathtub* of a boat. We never called anyone, you know . . . the police, anyone. There's no missing persons file on you or Océan. We could have put out a search for you. Interpol, the coastguard of Venezuela, you know. I listened to Clive. We *understand*, Gavin – the stress you've been under. We hoped you'd be back by Christmas. We told Océan's school that you'd taken her on holiday, to Miami, to see relatives.

I'm glad. Say what you like. Tell Clive I'm fine. Tell my mother I'm fine and will call soon.

Audrey is beside herself.

Tell her I'm fine.

You could have got help. Told us.

I did this instead. How is Claire?

Claire?

Yes. My wife. Océan's mother.

She is a little better.

Can she speak?

No. Gavin, she doesn't know you've gone.

Good.

When will you be back?

I don't know.

Clive says that *Romany* has a ghost on board. That she's haunted. That you and the old skipper, the one they never found, the owner before you, that you and he have done the same thing.

What's that?

Disappeared.

That might be true.

Clive says that old boat is *cursed*.

Jackie, I'm going to say goodbye now.

Oh God, Gavin. Don't just hang up. We . . .

Please take care of my wife.

She talks about you a lot.

Please take care of her.

CHAPTER TWELVE

CHOCOLATE CITY

By 27 December it is still raining, a light insistent drizzle on the turquoise pond. The salt damp has made everything oily. They haven't left the boat for two days. Meals, games, songs and the galley is now pockmarked with tomato sauce, the floor landmined with melted cheese and Froot Loops gone soggy. A fine layer of sugar coats the table and, weirdly, the V-berth. He suspects Océan has been taking sugar sandwiches to bed with her. There are no more clean clothes or sheets, nothing remotely dry or unsoiled left that he can lay his hands on and he's been considering whether it would be wisest to simply throw everything away and buy new clothes and sheets than find a Laundromat. The air in the cabin is now Jouvay morning, 5 a.m., Wrightson Road; the cabin is a mud band in full glory.

He is making coffee, the hatch closed up, when he hears a woman's voice.

Hellooooooo?

Daddy, there's a lady out there, says Océan.

Mr Weald?

This actually gives him a shiver. He hasn't been called 'Mr Weald' for a month, not since Petula. He slides open the hatch and gazes out into the humid gloom. A small woman is standing on the jetty, suntanned, with a short blonde bob, raincoat on, a guitar in a case strapped to her back.

Hello, he shouts from the cabin. I'm Gavin Weald.

I came to find you. About joining you.

I'm sorry, he says, coming out into the cockpit. I don't know what you mean.

Are you still looking for crew?

Crew? He only just remembers this. Yes. But he wanted a man. A small man with muscles, who can hoist sails, who can harpoon whales if need be. Not a blonde woman.

Uh, yes, I am.

I saw your message. I'd like to apply.

Oh.

I have certificates. From Sweden.

Certificates?

Qualifications. From Nautical College. I'm a qualified skipper. I have extensive sailing experience. The small blonde woman smiles. She looks about twenty-five.

He wants to say no, you're not right, not what I'm looking for. A woman?

Uh, look, best you don't come on board. It's a bit messy down here. Meet me in Taco Bell in the arcade. I'll be along in ten minutes.

Okay. She turns and walks back down the jetty.

He stares at her guitar, her sturdy brown calves. *Jeesus.* Then he says: Océan, quickly, get dressed please. We're going out for breakfast.

Taco Bell is all teak veneer and purple vinyl. It is still decorated in winking Christmas lights, red baubles and stars. They queue up and order classic chalupas and soft tacos, orange juice and coffee.

The young woman is sitting in a booth, a black coffee in front of her. He slides in opposite her and Océan slides in too. Suzy seems to intuit that this is some kind of panel interview and sits gazing attentively at the woman.

The young woman smiles.

He and Océan openly inspect her.

I'm Phoebe, she says, as natural as can be. Phoebe Wolf.

Her eyes are large and clear and blue and a little slanted upwards at the corners. Her skin is palomino gold, her hair is shock blonde, dead straight, held back in barrettes. Her lips are plump and pink. She is sleek and reminds him of a dolphin. She has shrugged off her raincoat and is wearing a much-worn black vest. Both of her arms are tattooed. On one, a curvaceous cerulean-blue hammer-head shark stretches from shoulder to elbow; on the other shoulder just one word in circus-type script: *further.*

He is afraid Océan will either start to drool like she did at the Virgin in the glass box or deliver a speech about her mother. He glances down at his child and realises how much she looks just like this young woman.

I'm Gavin, he says, this is Océan. Our dog is called Suzy.

Phoebe smiles at Océan. Hi, she says.

Océan stares unblinking, struck mute.

It's only then that he recognises something has changed. This is the first time he's met another adult and not wanted to blurt, or gabble, that he's run away. And this is because since the phone call on Christmas Day, they're no longer runaways. They have touched base; relatives know where they are. They are no longer *on the run*, no longer escapees from the asylum of the pink house. He's been released from his job; he and Océan even look different, wilder, and yet more relaxed. Now, he's just a traveller, like any other.

We're heading to the Galapagos, via the Panama Canal, he says, and as the words emerge, he realises this is the first time he has said his dream aloud. Until now, he has only made a reckless dash; this bigger step has been hidden away even from himself. He's not even mentioned the Galapagos to Océan. He is making his dream happen in this moment.

He continues: I know the crossing from Aruba to Cartagena is rough. Three days, more or less. I can't do it by myself.

She nods.

I've made this crossing once before, she says. My boyfriend is a sailor too. You're right; it's tough going. I'm trying to get to Panama to meet him. From there we travel north, to Mexico.

Océan's relief at the word boyfriend is visible; relief mixed with the thrill of enigma at the word, for 'boyfriend' is something she has already decided is her great future. And he has to admit, it's had an impact on him too. This Phoebe Wolf looks like Claire's younger sister.

Well, I'd like to wait till the weather clears, until after New Year. We could aim to leave in the first week of January. That would give me a few days to clean our boat, make any repairs. I'll buy the food – we can shop together, if you like, the day before. She's an old boat but very stable, 28 foot, a Great Dane.

Yes, I noticed. Her face goes soft, her eyes flash with knowing. My father owned one.

He stares. You're kidding.

No. She laughs. I learnt to sail on a Great Dane in Sweden.

That's *amazing*. So few were made.

She nods, hiding something else. They have a very good reputation, she says. I was surprised to see your boat in the marina. I never thought I'd see one in the Caribbean.

He nods. I think *Romany* must be the only Great Dane around these waters, he says. Wow. This Phoebe has just passed a test he didn't even know he was setting. Who in heaven is this woman? She's small and pretty, but a sailor; feminine but physically strong-looking.

I used to own *Romany* with my best friend, he explains. Sailed her all through my youth. The previous owner sailed it to Trinidad, across the Atlantic. He sold it in Trinidad – to us.

She nods.

His stomach flutters at his lie. Like the dream he is now making happen, he is inventing his future: one where his mother-in-law's words, *the boat is cursed*, do not exist. In his new life he is a travelling man, a man of the sea, and he is heading west, to a tiny archipelago on the equator. He is sailing on a boat with no ghost.

So, Great Danes. And Nautical College?

Yes. I grew up sailing, went to college to get my licence. I've been skippering all my life. It's all I know. When not skippering, I travel. Usually, I make deliveries.

Alone?

Sometimes, but only in the Med.

That's impressive. Very few women skipper boats.

Phoebe smiles.

Océan's face is lit up, glowing.

You have to pardon my child. My wife . . . and he pauses, realising here too, that he can now say the truth. He no longer needs to feel ashamed. It's the first time he has ever said it out loud.

My wife is in Trinidad. Our baby son died in tragic circumstances, a year ago. She is still . . . recovering.

I see. Phoebe's face softens again and he can see she knows something about loss.

I'm really sorry.

I think it's important that you know. If you are going to spend some time with us.

Océan clings to his arm.

We've been travelling a month now, and we are all good sailors. Even Suzy here, she loves the sea.

But not lizards, says Océan.

They agree to meet again in the New Year. Phoebe will come aboard and they will shop, consult the weather reports, decide when to set sail. They will be bound for wide-open sea, for Cartagena de Indias, the fabled walled city with wild monkeys in the trees, where emeralds are as plentiful as pebbles, where cocaine is sold, like sugar, by the pound on street corners. And he will be ready to meet the wide-open sea, ready for the next leap. Now they are regular sailors travelling forwards.

*

The skies clear and as a treat he hires a car and decides to drive to the south of Aruba, to Baby Beach in St Nicholas where the sea is flat and the snorkelling is supposed to be excellent. They choose a small silver Honda and when the rental man asks them where they're going, Gavin tells him.

Oh, says the man. He is Dutch and about thirty-five; he is bald apart from a tiny goatee on his chin. You mean Chocolate City?

What?

That's the local name for St Nicholas.

Really, why?

So many black people live there.

Gavin is so shocked he laughs. Open racism he's come across in Trinidad; it is a way of being. Everyone bears a grudge, the African man in the street, the East-Indian housewife, the Lebanese businessman, the Chinese shop-keeper, you name it; everyone snipes at each other here and there. This makes things both edgy and harmonious: if everyone can be crude then the truth is out, a tolerance can be bred into society. Trinidadians, weirdly, can be both racist and tolerant. But this? Chocolate City?

He grimaces.

No, really, says the Goatee Man. Even the black people call it Chocolate City. They all work at the oil refinery. They are all in one place on the island.

I doubt any black person will call his town Chocolate City, says Gavin. He is reminded of Océan's *Dutch arses* and feels impatient with this Dutch man.

No, I'm not joking, they do.

Never mind, he says, cutting him off.

He drags Océan out into the car park, hoping she won't repeat the words. He scowls down at her so she'll get the message.

She says nothing, just climbs into the front seat. Suzy hops into the back. They are a trio of seekers, explorers. They are off together again.

He drives south for an hour at least before the towers of the Valero refinery loom into sight. Behind the refin-ery is Baby Beach, where the sea, apparently, is calm and flat enough for even babies to swim safely. He figures this is the perfect spot for man, child and dog, somewhere he can relax. Baby Beach, from what he's read, is a shallow lagoon.

But it's still Christmas holiday time and the beach is packed with families who've had the same idea. They pass dozens of cars parked up on the side till they get to the end of the beach. Somehow, he feels robbed. Topless women everywhere, parched from the sun, some over sixty. Stray dogs trotting about, 70s music. *Knock Three Times* blaring from the nearby beach bar, posters of Balashi beer, brewed in Aruba. Half-domed yellow canvas pods all over the beach, people crammed into them. The water is murky, a milky turquoise, and to the left is some kind of rocky breakwater; there is a gang of people snorkelling out near this part of the lagoon. A gang. He considers leaving without even getting out of the car but Océan opens her door and is already fixated on the snorkellers.

Come on, Dad, she says, eager.

Okay, okay.

They make a camp in the shade of a grass-matted hut. He ties Suzy to a post and gives her a bowl of water. Good girl, he says; he will take her out into the sea later.

He plasters Océan with sun block and snags her miniature mask to her head, the mask he bought recently, because now she's mad about snorkelling. She has junior fins too. They march out, towards the lagoon, fins on, and he doesn't like the look of this at all. Hell is a sea glistening with Factor 15.

In the water they paddle towards the snorkellers by the breakwater and he notices the strong current. He reaches for Océan's hand; she is already face down, goggling at the underworld. Suddenly, she puts her head up and shouts, Daddy, *look*!

He plunges his head down into the sea, then grabs for Océan's hand and pulls her close.

There are hundreds of fish in the sea around them. Big fish. Fat fish. Oversized, overfed silvery reef fish. Aggressive-looking parrotfish with razor-sharp choppers, shoals of them swimming between their legs. He looks around and sees that people are feeding them chunks of banana and pieces of cheese. The fish are nibbling the human food from their fingertips.

Here, says an older Dutch man, standing waist high in the sea. He looks delighted at the frenzy he is causing. He hands Océan a piece of his banana. You can feed the fish, he says.

Before Gavin can stop her, she has plunged her head back in the murk and is holding the banana portion like a baton. In seconds she is rushed by dozens of fat silver fish, their gums bared.

Daddy, she squeals.

Good, huh, says the Dutch man. He makes a thumbs up sign.

No, Gavin barks, pulling Océan towards his chest, snatching her away from the pack.

Owwww. Océan holds her finger up for him to see; it is bleeding.

You *stupid* man, he shouts. You should *not* feed these fish. They are WILD, wild creatures. Leave them alone.

The Dutch man looks baffled. But they are only fish, he says.

Jeesus. Gavin finds himself storming clumsily out of the water, it's that or punch the old man down. He pulls Océan with him; she is wailing *Mummmmy.*

On the beach he rips off his mask and fins. He takes off Océan's fins and mask and hugs her tight. He is strangely overcome. Bananas, Jesus.

Océan's finger is grazed – he kisses it and wraps it in the end of a beach towel.

You okay, dou dou?

She nods but her face is watery and huge.

What was happening with all those fish, Dad?

They got greedy. Fish shouldn't be eating bananas or cheese, my love.

I'm sorry, Dad.

Never mind. You didn't know. But I think we should leave.

She nods. But there are questions in Océan's face. Again she is trying to understand it all and again he has no answers for her. He hugs her to him and feels wretched for the first time since they left Trinidad, lonely for his calm wife, the other half of the team. Claire used to have all the answers; she'd be there right now, for them both, making sense of the old man and his bananas.

They drive north along the eastern coast. All three ABC islands have the same eastern coastline, rugged, white-capped inhospitable sea. Each of the islands has a deserted east coast, the ground made of hard volcanic rock spotted with blowholes and caves and here in Aruba, the rough sea has sculpted natural bridges into the rock, one of which has collapsed. Each of the islands has this duality, the boutique Caribbean west and the bacchanal east coast, one side a seabath, the other a series of sucking whirlpools. He thinks of Claire, of her dislike of the water, her pale skin, her seasickness, her natural disposition towards the earth. He sailed off while she was away in herself. Now he remembers why he gave this all up, this affinity with such an unpredictable element; to be with her. Claire, who is usually so grounded, who was born to be a mother.

Strange constructions of rocks start to appear dotted along the coast. Small rocks piled on top of one another in totem poles. They are everywhere. Not natural forma-tions, but piles of rocks, like a child or an imp has been making castles in the night out of mischief. They drive along for quite some time, gazing at the curious piles, the rough seas behind them. Eventually, they come to a bend in the road; there is a man with a wheelbarrow, digging turf, near a pickup truck.

Excuse me. Gavin leans out.

The man turns round, he is sweating in the heat with his task.

Sorry to disturb you. But I'm new here. I was just wondering . . . about the castles.

Castles?

The little piles of rocks, you know, all along the coast.

Oh, he says. That's done for the tourists.

What?

The tour buses bring them out. Tell them it's a tradition here in Aruba.

Making rock castles?

Yes.

They tell them it will bring them good luck in the casinos. So they spend more money.

Is that some kind of Aruban in-joke?

Yes.

Gavin laughs out loud. Somehow it makes up for the mega cruise liners, for the invisible invasion by the USA.

They drive on, past a deserted gold mine and past a tiny church by the sea, and they come to a poor neighbourhood where there is a home like a junkyard, the family within seeming to hoard everything. Outside the house is a mannequin stolen from a shop, wearing a snow trimmed miniskirt and a red velvet hood. There is the whole nativity scene too, decorated with wispy brown banana fronds and a plastic man in a Santa suit and baubles hanging from trees and lots of candle cactus grown into sloopy clumps. A row of plastic children dressed in capes of crimson and sapphire foil guard the gate.

Can we stop? says Océan.

Of course.

She stares at this strange home with awe.

We will not be moving in, he says firmly.

Daddy, do people live here?

Yes.

Americans?

No.

Who, then?

Artists, probably. Or people who've gone mad.

I'm going to have a house like this when I'm grown up.

When you have a boyfriend?

Yeah. I will make my boyfriends stand outside in a suit like that.

All of them?

She laughs. Yes.

How many boyfriends will you have?

Ten.

All at once?

Yes.

And you'll dress them up and make them stand outside your house?

Yes.

He takes a picture of her next to the mannequin in the Santa miniskirt. Océan is six and a half and has got it all worked out already. Who she will be. The Queen of a colourful kingdom, suitors in kinky uniforms.

Let's go home now, mermaid.

To the boat?

Yes.

I like the boat these days, Dad.

I'm glad. But we have some cleaning up to do before we welcome our visitor. Our new crew member.

Phoebe?

Yes.

I liked her, Dad.

So did I.

Is she a sailor?

Yes.

She has tattoos. Mummy would never have tattoos.

No, she wouldn't.

I wonder if Phoebe has a mother.

Well, I'm sure you can ask her.

When they arrive at the marina the sky is pearl-grey and the boats in the harbour bob like pelicans. There are cars lined up nearby, each with a licence plate and the insignia: *One Happy Island*. But he has not been so happy in Aruba, the island with the fat fish. Soon they'll be in blue open water, heading for South America, not an entirely different spot on earth. Spanish ex-colonial, not Dutch. Mainland, not island. But nevertheless a land once taken by surprise, invaded and captured by the Old World, like it or not. Not only will the crossing be rough but the land will be difficult to negotiate. For South America was also dominated and its native people were hurt; an entire people don't recover from torture in just a few centuries. Recovery takes time; it is the story of the still emerging Caribbean.

FURTHER

CHAPTER THIRTEEN

GHOST

They prepare for the rough trip to Cartagena de Indias. The dinghy is deflated and stowed in the V-berth, the oars and small outboard engine in a cockpit locker, everything in the saloon is secured, nothing left loose. In a pet shop in Oranjestad he found a dog kennel with bars and a wooden frame, a bit like a chicken coop, which he secures in the V-berth and pads with newspaper; he also bought a net which will cover half the berth in the saloon, a harness for Phoebe. A new light for the mast. They shopped together too: plenty of fresh water and Pot Noodles and chocolate and chilli dogs. In the end he found a Laundromat and managed to wash and dry a month's dirty sheets and clothes before Phoebe climbed on board. Suzy will have to make the trip mostly in her kennel, Océan in the saloon berth; neither of them above deck, it is just too dangerous.

He and Phoebe agree the passage will be too rough for

the auto-steering. They will do three-hour shifts each at the tiller. It will be a hands-on passage. Phoebe travels light, arriving with her own foul weather gear, one small bag and her guitar. He is glad of her calm presence, that she has sailed a Great Dane before. A strong man, that's what he wanted, and from the neck down her body is compact and sturdy, like that of an adolescent boy. From the moment she's on board she exhibits the instincts and habits of a sailor, knowing where not to stand and what not to touch, possessing an easy familiarity with the boat. *Thank God*. There's very little chitchat between them and yet they say what is needed to be said. When they cast off the ropes at Renaissance Marina, they are off, business-like and alert. He lets Phoebe take them out while he sees to Océan and Suzy below. Both seem to understand there's been a change, not just a new crew member, but also a new type of sailing ahead.

You okay there, turtledove? he says to Océan.

She nods and sits tight in her life vest.

Big waves now, eh, Dad? she says.

He looks at her. She said it in a way which was meant to say, I'm okay, I'm ready for it. Are you?

Yes, big waves for a couple of nights. You've had your seasick pills, so you should be okay. But it will be like it was when we left Trinidad, so I want you down here, okay?

Okay, she says.

I want you to hang onto this if need be, he says, show-ing her the taut net he's strung up so she won't get thrown out of bed. With Suzy taking up the berth in the bow, she will have to sleep here. There are loops hanging above the berth. Hang onto these straps too, okay?

She nods and her eyes are large and serious.

By sunset, they've met high winds and he reefs the mainsail. First ten knots, then fifteen, then twenty-five, and it's thrilling to watch the little boat puff out her sails and take this wind as best she can. She is hurrying along, going as fast as she ever will, like an old lady moving in heavy skirts. Phoebe is keeping the mainsail and the jib trimmed. They chug along at six knots, riding and surfing down the swells. The winds shift and so does the jib and he helps her with the sheets, hauling together. They say little; this seamanship comes naturally to them both. The waves build, first three foot, then five foot; then waves start to take swipes at them, hurling themselves into the cockpit: *whoosh.* The bitch sea is at them again, grander than he's seen her before, a towering sea, her energy massive and intimidating and yet she is deciding not to clump them, douse them in one, like she could. These waves are regular in motion, and Phoebe keeps steady at the tiller and smiles at the waves and then at him and says: I like this.

Good, he replies.

She stands and keeps the tiller firm against her thigh, heading south-west, her hair drenched, her face wet.

This is fun, she says.

Yes, he laughs.

Phoebe makes him feel better. She is wearing a harness and a lifeline; she cannot get swept away. His spirits are jangling up around his ears. Somewhere inside, some part of him remembers just how much he likes difficult seas too.

Night falls around them and then it is black sky and jet-blue waves like mountains. *Romany* climbs them slowly. What is going on, deep down in the bulging heart of this great element? Why is she so troubled right here? It's as if she is shifting about in her sleep, trying to get comfortable. *Jump*, she shouts at them, jump into my willowy arms, into my swells, my curves. The sea moves him. For the first time in years he wonders if he will be seasick, spill his guts. He can feel his insides shift, his organs swaying about. He remembers the barracuda on the jetty in Spanish Water, its innards sliding into the sea, its dead eye fixed on him. He remembers his son, his baby boy, taken by a vanquishing wave.

For hours they man the tiller, taking turns, making tea, noodles, Cup a Soup, checking on the child and the dog, negotiating the head, pumping water out, keeping the valves closed, trying to pee in that rocking-horse of a cupboard. It is almost impossible to walk down below. They stagger to and fro, clutching at whatever they can, banging knees and elbows, holding onto corners and knobs, the bones of the ship creaking. Downstairs Océan is white and silent and clutches at the net.

Hang in there, sweetie, he says.

She nods.

Suzy is sitting like a monk in a cell, penitent, head bowed, safe. Mumbling to herself.

Good dog, say your prayers.

Big sea, he whispers.

You try and get a couple of hours' sleep, Phoebe advises. He stares at her. *Really*? This sounds crazy, but he sees that she means it; she will be okay for a couple of hours, more than okay. He realises she isn't just younger but fitter than him, springier with youth; she has more élan, more grit. He's almost out of his depth, but she isn't.

I'll wake you at 5 a.m.

Are you sure?

Yes, I'm fine. He looks out to sea. The waves are large but have become more even, the swells heaving with a predictable grace.

Okay. Get me if there's any kind of problem, he says, knowing that a rest will be good, but sleep impossible. He will lie next to Océan, keep her safe. He goes into the cabin and lies down, near his child, feeling his eyes heavy, his fibres soft. The boat rocks him, rocks the child in his arms. Images come to him, all tumbled up, of the wave, the big brown wave, the water rising, breezeblocks flying forward, the garden walls erupting with water.

*

When he opens his eyes it is light. The saloon is heavy with salt air. His child is asleep next to him, her face is serene, her ribcage moving up and down in gentle swells. He checks his watch, 6 a.m.

Shit, he gasps.

He jumps up and climbs the stairs to the cockpit. Dawn. Lavender skies and a massive white sun behind them. The seas are still like mountains and Phoebe is sitting there, smiling lazily like the sea. It has happened to her too, overnight, her blood and the sea have aligned. She looks feline and saline, like she has been to a bar, slowly got drunk on red rum.

You okay? he asks.

She smiles. He left her to skipper a boat like the one her father owned, like the one she sailed as a child.

I can take over now, he says.

Sure, she says, and they swap.

Anything to report, he asks, as she is about to disappear into the saloon.

Yeah. I saw a black tip shark jump from the sea. Oh, and . . . She looks at him, her expression careful, serious. I kept seeing something . . . Another person. I mean it. I know how you can hallucinate at sea. But this was real. I kept seeing a *man* or the shadow of a man on the foredeck.

A man?

Yes, he looked like he was hauling down the mainsail, a man. I saw him all night.

Up on deck?

Yes.

Oh, says Gavin, shivering. He doesn't want to press her for more. But she gives him a look like Océan gives him sometimes, like his wife used to give him too, a look which means let's talk about this later.

*

Early morning, the sea is the same. They are traversing a valley of blue mountains; they are climbers as well as sailors. He holds the tiller steady, the main is full, the jib pulled close, the boat still pushing six knots. The swells are even, nothing too tricky is happening at all. A pod of dolphins joins them and they dance and somersault close to the bow, taking turns in dipping under or flipping over it. Miles away another supertanker is heading towards them. His straw stetson-sombrero is tied to his head with string. He sings to himself, an old Sparrow calypso, something about a sailor man. *Oh God, I nearly die of tabanca.*

He sits for hours in quiet morning meditation, many people appearing in his thoughts and vanishing in a haze: his wife, his son, his home, Clive, Paco, Jackie, even Petula. They all pass before him, his old life, his real life, they all come to say hello. His mother Audrey too, and the iguana which falls every day from the tree in her garden. His mother is a good woman, accident-prone in her old age, her bones brittle now, eighty and smoking a pack a day, glued to Facebook and daytime TV. What will he do in his old age? Or will he throw himself into the sea long before then? He fingers his beard and still has no answers for Petula or Clive, or himself, nothing to say: only, maybe, okay – you were right, Jackie, this boat has a ghost, the ghost of the man who fell into the sea while he was hauling down the mainsail.

Phoebe appears with Océan.

I've fed her, she says, and the dog.

Thank you. *Do you want to be a mother*, he wants to ask. But instead he feels himself blush. Too soon for such personal questions.

They swap places next to the tiller.

The three of them sit together in the cockpit, each of them attached by a line to the jack lines laid down on deck, each in foul-weather gear. Océan has on her Snoopy sunglasses, but she is still quiet and watchful, her eyes on the mountains of sea; she is so different to the day they passed the tooth, sailed away from Trinidad.

Will we ever see a whale, Dad? she asks, as if this question has emerged from whatever she is dreaming behind her shades.

Maybe. Probably not here, though.

Where then?

On the other side, in another ocean.

What is *this* ocean called?

The Caribbean.

What is the other ocean called?

The Pacific.

That's where we might see a whale?

If we're very lucky.

Dad?

What?

You named me after which ocean, then?

He laughs. I named you after them *all*, sweetie.

Why?

Because the ocean is full of wonders, and so are you.

She purses her lips, flummoxed at the compliment.

Okay, then, she says after a while.

Hours of it, all day. High seas. Suzy becomes restless downstairs and barks and for an hour he lets her out for a bit of exercise and a crap on some newspaper. He gives her something to drink and strokes her and pats her and they have a conversation, but he doesn't let her up into the cockpit.

Hours, a whole day of unrelenting seas and seamanship. Phoebe is never once thrown. She knew what to expect of this sea, what was needed of her. Now, he realises she knew so much more than he did about this crossing; he feels a sense of shame thinking of the way they stared her down in Taco Bell, inspecting her: *was she good enough?* She was the one who'd asked these questions first, made an assessment – before she even made contact with them, is his guess. She'd had a good look at *Romany*, eyed her up in the marina. A Great Dane – of course she wanted to skipper his boat, take her across rough seas. Phoebe wouldn't have offered her services if she hadn't thought it would be okay. Turning up with her guitar, how he'd underestimated her. How he was romanced by her blue eyes, her soft feminine nature. A small blonde woman. She is taking them across, not the other way around. She was up for the challenge of this old boat. He feels odd around her, nice. Phoebe is the seafaring version of his wife.

They eat noodles and cheese sticks, drink chai tea. Nothing more is possible. Late afternoon and the sun drops, the wind picks up and they plough across the waves. *Further*; she has the word tattooed on her arm. What does it mean? Maybe he should get himself tattooed too, an anchor or a rose, his wife's name. Or an interesting word which will make him seem enigmatic, like the sea. Phoebe is watching him.

You are very far away, she says.

Yes.

Me too, it's the sea, it makes you contemplate your life.

You're right, it does.

It makes you ask yourself how you are doing, so far.

They stare at the steep dunes of blue.

How are *you* doing so far, he asks. It feels rather daring to make this enquiry.

She laughs. I'm okay, so far, I think.

No marriages, no divorces?

Yes, I've been married.

Really? He is genuinely surprised.

I got married at eighteen.

Wow.

Yeah. No one thought it would last. And it didn't!

Good grief.

He was a lovely man, a boy really. I was a girl. We're good friends now. We grew apart; both of us went to college. He never liked the sea much.

What happened to him?

He joined a commune in Spain. I'm divorced now. I doubt I'll marry again in a hurry; but it was so romantic at the time.

How old are you, if you don't mind me asking?

Twenty-eight.

I married late. I was thirty-five. I didn't meet my wife till I was thirty. We left it for a while, or at least I did. I liked the sea too.

The sea likes to make you single, she says.

Yes, I think she does.

She is jealous. The sea is full of lonely men. Men own boats, women don't. Men go to sea, women, well, very few do. Men go to sea because the sea challenges them the way a woman can. And the sea wants them for herself. Thousands of men out there. I used to boat hitch. Every boat has a man on board as skipper. Thousands of single men out there, making love to the sea.

He feels shy, embarrassed.

I guess you've seen it all, he replies.

I've seen a lot. I've met a lot of men who like to sail. Most are running away from something. Apart from the ones who race or deliver or who have a profession at sea, the cruisers are all amateurs leaving town. Adventure, she says, flashing her eyes. The sea calls them, or so they feel. Some are bohemians; take their guitars, like me.

I ran away, he says, bluntly.

She nods.

I guess I'd like it to be different. I'm less running away now than I was. But yeah, me too. I cut and run. I left my job, just walked out one day. It was dramatic at first – but now, I'm here.

It's okay, you know. To do that.

Have you ever run away?

I ran away from home. I ran away from my father. He beat up my mother and me and my little brother. I left home at sixteen.

Good God.

Yeah, she smiles. I'm better off on my own.

I'm sorry.

Well, I'm sorry for you too.

You are brave coming on board men's boats.

Not really. It's always women who choose. I chose to come with you, not the other way around. You have a good child, a cool dog and an excellent boat.

I know, he laughs.

She laughs too, this Phoebe Wolf with the tattoos.

Night falls. Océan passes out below. More high winds sing in the sails; they are incessant. They sit in the dark and don't say much, each lost in the motion and shapes of the waves. Phoebe has hold of the tiller.

So, she says. You never told me about the ghost.

Ha, he groans. Well . . . I've never *seen* a ghost on board. Never once, in all these years. There is some kind of legend, though.

And?

Well. I lied.

You *lied*!

Yeah. Sorry. Got carried away with myself.

What did you lie about?

I did own this boat with my best friend, Clive. But we didn't buy it off anyone. We didn't buy it from the owner.

No?

No, *Romany* was found. Adrift. These things happen. She was found abandoned, flapping sails, unmanned. Some local fishermen brought her in. Then she was going to rot; she'd been on the hard for over a year. They were going to take her out, moor her in the back of the bay in TTSA, let her fill with water until she sank. So my friend made an offer; we bought her for very little. We were your age, maybe younger. It was a dream to own a boat so young.

You never found out what happened to the skipper?

No.

He must have gone over, rough seas. Like these.

Yes, poor bastard. And he means it, poor man, to go over into the ink. No harness on. Not a chance of rescue. The boat would leave you behind in minutes.

They sail for hours, winds at their backs, howling in the sails. Twenty-five knots behind them, thirty at times, and *Romany* climbs the black cliffs in her own time, no fuss.

She's so sure of herself, says Phoebe.

Does she remind you of your youth?

Yes, my father used to sail his boat a lot. But I was the only one in the family who also liked the sea. He used to take me out when I was a kid.

Like Océan?

Yes.

Does he still have his Great Dane?

No, he sold it eventually.

Well, I'm glad you're here, that you found us.

All night they take turns again. This time it is Phoebe who goes down to sleep for the longer shift. He is left in the cockpit at 2 a.m. Now he wishes he had a pipe, something to puff on while he is out here in the dark. Plenty going on, both inside and out and he is on edge. *Romany* chugs up and down the waves, like a steam engine or a bicycle or something very simple in its intent. The sails hum and the bow snuffles in the waves, in out, up and down. His body is rigid as he scans the waves, the boat, her sails, as he trims the main, makes tiny adjustments. *Romany* needs constant attention and care; it's impossible not to be aware of the precarious dynamic of small boat and big sea. Instinctively, she is responding to the sea and the wind and instinctively he responds to her needs. And she is perfectly fine, this old boat, happy to be out here.

All night he sits or stands at the tiller, eyes peeled on the blackness ahead. *Baf, baf*, as the bow hits and ploughs the waves, *sloosh*, the occasional swiper into the cockpit. *Baf, sloosh*, salt on his skin, stinging him, his eyes like radars in his head. A pain in his chest, the pain of abandonment; the pain feels more alive because of all this sea around him. The salt sea could either cure him or drown him, take him away from all his failures. His wife with her heart broken in two, oh how I love you. I understand, I really do. Where is Claire now? In that room upstairs in his mother-in-law's house, the one with the windows looking out onto the tall chaconia plants? Is she sitting there all day, still, knitting and staring at the TV, growing whiter and thinner, not eating, not speaking?

All night he keeps the tiller on course and contemplates the possibility of a new life for himself, out there, on the horizon, a new way to live. And he sees no man up ahead, on the bow, hauling down sails, struggling with the main. No dark shape appears, nothing moves up on the fore-deck. All he can see is the sea, nothing else, hills of black-blue, like he's arrived somewhere unfathomable, unstable. This place on earth is dangerous. Finally, he's here, out in great depths. But also, he is part of it. He is a man in a small boat at sea, and the waves are so much bigger than he ever imagined and he is becoming a sailor man again.

CHAPTER FOURTEEN

MIRA

They arrive at Club Nautico, Cartagena, early on Thursday evening. It has taken over three days to get across. Here the boats are protected by a curved hook of reclaimed land, Boca Grande, and on this curved coastline the Colombians have built their version of Manhattan. The marina is encircled with high-rise buildings which stand like a crowd of glittery partygoers on the flat grey sand behind the yachts. They arrive exhausted, all of them, even Suzy. They anchor and release her from her kennel, snap themselves from their harnesses, pour bottles of fresh water over their heads. Land, earth. It feels like a miracle to be here, safely moored.

Thank you, he says to Phoebe. You saved our arses. Let me buy you dinner while we're here.

Great. How long do you plan to stay?

No idea. A week?

I have a friend who runs a hostel here, in Getsemani. If

you don't mind, I'd like a few nights in a room, with a shower and hot water and TV.

That's fine.

Why don't you get a room too?

Us?

Yes. When was the last time you had a shower? Slept in a bed, you know.

God, over a month.

Well, maybe it's time for a pit stop.

Maybe. What about Suzy?

I'll ask my friend. I'm sure he can make an exception for a few nights, my friend is cool.

They all fall profoundly asleep that night, like babies in the arms of Cartagena de Indias. His dreams are barren, his head tight with being over-alert, over-active. His dream-life, his inner life, since leaving Aruba, has shrivelled from nervous exhaustion, from exhilaration and from caffeine. They were relaxed when they left, now he feels anxious again, on edge. Three days – the passage has left him exhilarated and confident. Again, they made it. This far, this is how far they've come.

In the morning, they inflate the dinghy, attach the small engine, pack a bag for a few nights, ride across to the jetty and tie up. They clear through customs, then eat breakfast in Manga at a café, milky coffees and croissants. Phoebe and Océan play Scissors Paper Stone with their fingers. Phoebe feels like part of their team. She has established herself by action, as someone like them. Océan still stares at her, curiously, taking note, as if she has found a role model of how to be. He realises he hasn't had any sexual fantasies about Phoebe probably because she hasn't wanted to be seen like that, not by him, anyway. She has slipped into their knot without fuss; she has accepted them and vice versa. He'd expected it to be harder, more awkward with another person on board. But Phoebe is like them; she *gets* them.

After breakfast, they walk across the bridge from Manga to Getsemani, a rougher part of the city, named after the garden at the foot of the Mount of Olives where Christ prayed the night before he was crucified.

Here, the streets are narrow and crowded, a sign saying *LLAMADAS* on every corner, where a person is standing selling calls on a mobile phone. The buildings were once grand but have now fallen into decay and here and there magenta bougainvillea spills from ornate balconies. They walk past a park with desiccated grass; dark cafés with high ceilings filled with men smoking and drinking coffee. They turn down a street and all of a sudden he knows that for the first time in their journey they are in a place which isn't safe. Here, people are lanky and look wily, more so than in downtown Port of Spain; the locals look at him in a direct and assessing way.

Phoebe guesses his thoughts.

It's not safe here, she says. Not after 9 p.m. Be careful. Never carry anything valuable on you. And you will get stopped by the pushers.

Pushers?

Cocaine.

They stop at some wrought-iron gates and Phoebe reaches inside for the buzzer.

The gate opens.

Inside, there is a dimly lit TV room full of listless backpackers, a Colombian man on the desk, bald as a marble under his cap. His eyes light up when he sees Phoebe and they greet each other in Spanish. Then she turns: *Si, Franco, este hombre es mi amigo, Gavin, y su hija, Océan, y Suzy.*

Gavin feels suddenly awkward in his straw hat and new bushy beard, with his child and his dog, like they are a group of refugees or they have come from a festival on the sea. Now they look like hippies. Océan's hair is pearl-silver and she is giving Franco a six-year-old's cut eye, like she is the child of a drug lord or a pirate. All the adventure has gone to her head.

Franco proffers his hand. He and Phoebe speak in Spanish and then Phoebe says, yes, he has a room and the dog is okay, a room with a shower, upstairs. Nothing fancy. I'll be sleeping downstairs, along there, she points. I'm going to unpack and have a shower. See you later.

When Franco shows him the room, it's both the worst room he's ever seen and the best. The walls are unpainted and the floor is red chipped terrazzo, not even a ceiling fan. No curtains either, just wooden shutters to close at night. Two beds, a double and a single, and a small bathroom with a shower.

Thanks, he says. This will be fine.

He, Océan and Suzy immediately climb onto the

double bed. He switches on the small television and they stare at CNN. He opens a packet of Doritos and they stay in a huddle like that all morning, watching TV as if they've never seen TV before, never slumped together like this. They fall asleep and don't wake until much later in the afternoon, the TV still on, CNN reporting something about floods in the countryside, thousands stranded and flooded from their homes. Images of crowds standing huddled, rain-soaked, houses broken and bobbing in water. He and Océan register the images and she snuggles under his arm, hiding her face. He puts his hand to his chest to check his heart and whispers a prayer for those who have lost their homes. Trinidad, Venezuela, the rains in Aruba. These floods are here in Colombia, too; they're everywhere.

*

Late afternoon they walk from Getsemani to the walled Old City. On the way they pass a street market of second-hand books and men pushing glass boxes of fresh tamarind juice. They duck down a street where there is another market, people selling slices of watermelon and mango in cups, men filleting fruit, paw paw, oranges, an open air canteen, many people sitting eating fried fish in the early evening haze. Further on, there's an arcade of silk flowers, and men sitting in rows, in front of typewriters. They are the city's scribes, offering to write letters to various authorities. Everywhere, there are men shining shoes, their customers sit on a colourful wooden chair and rest their feet on a metal footstool.

The Old City is hidden behind high walls, behind which is the sea they have just crossed. They walk under an arch and find candy sellers, rows of them, hawking homemade confections in jars and shops changing money. He changes some US dollars into pesos. They walk the streets holding hands, Suzy on the lead. There are men standing still as statues on street corners, blacked up with boot polish, buskers miming for money, young police-men everywhere. Here the buildings are restored to their colonial glory, every balcony dripping with rapids of lilies and bougainvillea, every building chalk-red or violet, sky-blue, lemon.

This is the city the Spanish built and fortified, from the sea and from pirates and invading fleets. This city fought back a massive British invasion, hundreds of gunships. The Inquisition was here in Cartagena de Indias, and they brought contraptions to squash skulls, disfigure genitals; they tortured the native people into Christianity, hoisted them from ceilings, filled their gullets with water, damned them as witches unless they denied their heathen faith. Cartagena has been painted to appear gay and pretty, romantic, but it feels old and lonely, tragic.

They wander for an hour through narrow alleys, everywhere emeralds for sale. They linger at one shop and are quickly shown rough jewels the size of Gavin's thumb.

Océan loves the green stones, her eyes glow at the collection shown to them. Can we buy one for Mum? she says.

The sale takes minutes.

He buys his wife a ring with a dark green polished emerald. With it comes a certificate of excellence and he wraps both together and slips them into his bag.

They arrive at a large square with dancing fountains surrounded by cafés and find a table and sit down. Horses drawing carriages clop around the square, on the far corner some sailors in navy uniform have gathered. A waiter comes out and hands them menus; they order pasta. It is 6 p.m., the sky is fading to night. Men and women pass them selling jewellery, watches, paintings and etchings of the city. It takes a very firm no before they move on.

A little girl appears at their table. She arrives from nowhere, from the street. She has long brown hair and must be the same age as Océan. At first he thinks she is trying to sell him something and casts his eyes away; then she says something in Spanish.

Mira, she says, and holds out her arm. *Look.*

He is a little frightened to look at her but he glances down and sees she is carrying a brown creature on her forearm, a baby sparrow or a bat.

Mira, she says, emphatically, holding out her arm so both he and Océan can see.

Océan cranes her neck and stares.

He looks closer.

It's not a bird or a bat. It's a moth, huge, brown and furry, its wingspan several inches across.

The little girl smiles, smug once she realises they have understood. Sitting on her arm, tame, ugly, is a moth as big as a bird.

Go away, says Gavin, his voice gentle, but firm.

The little girl backs away, grinning, pleased she has showed them something of her city.

That was horrible, Dad, says Océan.

He nods. He looks up, to search for the little girl; but she's gone, vanished, round the corner past the fountains. From nowhere, he feels a strong gust of homesickness. *Look*, said the little girl, as if to say, look at yourself.

They eat their pasta in silence.

Suzy mumbles, asking for her share, and they feed her under the table.

The sea has leeched all their energy. The city around them is a fairground of splendid attractions and they are like hobos, too travel-weary to get on the rides. He thinks of *his* city, Port of Spain, also a city by the sea. He thinks of how well he knows Port of Spain, and how, oddly, it attunes him to this never-before visited Caribbean city. Somehow he knows Cartagena, its layers of history, of being invaded and handed over, fought over again and again. He doesn't entirely feel like a stranger here.

They walk back to their hostel in the rougher part of town. It is because they have left *Romany* behind, he decides; that is why he is feeling out of himself. They have been on the boat for so long it has become their home. The child with the moth, the ghost on the fore-deck, hoisting the main: all of it, jumbled up.

Their real home was knocked down. He built it back. But he and his child didn't take to this new home. Those pink walls, Pepto-Bismol-pink, they made his stomach heave. And the rain which still walked down the mountains all around. He could not stop the rain from falling, from scaring his child. And so they got on the boat and that has been some kind of home, and now they are here in a city which reminds him a bit of Port of Spain, and it is okay, he reassures himself. Océan, he marvels at how she has taken it all in. She is like a super-heroine, Mermaid Girl. How he has underestimated her too, and how he still has a sense that she is supporting him.

They arrive at the hostel without being approached by cocaine pushers and buzz to be let in.

He puts Océan in the shower, hands her the soap and says scrub yourself clean. Then he puts Suzy in the shower and scrubs her down and dries her off. She gets into the single bed with Océan and the two fall asleep instantly.

He gets into the shower himself and when he does, it is like being hit by rain, pelting cleansing rain in his face and tears fall too. Tears for his wife and his baby son and tears for the man he has become, the man running away. He sobs in the shower and it is a relief. He has been waiting for it, this weeping. The door is closed and the sound of the shower muffles his sobs; his body heaves and he weeps for something lost that will never return. One part of his life is now gone. He will never go back to that time. It didn't work. He thinks of Phoebe being beaten by her father and he sees the little girl with the moth on her arm. *Mira,* she says to him. *Look,* she says and with that he sobs like a child, saying help me, oh Lord.

CHAPTER FIFTEEN

GETSEMANI

When he lies on the bed, clean, his eyes burning, he remembers it all. It had been raining hard that afternoon, from four till six o'clock. Rain without pause. Rain so loud it drowned out all other sounds, so heavy it short-circuited the world, like when black-and-white TV was first invented, and occasionally there was an almighty clash in frequency and the screen went wild. It was like that, frenetic and agitated, and it had the effect of stirring panic in the blood. From his office window he watched people in the streets of Port of Spain running with umbrellas breaking and bending in the onslaught. Gutters filling, the roads raging with brown water, and when the rain stopped, suddenly, he went straight home to check on his house; there'd been a problem with flooding the last two rainy seasons. They were building condos up on the hill behind his home, denuding the forest and this had caused flooding at the bottom of the hill in his neighbourhood.

And so he went home and found inches of water in his driveway up to the kitchen door and he got a broom and swept this water away into the drain out back. These smaller floods had already been happening, seven over the last two years, and there'd been nothing he could do. Fight who? Fat cat developers, the government who had no laws around private planning?

At 8 p.m., the rain started again, just as hard. Claire had fed Océan potato waffles and baked beans, and Océan was still watching cartoons on TV in her pyjamas. Alexander was in his cot under a mosquito net, asleep. His bedroom was at the back of the house, the door ajar. They'd been preparing for a quiet evening, when the rain started up again. Josephine was there, in her room next to the kitchen. She was also watching TV. Suzy was inside, under the coffee table, moaning with unease at the rain. The Christmas tree, winking with lights, stood in the corner like a lighthouse of good cheer. All their wrapped presents were under it.

Half an hour ticked past, the rain was a solid wall of water falling from the sky. He began to fret. The ground around them was already sodden from the afternoon's downpour. There was a storm drain behind his house already full of churned-up water. His neighbour rang him, also worried. His neighbour's house was even closer to the foot of the hill with no trees.

We're sitting ducks, Gavin said, on the phone. You okay?

Not really. It like a pond in mih garden.

Rain like war. He put on gumboots and went out and stood on his porch and watched. *Fuck*.

Rumbles in the sky, great tearing sounds, and the clatter of an army marching, soldiers roaring. Trinidadians live with the rainy season. This happens every year, half a dozen or so downpours this violent between June and December. Every year his neighbours ring him, especially the last few seasons. He shouldn't worry; this will be okay, it is not unusual. He put on a waterproof jacket and dragged a kitchen chair out into the sodden garden. He climbed onto the chair and peered over his garden wall. *Oh, God*.

Brown water, a river now raging down the denuded hill, water spraying and buffeting off his neighbour's wall. The street outside his house was a swollen river of brown. The floodwater was rising, rising up the thin garden walls of his home. He jumped off the chair, went back inside and poured himself a rum. He knocked it back, then poured another and knocked that back too.

Claire was sitting with Océan on the sofa. She didn't want to look over the garden wall. She sat calm, her face composed. At one point she got up and went to the back room to peer in at Alexander; then she returned and sat again.

He's okay. Best we don't wake him, she said.

Gavin guessed she was weighing things up, coping. Claire always knew nothing bad would ever happen to her or those she loved; God was on her side. She'd had a tranquil and blessed life until that night.

But he was fraught; his own fear was also rising; the world outside was turning to water. Claire sat on the sofa as he paced the porch; she was holding her daughter's hand.

Another of his neighbours rang, same story.

Shit, man, said Jeremy from across the road. His father lived with them, his father who was blind and autistic. Mih father gettin upset.

Gavin considered getting down on his knees and praying.

More phone calls. Every person he spoke to was alarmed. Eventually, he could bear it no longer.

Claire, I'm going to ring Clive. It's time you all left. I don't like this at all. You, the kids, Josephine, Suzy. I'm going to ask him to come in the Jeep.

And leave you behind?

I'll be fine.

She shook her head.

I'll climb onto the roof with a ladder; it won't be hard. You better get Alexander.

But Claire didn't move. He saw that she couldn't. Something inside her had already shut down. She was sitting still, on the sofa, Océan next to her, when it happened.

An almighty *crack*.

He turned in time to see the concrete garden wall break open and bricks fly into the floodwater, the wave of water like an athlete taking a hurdle, landing tight and then springing forward, racing towards them.

Run, he shouted and he fled, seconds ahead of the brown wave.

Claire sat rigid, clasping her daughter's hand. Océan turned to face the wave, her face lit up with terror.

Run, he screamed, and then he was with them and had picked up Océan by the hair and swept her up and over his shoulder and dragged his wife from the sofa. Then the brown wave was in the house, sweeping through, and he was hurled against a wall, thrown flat, water up to his chest. The Christmas tree was bobbing in the water and Suzy was howling – he saw her paddling and gargling and snapping, and then she disappeared, swept away around the same wall he was pinned against. He heard Josephine in her room wailing, *dear God ah ent dyin alone*. Water up to his neck, and Océan held above him on his shoulders, screaming *Daddyyy*, and his wife also pinned against the wall. The water was gushing, moving through the house like a herd of cattle, swirling up against the windows. There was the sound of the porous inner walls cracking too and the rain doubling in intensity.

A new roar, louder, like a machine switched on, a chainsaw revved.

Minutes passed with the three of them flat against the kitchen wall, the brown water holding them there. In those minutes, a lifetime; images came, of his first bike, his first dog, his first kiss, his first trip on *Romany*, their wedding day, the moments his children were born, his famous recipe for rum punch, his telescope, the time he had a molar extracted and it bled for days, and he thought, why this and why us? He prayed then, Dear God on earth and in heaven, help us, help us now. And he thought of his son, in his cot, that he must rescue his son.

The flood had caused a river torrent in the house and he could hardly move until the waters slowed and even then it was difficult. He managed to inch towards the kitchen where there was an island of countertops and he hauled Claire onto one and said, stay here, don't move, stay with Océan.

She nodded, sodden, holding Océan to her waist. Océan was blue with cold, her eyes wild. The flood was still agile and swirling, but the initial surge had subsided. The water was chest high. Claire was shaking, clutching her daughter.

He moved forward slowly in the murky cold water, down the corridor, towards his son's bedroom. The door had burst open and inside he could see the room was full of water, black and brackish, like a dark sea. His heart was yammering, a pulse of unbound energy leaping about his neck, his face. His boots were full of water and he strode forward as best he could, but the water in this room was deep. He saw the mosquito net drenched and sagging into the brown silt and the cot in the corner submerged. He thrust forward and dived down, his arms outstretched and dimly he saw, through his wide-open eyes, that the cot was empty. He burst to the surface for air and plunged into the water again, searching every part of the cot, turning the mattress over, coming up again for air. He realised he'd have to search every part of the room and then he was so panicked he was yelling and his heart was seizing up. *Alexander*, he shouted, *my son*, and then, in the far corner by the wall, he saw his son, his tiny body lifeless and his clothes brown with mud, face down.

*

Later that night, he finally called Clive on a neighbour's mobile phone. Clive came in his Jeep when the waters had subsided and took away Josephine and Océan and Claire and the body of their son wrapped in a blanket. There were walls down everywhere in the street and lost dogs running around, excited, barking in the sludge. Suzy wasn't one of them.

In front of his home, the waters still raged; the river was smaller but it still poured down the hill. His home was stiff with silt, but the waters were now draining from the rooms into the already rain soaked earth all around. The neighbours were walking about, stunned, exchanging stories. There was one house worse hit, the house at the end of the street, square in the path of the floodwater. They had thrown their children over the wall, jumped over it themselves and run down the main road, barefoot. He told of his loss and everyone said *Jesus, Gavin, I'm so sorry*. One woman cried. They were shocked and sorry but no one said much more.

He was dazed and unable to think straight. Someone

gave him a dry towel to wrap around his shoulders. Everyone was incredulous, as he was, that the neighbourhood could be flattened in an hour. Rubble. Trees down. Furniture swept into the road.

Audrey, his old mother and her best friend Marguerite, and his sister Paula turned up in a Mini, armed with flimsy house brooms and dustpans. They quickly got mired in the mud and screeched with fear but couldn't drive up the road to his home. They called out to him, sent him love and kisses; all were in tears. They said they would be back at dawn. He didn't tell them his son had drowned. It was impossible. He said he would stay at the house till then; he wanted to guard it, somehow. Even now, thinking back, it's hard to know why he wanted to stay there all night, a sentry in his devastated house. Only now he knows why he didn't leave with Clive, go back to Clive's home. He didn't want to be with his dead son. He wanted the body gone, taken away, so he never had to see it again.

He sat alone, on the porch of his muddy home, and he cried all night. At dawn his sister turned up in gumboots, Paula who was a journalist and lived in London, and had flown in for Christmas the night before. He was standing outside the rubble of his home and his clothes were still soaked and he was blue and shivering. When his sister saw him she wept and said *oh Christ*, and put her arms around him and said *I'm so sorry. I'm soo so sorry*. And he let himself be held and let himself cry in her arms. They sat for a very long time, doing little. She had brought a flask of coffee and he told her what had happened. He told her about finding his son in the water.

*

Claire and Océan stayed at Clive's for days. Claire didn't want to come back to see the house and Océan was traumatised. Suzy turned up the next day, barking, wild with joy at seeing him. He patted her down and fed her but it took some time to reassure her. In the end he had to chain her in the garage she was so jumpy, she kept climbing onto him.

From nowhere, friends arrived, people from other parts of the neighbourhood too. Some even came with shovels, ready to work. His sister went to buy breakfast for everyone and more shovels from the hardware store and they began to dig away the mud. It was a lost time; he was dazed and forgetful. Once he lost his shoes for hours, only to find them where he'd left them, in the bathroom, in front of the toilet. Gangs arrived, teams of workers paid by the government, a gang of men turned up with JCB diggers and a small Bobcat and they scooped away the mountains of rubble blocking the drains. They began moving away the trees which had fallen and shoring up power cables and posts which had fallen.

For days they dug in the mud. For days he couldn't think straight and felt tired and distraught. His sister had hoped to take charge, but his state was contagious and every time she tried to make a methodical attack on one part of the house, she too got lost. Everything was in the mud. While digging they came across alien objects: one leg of a Barbie doll, Océan's tricycle, a potato peeler, toothbrushes, the dead goldfish from the broken tank. The fridge and the oven were thick with mud, the cupboards too; mattresses soaked, doors swelling, everything stank of rot. The Christmas tree was ruined. Untangling the lights was when he almost cracked. His sister looked at him as she held the other end and said: *Gavin, look at me. Breathe. Look at me.* His hands were shaking.

For days his bowels quaked and his hands shook. He didn't sleep. People came and went; they brought pots of pelau, hops and ham, macaroni pie and Carib beer. They dug mud from all the rooms of his house in wheelbarrows and sprayed everything with power hoses.

A television crew turned up, and a reporter from the CNC, the local news channel. They interviewed him and filmed his house. Hundreds living in wooden houses in rural areas had lost their homes, too. He couldn't imagine that things could be worse, but they were, elsewhere. But he, a white man from a gated neighbourhood, made national television because he'd lost his son, the only death. People he only vaguely knew called to send their condolences because they'd seen him on TV. The local MP, Harry Winslow, turned up and walked through his house with his little daughter, Océan's age, who took pictures on her pink plastic camera.

Little girl, put that *away*, his sister snapped. This is not a tourist attraction. Put that camera down. He thought Paula was going to hit the little girl.

Paula scowled at the MP and said what the fuck are you going to do about those people building condos up on the hill? My brother's son is *dead*. Drowned. He was just a baby. Just what are you going to do?

Then she lost her temper completely and shouted I'm going to sue your balls off, you fucking creep, you macho fuckface. She shouted this and worse at the local man from the government.

Paula cussed him like a devil because she was from England, where democracy is better than in the Caribbean and where MPs are held accountable for anything bad which might be associated with them. The MP stood there, nodding, listening with intent, but said nothing.

*

Gavin barely saw or spoke to his wife during those first few days after the flood. She moved from Clive's back to her mother's. He stayed at the house. They spoke on the phone and he went over once or twice but didn't know what to say to make things better. He felt angry that she didn't try to help him and she felt angry that he didn't come to comfort her; they left each other alone. Someone from their insurance company visited and assessed the situation and assured him they would cover all costs and pay for another house to rent for a few months. Mr Grant called and gave him two weeks off. His mother cooked for him, neighbours continued to come round.

After the funeral, the three of them went to live in this other house, a townhouse in a community of townhouses in La Seiva which all looked onto a swimming pool and a children's playground. There were lots of children around for Océan to play with, but she didn't want to go out. She watched them through the window.

It was then, in that cold new bed, the bed that wasn't theirs, that he held his wife and felt her body stiffen and knew that something had already set in; it was then his old life ended. He and Claire didn't manage to speak about their son's death; her grief was turned in on itself. It was like she'd lost her wiring, the electricity that makes a human spark, live, talk, smile, sing. Her soul had vanished. And, to be truthful, he had a similar feeling in his heart. How could this happen, and what would they do now? They'd been working hard to live a small good life and it wasn't enough. The flood was random, a rare occurrence. But what troubled him most, then and still, is that the flood had no meaning, no order; it was a catastrophe to him and meant nothing to nature.

CHAPTER SIXTEEN

HALF A MAN

They set sail in *Romany* a week later, bound for the San Blas archipelago, a group of islands off the Isthmus of Panama. The island chain is either known as the Kuna Yala, its Indian name, or San Blas, after a fierce Spanish admiral, Blas de Lezo, who lost an eye, an arm and a leg in the course of his navy career and was also known as 'half a man'.

Leaving Cartagena was easy. He didn't feel comfortable for one moment in the city. He had his shoes shined while sitting on a fancy chair; they ate at long communal tables in the market every day, fried fish and plantain, and they drank fresh tamarind juice from the glass tanks on the street. They ate once with Phoebe in a restaurant opposite the grand Hotel Santa Clara. But he found the place inhibiting with its balconies and trailing lilies and horse-drawn carriages; it was one of those cities for lovers, just like Paris. It gave him the heebie-jeebies. But the hostel bed was good enough and so were the shower and the TV. They spent most of the time in their dingy room, watching movies. They were on their raft again, like old times.

Now, it is late January, still the windy season, and again they are sailing on following seas, but they are rough. Everyone on board is harnessed up, Suzy stowed in her coop. Phoebe again skippers them out, into the open blue water. He ties his big straw hat to his head and settles next to her in the cockpit, alert, scanning the waves. The balancing of the waters in his body and the sea now feels like a conscious tuning in; it is palpable, some inner balancing. Phoebe smiles and nods, yes, she knows about this too. Sailing in open water can be many things: laborious, monotonous, exhilarating, dangerous. Acres of blue with little else to see. Little to say, but plenty to watch, plenty to sink into.

Again, they are climbing dunes; all day they climb up and down these steep cliffs, taking turns at the tiller. Up, down, tea, coffee and noodles. Winds behind them, they are on a broad reach with the main and jib out. It is simple sailing in this old craft. In the saloon things are being thrown about, impossible to keep everything neatly stowed. Océan clings to the netting, to the loops above the berth. Hang in there, mermaid, he calls down to her. She is good, oh so good, his daughter; she is becoming a sailor.

All day, then all night. Tight seamanship, both of them in sync with the boat, both aware of a million things which could go wrong with the sea which is visible and the winds which are invisible. It is a fluid effort of rigour, mental and physical. Each of them takes frequent short naps, each of them fizz with nerves. The sea around them could catapult the boat stern over bow, or swallow her whole; it could form a whirlpool, suck them under, or it could behave well enough for now. His skin crawls with an erotic terror; this kind of sea is a horror and a turn on. And they work together: woman man, boywoman man, and sometimes he feels like a boy and sometimes he cannot see which of them is the woman and sometimes he feels big and sometimes he feels small. And he can see the best of Phoebe and the best of himself too, how they can handle this old boat.

And they sail all the next day too, and then all night again. Forty-eight hours straight. He sings a lot, into the winds, the words he can remember of the Sparrow calypso, *A Sailor Man*:

> *It's the same behaviour,*
> *Horn like fire, I can't take it no longer,*
> *You know I nearly died with tabanca.*

Tabanca. It's one of his favourite words, what Trinidadians call heartbreak. *Tabanca fer so*, a man or woman will declare when gripped by this particular emotion. People laugh or smile at the word because it rolls so well on the tongue; it could be the name of a cocktail, or a flower, something enjoyable, but no, there's nothing enjoyable about being in a state of tabanca, this soft mournful feeling in his chest. It is killing him, getting the better of him over so many weeks and months, wearing him thin. He's been dying, slowly, of tabanca – that's the truth of it. The sea makes this feeling both worse and better.

On the second night he is at the tiller. It is 3 a.m. The sea is black and in a state of argument, the roughest seas yet. Sleep isn't possible. Everything downstairs is pitched about; Phoebe is in the saloon with Océan who is hanging onto her bunk. He has his eyes on the sea; he feels calm and also fearful. *Romany* does well in these conditions, and he knows this, yet his testicles have scrunched up into his body, they are hiding behind his arse. He imagines whales rearing up, freak waves, even a giant squid gripping the boat in its tentacles, the boat dismasting or worse, rolling over. He's imagining all these things, and staying calm, when he hears a chilling sound from the saloon: his child screaming in agony.

Phoebe sticks her head up from the hatch. Her face is bleak.

Océan fell, she says, fell badly. The netting broke. She was flung out.

Quickly, they swap at the tiller and he flies down the steps. Océan is on the floor, streaks of blood on her face. She is wailing, her mouth wide open, her eyes rolled back in her head. She is clutching her lower leg.

Jeesus, sweetheart!

He dashes to his daughter's side and almost gags. There's a wound on her leg, a star-shaped gash, the flesh on the shin all this way and that, and he can see yellowy muscle and a deeper paler tissue flapping. The wound is vicious-looking, gaping, the blood crimson and beginning to gush.

Shush, dou dou. He tries to soothe her. You'll be okay, we're gonna make this better. But his words sound thin and don't seem to matter. He tries to press the flesh back over the gash, but the skin moves away, like there's grit in it, or something folded up.

Océan glares at him, in shock. She is horrified, and, he realises, so is he. He looks about. Yes, the netting snapped and Océan was catapulted out onto something sharp.

Sweetie, I'm going to get the first-aid box, be brave. I'll only be a minute.

In the V-berth he pulls open the drawer, pulls out the box he bought at Peake's, returns with the kit. But already his heart is banging in his chest, his hands are shaking as he kneels down next to her and flips the lid open. In it, rows of bandages, bottles of ointment. Océan is sobbing, the wound is messy and gaping again.

He opens a bottle of antiseptic ointment and dabs it on a gauze pad and he finds himself drawn to looking into the wound. His stomach heaves and his head goes light and fluttery. The lights in the cabin seem bright, like fireflies, buzzing around him.

Daddy will fix this up, he says, nodding, reassuring her. But her face is swollen with tears. He cannot move his hands, they feel stiff and clumsy. He dabs more ointment on the pad and dabs the wound, touching it gingerly, but he cannot make the skin go back as it was. She winces and whimpers. *Ooooh*, Dad. It's like she's been cleft with the claw end of a hammer, or gouged by a rake. And then he doesn't feel well at all, like he's drowning, going under; he shouts for help, *Phoebe*.

He wakes moments later, on the cabin floor, with a thick head.

What happened?

You fainted, Phoebe says, a flinty impatience in her voice. Go upstairs, I've lashed the tiller, it won't hold long. Get some fresh air, I'll finish bandaging her leg. He looks at his child and she is clearly amazed. Adults faint?

He feels sick and ashamed. He kisses Océan on the forehead. His legs are weak and he tries to get up but his head is still swirly. He's never fainted before, at anything; he feels old suddenly, like he might shit his pants. The boat is bucking and it is hard to get onto his feet – he *must* get back to the tiller, or *Romany* could roll over in these seas. But he's as heavy as a bag of cement.

Yes, he says, I'll get back to the boat.

Phoebe nods and doesn't look at him; she shows a human quality he associates with people who come from countries of the northern hemisphere, countries which have snow, an extreme hardiness.

I'm sorry, he mutters.

Outside, the salt air slaps him in the face. From the square light of the cabin, Phoebe thrusts out her hand, in it a small bottle of rum. *Drink some*, she shouts.

He grabs it and thinks, rum? Where did she get this

from? It feels like another of Phoebe's mysteries. He is ashamed and scared. He knocks back a hard slug and he pours some into the hollow of one hand and slaps it onto his face like cologne. He knocks back another slug. The boat is surrounded by steep hills. *Romany* steps up them carefully, like a mule taking a sheer wall face. He can hear a low rumbling from the sea, hahahaha, you foolish man. You're only half a man, half the man you think you are. He sits at the tiller and watches his hands tremble. He feels a rolling throbbing terror at the thought that Océan could ever be hurt, that another of his children could die.

*

At dawn, the sea is different. Calm. Tufts of islands are spread everywhere, like they've sailed into a lake of upturned toothbrushes. The islands are tiny, on each a crush of green palm trees, nothing else. His charts show reefs and there's plenty of evidence that they are treacherous. The rusted carcass of a cargo vessel is still crunched onto a reef to the east, and somewhere up ahead, off the port bow, he can see the listing spike of a yacht's mast, the boat sunk only metres off one of these islands and recently, or so it looks. No rust. He radios in on the VHF and Phoebe speaks in Spanish and finds that yes, there's a medical centre on one of the bigger islands in the centre of the archipelago. He switches on the motor and keeps the sails up; they forge on. Océan is asleep. It has been four hours, now, since the accident; she will need stitches fast. They head for Rio Acuzar, where there's a clinic and doctors.

There are houses on the island, made of grass. Cone-shaped grass huts faded to a silver ash-brown. There are fishermen in the small cove, paddling about in dugout canoes, Kuna Indian men. They wave at him. He waves back from the deck of *Romany*. There seems to be one concrete building close to the shoreline, painted green. After they anchor, they take Océan and Suzy in the dinghy to the shore. They tie it to a big stone and hop off onto more stones; there's no jetty here. On the land they meet two women who seem to be waiting for them. Gavin is holding Océan in his arms.

Necesita un medico, says Phoebe.

Both the women nod. We are the doctors, one replies. We heard your message on the radio.

These women are also Kuna. They wear jeans and T-shirts; their hair is black and long, tied back.

You speak English? Gavin tries.

A little bit, says one.

This is the clinic, then?

Yes, come this way.

They follow the two women into a yard overgrown with weeds and there are chickens pecking about, stray dogs sizing them up. At the door there are three women who smile in greeting. They are wearing the Kuna traditional dress: colourful patterned headscarves and appliqué cummerbunds called *mola*s and their legs are encased in beaded chains. They wear gold rings in their noses, gold in their teeth, they have tattoos across their cheeks. He smiles at them. They smile back. Océan stares.

Daddy, what are they?

Indians.

I'll stay outside with Suzy, says Phoebe.

He nods, and carries Océan up the corridor. The ceiling has stains and missing squares. Rusted dusty filing cabinets and an atmosphere of damp and decay which comes from being so close to the sea.

The women bring him to a room with some kind of operating table. A man appears, a Kuna man, dressed in a green hospital gown. The man smiles. I am Anton, he says.

I'm Gavin. Here? he asks.

They nod. He lays Océan down on the table. He stands, awkward, holding her small hand, looking around. The clinic is like Toco, fifty years ago. Everything fragile, ramshackle, red with rust. The women start to unwrap Océan's bandage and she flinches; *owww*, she whimpers.

Blood has seeped through the bandage overnight. They use a bottle of water to ease the layers off, then carefully prise away the gauze. The nurse has hold of Océan's other hand and smiles down at her and then at him. Big cut, he says.

No, says one of the female doctors, it is superficial.

Again Gavin can see the yellow muscle and flaps of skin. The wound is meaty.

It doesn't *look* superficial, he says, grimly.

It didn't cut to the bone, says the Kuna doctor.

Can you stitch her up?

They nod.

He can feel his stomach begin to move, like an octopus inside his guts, pushing around, trying to get out. He grins at the nurse. I'm okay, he says. Just a bit squeamish. You know, he gestures. My stomach.

Anton nods and smiles with amusement.

One of the Kuna doctors snaps on surgical gloves.

Er, you do have anaesthetic, don't you? Gavin enquires, realising this isn't a stupid question.

She nods.

He turns his back to them and looks down at Océan.

Now, you have been very brave, my love. There will be some pricks, some stings, but after that, you won't feel anything.

Océan nods and clamps her mouth closed. She shuts one eye and keeps the other open, then uses her open eye like a telescope and scans the room. She holds onto him with both hands and he can feel her palms are sweaty. He looks back over his shoulder and sees that the Kuna doctor is tapping at a syringe. She nods at him, as if to say, *ready*.

Okay, mermaid, hold on tight.

The doctor makes a stab.

Océan wails. The doctor is jooking her with a big needle. Gavin cannot watch.

She screams. The needle is stabbed into her leg quite a few times, all around the wound to numb it.

Daddyyyy, his child bellows and tears fall in sheets down her face. His hands are sweating too. His child's terror is his terror; it is excruciating to see her in pain.

Is there anything you can do? he says to the nurse.

Anton smiles and shakes his head. Océan's face is slippery damp with her tears and her fear.

A sound erupts from the nurse's chest, his mobile phone in his top pocket. He answers it and begins to speak in Kuna and for a moment Océan is distracted. Then he smiles at her and passes her the phone.

For you, he says.

Océan is delighted and not the least bit surprised.

Hello, she says, like an efficient secretary. Gavin stares, incredulous; the Kuna man laughs.

My brother, he says.

Océan looks puzzled but she is listening, trying to work out what is being said down the line.

Dad, I think this is a person speaking Dutch.

He raises his eyebrows and stifles his amusement. He peers back over his shoulder. The doctors are pressing around the wound. Océan doesn't seem to notice because the anaesthetic has already kicked in.

Thank you, he says to the nurse.

He smiles.

Océan is still listening to the man on the phone who thinks he is still speaking to Anton.

I think he has the wrong number, she says. She hands the phone back to the nurse.

After that, it's easy. Océan lies back and turns her

mouth down again, like she has sucked on a pickled pommecythere, her eyelids flickering and closed and she makes out that she is suffering an ordeal, even though now she cannot feel anything. He wonders from whom she's inherited all her tendencies. Before the flood she used to play karate with the neighbourhood boys, race them on her orange tricycle, give them Chinese burns on the arm. She was always in the thick of what was going down in the street, joining in with the older kids, and their games of Cowboys and Indians. She has been acci-dent-prone too; once she fell out of a mango tree, taking with her a fruit wasps' nest; she has sat on a tree trunk full of bêtes rouges and scratched for weeks. She once cut a classmate's plaited pigtail off and came home with it in her school bag. She is passionate about Suzy, about Willard Price adventure books, about her collection of pink skirts. She is always exhausted by dinnertime, will eat anything and fall into a heavy sleep. She is a born conversationalist, comical, sometimes ridiculous. She runs around barefoot, dirt on her dresses, on her knees. She gets great reports, already, at school, 'a sociable and intelligent child'; A's for everything. The brown wave knocked quite a bit of this gusto out her, for a time; but now it seems to be back, her spirit. She will break hearts, his little girl; and have her heart broken too.

When the doctors are finished stitching, they bandage her up. She is silent and grim-faced. Her left leg is now white with bandage and surgical stocking. They give her a course of antibiotics and a tetanus shot in the arm.

Take her to a hospital when you get to Panama, one advises. Gavin pays them fifty US dollars for their skills and time. Outside Phoebe is chatting to the Kuna women in Spanish. Suzy whines when she sees Océan's white leg. The Indian women chatter and make a fuss over her. For the first time in weeks he feels a tug in his chest, homewards, that's what he should do next; take her home, back to the pink house, put Océan to bed in an air-conditioned room, and then sit in his hammock on the porch, with Suzy, watching the corn birds in the trees, sip a spicy Malbec to steady himself. He is hit by a wave of tabanca, for home, for those green hills which nestle around his house, curled up and close, like a colossus asleep on her side, his home which lies at the foot of the green woman of Trinidad.

*

He and Phoebe sit in the cockpit of the old boat. Océan lies downstairs, her leg up on pillows. Suzy sits on deck, panting, her wise eyes squinting into the sun. Cool dog, cool kid. But Phoebe is not so okay. The accident had an impact on her too and she has turned oddly moody, as though cross with herself or unsettled. She has hitched a ride, tried to get from A to B, but she has found herself mixed up in a more personal way, with strangers. Blood, tears, a screaming child in high seas. He thinks of her violent father; what must she be thinking?

I'm going to make pasta for lunch, he says. We could all do with a hot meal.

She nods, says nothing. She is wearing a vest top and shorts, her shark tattoo swimming down one arm, across the other, the single enigmatic word. *Further.*

He does a flash clean of the galley and the saloon, then sets to chopping onions, garlic, fresh tomatoes bought in Cartagena, red bell peppers. Everything sizzles in the pan. He puts water on to boil, grates some cheese, washes and slices a head of lettuce, thinks, how do I feel about Phoebe? Weird, all of a sudden fatherly, concerned, like their roles have shifted. But also something else, comfortable. Himself. It's okay that he fainted, that she's a better sailor, that she is younger, prettier, has more tattoos. For a time, she seemed more capable, maybe even more stable than him, more at peace. Now, he is the quieter one, more sure of things. He is a man, and she cannot be that; he is older too, and she cannot accelerate her time on earth to catch up with the years he's lived; and he's a decent father to his daughter.

The sun shrinks behind the clouds. When he serves lunch on the roof of the hatch, it is shady and cooler. Suzy rolls around on her back, her legs in the air, and waggles her paws at the clouds, groaning.

He serves up the hot pasta in bowls, sprinkles cheese, and they eat in silence.

Océan has sauce on her face. She has also gone a little off mood. They are all a little off mood, he feels, even the sun.

Phoebe, says Océan, her mouth full.

Phoebe stops eating and looks at Océan as if she were an adult. Like she might be about to ask something unwelcome.

What does 'Further' mean?

Oh, she says, relieved. Oh that, it's the name of a bus.

A bus?

Yeah. A bus full of hippies, of free spirits, free thinkers, who travelled around America in the 60s. They were writers and poets and wanted to make their own way around their country.

A bus could have a name?

Sure, just like a boat, like *Romany*. It means something. *Romany* means gypsy, a traveller. It's a one-word poem.

A poem?

Yes. This word has two meanings. Further was a destination, in actual terms, but it was also a broader way of thinking, you know, keep going, even when things have broken down, keep on moving, exploring and going on down the road. That's what a poem is. Words which have a hidden meaning. A poem is like a secret.

Océan is glowing, trying to understand. She keeps chewing her pasta. She doesn't reply, she just eats and stares into her bowl with her bandaged leg, like maybe she is but maybe she isn't going to keep on moving forward. She is having a think about it. And Phoebe, he can see, is having a think too, about the poem she has had etched in indelible ink on her arm, a brave declaration of intent: I will keep going. Has it been her motto, this tattoo, her way of dealing with the past? If so, this idea isn't so bad.

CHAPTER SEVENTEEN

GRINGOS

They keep sailing, on through the Kuna Yala archipelago. Exactly thirty-six islands are inhabited and there are several communities amongst them, each with its own spiritual leader. Every island they pass is a miniature world: sand, shore, palms, some are deserted; others have grass shanties with palm fronds for roofs which stand close together, metres from the water. Each island sits in a swirl of turquoise. There are Kuna men about, men with red skin and straight black hair cut short, paddling canoes. There are other yachts too, sailing through like they are, staring at the natives, who stare back.

They put out a fishing line and trawl for fish. Phoebe gets out her guitar and strums, singing Swedish folk songs. Océan sits next to her, listening and staring at her feet and trying to understand everything again. She has on her hat and sunglasses and there is something about her attentiveness to Phoebe that makes him soft. His little girl is like an adult trapped inside the body of a six year old; she exhibits a sense that she knows she'll have to wait quite some time till she can be like Phoebe, grown up and singing songs on a guitar, until she can burst out into her full glory. Océan smiles up at Phoebe and Phoebe smiles back, and she taps her toes to the songs.

The fishing line goes taut and zings.

Quick, Dad! Océan points.

He scrambles for the rod and yanks at the line. He realises he has something heavy on the end of it and thinks *oh God, a battle* and he remembers Hemingway's old man and the sea, and how those massive marlin no longer exist. That old man should have known better about the sharks if he was such a wise dude. The fish dives deep and he can feel it's big.

Jeesus.

He pulls back on the rod which bends, as it should, and the line goes like wire, tight and steely, down into the sea. Phoebe stops singing and comes to stand next to him. You got a grouper, she says.

Yes, maybe, they are shallow enough. But not a turtle, he hopes. And not a wahoo, because it would have already bitten straight through the line. He pulls again, leaning backwards, and Océan is now watching too, and he doesn't know how he feels about fishing any more, tugging a fish out of the water. The fish is now hooked and struggling, causing adrenaline to buzz in his veins and he has a daughter and this young woman looking on and to cut the line also feels wrong. He curses Hemingway as the fish fights him and stakes its claim to be alive. And then the pull of *Romany* and the line is too much and the fish breaks the surface, beating up its body against the sea and hopelessly hooked. A twenty-pound grouper, solid as a side of beef.

He begins to reel the fish in.

I'll get the rum, Phoebe says.

No, get the gaff hook. It's in the locker.

He pulls backwards and then allows the line to go slack and then pulls back again; the fish is now arrowing towards them like a missile released from a submarine. He saws back and forward, back and then forward. There is a sweaty battle, him against the fish, a growing despair in the pit of his stomach, knowing that he will win. His heart rate soars and the sun lashes down on him struggling with the beating fish. Then it is truly snared and thrashing on the line, hooked, trying to release itself. He leans backwards to reel the fish in.

He yanks again. Phoebe comes forward with the gaff, an ancient thing, a wooden stick with a steel hook at the end. He reels the fish closer, until it is struggling alongside the hull, and then he hands Phoebe the rod and does what he hasn't done in years; he bends over the side with the gaff and clubs the hook into the flank of the big fish, piercing the flesh, *thunk*. It's like stabbing an animal. The fish stops moving abruptly from the shock of the blow. Gavin yanks upwards. The stunned fish comes up out of the sea, on the gaff, a marine creature, dashingly silver in its sequined suit. Its eyes are still alive and furious. It is already bleeding heavily.

Then it is on the floor of the cockpit, bloody and curving its body upwards, thudding its tail fin against the lockers. The fish is a brute, its gills billowing in and out with the exertion of the battle still going on, and then Phoebe is pouring rum into its gills to drown it.

He puts his hand to his chest to check his heart.

Océan jams her hat down over her eyes to block the sight and her knees quake. Oh no! she cries. Daddy, put the fish back in the sea, put it *back*.

The fish is still bucking and hefting its weight about, unable to flip itself over, back into what might be the sea, its mouth turned down in a grimace. This is not a noble way to die for this noble creature – it will take half an hour to expire. Océan is standing on one of the bench seats, her eyes now cast down on the fish, her face lit with revulsion. He wants to hurl the grouper back into the sea to make it better for her, hide it. Oh, God, forgive me, fish, forgive me.

Phoebe is calm throughout. She is no vegetarian, not squeamish at all; she continues to drown it with rum, the amber liquid running through its gills like a poison. Between the rum and the air, the fish dies slowly, in spasms, in the sun, on the cockpit floor, its big plate eye never losing sight of him, and he feels wretched, watching. Océan watches too, folding the brim of her hat over her ears as if it is offending her hearing. But no, my mermaid, a fish cries in silence.

Daddy, what will we do with it? asks Océan, uneasily.

We're going to eat it, for dinner.

*

That night they drop anchor near to one of the inhabited islands and go ashore with the dinghy. Phoebe shows the Kuna people the big grouper and asks if they can cook it on their island.

He and Phoebe search for big stones to line the pit. They dig a hole in the sand and gather fallen coconut fronds and other dry driftwood to light. When the fire has cooled a bit and the stones are still hot, they wrap the big fish in tinfoil with some garlic and olive oil. They lay the fish amongst the stones and cover it with more fronds and leave it there to cook. There are dugout canoes pulled up onto the beach, each made from a single tree; children and chickens run wild. Two huts stand right on the beach, each looks dark inside, and there are a few more huts towards the back. The whole island is smaller than a football pitch. A young white dog makes friends with Suzy. The dogs tumble and cavort on the beach, tearing in and out of the sea.

One of the fishermen comes to talk to them by the fire. He is wearing jeans and nothing else. Océan sidles up to him, staring at the tattoos across his cheeks. Gavin fears she will reach out and trace them with her fingers, she looks so curious.

Where did you get your dog? she asks him, in her Trinidadian singsong.

But the Kuna man doesn't understand.

Phoebe translates in Spanish.

Ahhh, he says, pointing at the sea. He stoops, close to Océan and points again.

The sea? she asks and points.

The man nods.

Boat come, he says. Pass by. Man throw dog away.

Océan stares at him like he has just told an enormous lie.

Gavin winces. He and Phoebe catch each other's eye.

A man threw a dog off the boat, he whispers to Phoebe, as if he didn't get it right either. She nods and checks if this is right with the man, who has stood up again.

The man makes a paddling movement and says in Spanish that he saw a man throw the white dog off a boat, and went paddling out to save it in his canoe.

Now we have dog. Good dog.

Jeesus, says Gavin. What kind of man?

Gringo, says the Indian.

Gavin finds his sleeping bag and takes it onto the fore-deck of *Romany*; he'll sleep under the stars tonight. He wraps himself up well, padding himself with cushions from the cockpit, zipping himself into his fleece and the downy bag. He gazes up at the stars and remembers his wife and talks to her, saying: God, I wish things were different. Claire stayed in the townhouse for only two or three months after the flood. There was never any discussion or debate about her going back to live in the pink house again. And he never quarrelled with her over this; he never fought her mother either. Jackie knew best, and he said *okay*, because a part of him knew he couldn't cope, not with his newly broken wife, his badly destroyed house, his job, keeping Océan fed, dressed. A year ago he was scared of his wife, of catching what she had, that she'd spread it; that he was already a little contaminated.

Depression ran in her family. It did not run in his family. But these things can catch and he didn't want to get what his wife had. And so he didn't make a fuss when Jackie said, *she should come by us. She should come home, for a while.* He let her go back to her mother's house; no question of a nursing home; not the expense, but just no way she would live somewhere like that. He never fought for her, that's what happened in the end. He was afraid of his wife, of her remoteness. Two of them couldn't be like that; they couldn't abandon Océan to their separate depressions. And so he let Claire disappear; they separated.

Tears fill his eyes. He hugs himself and feels like he will never rid himself of this feeling of heartbreak, like he will never recover from what happened with the brown wave, no matter how far he sails away from it. Things could happen to a man; things could happen just like that.

Sleep comes, it is a heavy thing, drawing him into a dark tomb and he falls unconscious with his fingers knitted on his chest, like a pharaoh prepared in death for the afterworld. Sleep delves his tissues, depositing parcels under the skin, weighing him down, healing him, just like sleep is healing his wife. Sleep, tender sleep. Sleep and sea all around him, and when he wakes in the middle of the night to soft rain on his face, he cannot move. The salt air presses on his face, the rain shakes down in a slow haze, the galaxies above appear dazzling and crystalline. He can only open his eyes and gaze upwards. He finds he is surprised with all this activity going on around him while he's been inert. The black sky is alive, twinkling with a fierce intelligence; the world doesn't switch itself off, ever. It revolves eternally: busy, electric.

He wakes again at dawn, stiff as a tree. The turquoise sea is placid, a becalmed oasis; the island resembles a small sleepy village. On the beach the white dog is running around. Suzy is a white dog too, apart from her pink nose, the flecks of grey spots under her fur; but this dog is different, smaller, more sprightly, a wily pot hound. He watches and cannot understand how it doesn't remember. He feels the need to go and be with it, so he strips to his underpants and lets himself over the lifelines and slides into the dawn sea. He swims towards the beach. The dog trots up and down nervously, waiting for him. When he gets to the shoreline he sits half in the water and the dog comes to him, pressing its muzzle into his ribs, nosing him under the armpits.

I am a man from a boat, he says to the dog. I am a man from a boat. He jostles and plays with the white dog for a while, admiring its youth, its sleek coat, its new sharp teeth which gnaw at his fists and he sees that no, by some miracle, the dog doesn't remember being tossed from its boat like a piece of garbage.

*

They set sail again and engage the auto-steering. The whole archipelago is two hundred miles long and a steady breeze carries them through it. The world around is every shade of blue and the sun laughs down on them, ha, ha. For the first time on the trip he feels like a cruiser, or a tourist. He is looking, gazing at another world. He is modern and this world has chosen to stay as it was a long time ago, civilised and ancient. He says goodbye to it; he cannot understand it but it is not important that he does. Goodbye, he says and tells Océan to wave goodbye to Kuna Yala and the Indians.

Where are we going next, Dad? says Océan.

Towards Panama and then we will sail through a piece of land, through a canal.

What's a canal?

It's a passageway, like a short-cut.

We're taking a short-cut?

Yes, through a country.

Wow.

Yes, you'll like it.

By now he is so relaxed with Phoebe they speak without having to cover anything up. Océan's leg is still dressed and the scar underneath covered with a solid cake of dried blood. He can tell there's something on his daughter's mind.

My mother fell asleep, Océan informs Phoebe.

Phoebe nods.

Gavin no longer cares what she might say next. It feels easy and natural between them all.

Do you have a mother? asks Océan.

Phoebe crosses her eyes.

Gavin laughs.

Yes. But she passed away three years ago.

Océan nods, but there is an expression of incomprehension in her face.

She died from smoking too much and from worry.

Océan still looks thrown. She died?

Yes.

Like the fish died?

Not in the same way, but . . . yes, she stopped breathing.

Oh. She fell . . . dead?

Yes.

My mother fell asleep, what's the difference?

In one you wake up, in the other you don't.

She never woke up?

No. Phoebe smiles.

My mother is going to wake up, says Océan.

Yes I'm sure she will.

I'm sad about your mother, she continues.

It's okay, says Phoebe.

I can be your mother, if you like.

Phoebe laughs. You?

Why not? I will grow up one day – and then I can be like your mother. It's not funny.

Okay then, says Phoebe. I'd like that.

They sail on. He and Phoebe take turns at the tiller. The sea turns green and the coast becomes rugged and looks like the north coast of Trinidad. Trinidad was once part of the mainland of South America and all of a sudden he feels a surge of confidence born from familiarity. Like they have come pretty far, but not so far as Japan, or parts of the world which will look entirely different. Japan, now that would be weird. He cannot imagine sailing in those cold seas.

It is later that evening, moored off the coast in a tiny bay, when they have The Talk. It goes like this:

Tomorrow, I'm getting off the boat, says Phoebe.

Gavin is surprised. They hadn't yet discussed when and where she would depart from *Romany*, but he knew it would come. Tomorrow he was going to make a call, book his toll fee through the Panama Canal, which has to be done two days ahead; he will be assigned a pilot to guide him through. He knew she was going to leave any day soon, that she wasn't going to travel through the canal with them; *to Panama* was what they agreed. He will have a pilot, he'll be okay. But even so, when she says this, his heart sinks. Tomorrow? He looks away, out to sea. Then he glances at his daughter sitting in the cockpit.

Yes. Puerto Lindo. I'll get off there; it's the next port. My boyfriend Daniel will be waiting for me and we'll get the bus the next day down to Panama City.

Bus? says Océan.

Yes, we're going there for a few days, to meet with friends. Then we'll head north to Mexico.

Are you getting on the hippie bus? The poem bus?

No.

What kind of bus, then?

A regular bus. One that goes to Panama City, a public bus you can flag down in the road.

She is saying all this very carefully, looking Océan dead square in the eye. But Océan still hasn't understood. Gavin realises that probably Océan has no real concept of where they are or where they've been, let alone where they're going. What matters are people, or who she feels safe with: Daddy, Suzy. And now she has come to trust Phoebe.

Océan stares at her bandaged leg. Her eyebrows knit together, her lashes flicker, and he can see that it has started to come, that she is struggling now to cope with the idea that Phoebe is leaving. She sits with her toes together, her face acrobatic with arriving pain. She doesn't say anything, but her small chest begins to rise and fall noticeably. She doesn't cry but he can see there are hot tears behind her eyeballs.

I'm sorry, says Phoebe. I'm leaving. I . . . and she begins to try to make a loving heartfelt speech when a ripping sound breaks from Océan, half-roar, half-gargle, as a pure and virile anger tears through her. Océan flings herself down onto the floor of the cockpit and begins to scream and beat her legs and arms in a mighty hurricane of feelings. They sweep through her visibly, fury, disbelief, her small body unable to contain them. She wails and screams. *Nooooo*.

He doesn't pick her up or try to soothe her. Not yet. Because, dimly, he is also suffering pangs of Phoebe's abandonment. He didn't see this coming. He needs his wife so badly, misses her so much, loves her, has found the pain so excruciating, the longing so intense, her disappearance so devastating that he is watching his own long-held pent-up feelings explode in his child. He knows they have shared the same suffering. She left us, went away. Everything went away. He cannot bar his daughter from this wild state.

Océan goes into a tirade. Noooooo. No bus! Where are you *going*?

Phoebe flattens her hands to her face.

I'm going to see my boyfriend, Phoebe almost pleads.

I DON'T CARE.

Phoebe stares, words unable to flow. She looks at Gavin, as if for help.

I don't want you to go, I love you, where are you going?

Tears in Phoebe's eyes.

I love you, Océan wails. Where are you going, I hate you, why are you leaving, why can't you stay here?

Phoebe puts her hand to her mouth, bites her knuckles.

He kneels down and picks up his daughter. She is hot and rigid, her face puce, snot and tears swamping her. She wails louder. *Why*, she bawls. He holds her to him, her body against his, and he rocks her and shushes her, like he did when she was a baby, and he says, Océan, we are going to ring Mummy tomorrow, okay? We will call home and you can speak to Granny Jackie and she can tell us how Mummy is and then we'll say goodbye to Phoebe. I'm here, okay.

Her little body goes into convulsive hiccups. No, she says, her face now plump, moist, like a tapioca pudding.

Phoebe has no mother, says Océan. She has no mother and she said I could be her mother and now she's going and she doesn't have a mother and she could be here with us, all together.

Phoebe's cheeks are striped with the silver tracks of her tears.

I'm so sorry, she says.

*

They arrive in Puerto Lindo at 9 a.m. the next morning. It is a tiny port, a small strip of sand, green jungly mountains full of howler monkeys close behind. It is a desolate spot, not much going on, but there is a hostel a little way up the one road and the bus to Panama City goes past twice a day. They moor the boat and take the dinghy to the shore. Phoebe has her rucksack and her guitar and an air about her of moving on. He understands this. Further, that's where she's going.

Four weeks. That's how long they've been together, most of the New Year. Aruba seems like a long time ago, another life, those aggressive iguanas on the jetty. The greedy parrotfish, Baby Beach. Phoebe has helped them and he is grateful. Océan is sullen and still weak from her storm of tears. She wheezed and hiccupped through the night. Now she clings to Suzy who is oblivious, her tongue hanging out and waving in the breeze. There is a small rickety jetty; he ties up and Phoebe hops off. He hands her the rucksack and helps Suzy off and then he helps Océan off who cold-shoulders Phoebe and marches off with Suzy down the bumpy jetty. There is a small café restaurant to the right of the jetty, and in front of it many dinghies tied up. A man is sitting at one of the tables in the café.

Phoebe turns. On seeing the man she waves and blows kisses and shouts *Daniel!*

Gavin feels fat all of a sudden, fat and a hundred years old. Phoebe leaves her rucksack where he put it; she doesn't even try to pick it up. The man stands and waves back and then she is sprinting down the jetty, past Océan and Suzy, who are heading in the opposite direction, running towards the café and the man standing there, his arms open.

Gavin picks up Phoebe's rucksack. He cannot help his reaction, how his body and face prickle with discomfort. Have there been fantasies? Lost dreams? Somewhere, yes, somewhere between feeling fatherly and feeling grateful for her help, he has seen her as a woman, a person he could be intimate with; yes, she is as good as the woman he chose for himself. He will say goodbye and it will be okay, and Océan will bear up. Now they will meet the boyfriend, now they have to go and say goodbye properly. He forces himself forward, down the jetty, his big straw hat shadowing his face, and he calls to Suzy and Océan who are walking away from the café and says, this way, guys, we are going to say goodbye before we make any phone calls.

He swings the rucksack onto one shoulder and the child and dog stop in their tracks. All three walk towards the café and when he gets there he extends his hand warmly to meet the younger man.

I'm Daniel, the younger man says. He is an olive skinned Latin American man with long dark hair and a direct gaze, full of an easy natural machismo. He is about thirty-five.

Gavin. This is Océan and Suzy.

The strong handsome man gazes at them all appraisingly, looking each one of them in the eye. Gavin realises this man is good enough; immediately, he knows this, sees why Phoebe ran to him.

Daniel bends to say hello to Océan who is standing with a blank face. He has enough charm, enough self-knowing to pick her up and sweep her into his arms.

Hello, he says in a thickly Spanish accent; he kisses her cheeks.

Phoebe blushes deeply. She winks at Gavin.

We are going to miss you, Gavin says.

I'm not going to say goodbye, just good luck. This is my phone number. She presses a scrap of paper into his hand.

Then they all walk away from the café, up the spare concrete road through the jungle, towards a hostel tucked away in a recess, huddled onto a riverbank. Daniel carries Océan up on his shoulders. Suzy snuffles and trots ahead. Gavin carries Phoebe's rucksack.

At the hostel they don't really say goodbye. He goes

forward and hugs Phoebe close, squeezing her tight. Daniel lifts Océan down from his shoulders. She looks upwards at them and spins around as if conscious that she is so small compared to them, a little annoyed to be so small, just a child.

Then she says: Goodbye, Phoebe. She shakes Phoebe's hand like she might shake the hand of a lawyer, very formal and courteous. Phoebe bends and kisses Océan on the cheek. And then the three of them go up the road to find the telephone at the post office.

CHAPTER EIGHTEEN

GATE

The pilot is called Eduardo, a plump middle-aged red-skinned man with round cheeks and big square teeth. He is a married man, with a wide gold wedding band which looks like it has been polished, and he has a constant contented grin. Eduardo joins them in Colón, the town at the top of the Panama canal, on the Atlantic side, a place like Chicago eighty years ago, a gang dominating every street. It is such a violent city Gavin was advised not to get off his boat. Instead, this pilot was ferried out to *Romany*. Eduardo speaks broken English and what with Gavin's broken Spanish, they get along well enough. Océan is still lost in her reveries. He can see she is puzzling: how could Phoebe come and go so fast; where did she disappear to with that handsome man? *Daddy, I will never see her again, will I?* She is quietly working out how many different types of loss might exist. Many, my little mermaid. Many.

And so she is indifferent to Eduardo, barely mustering a glance his way. She has gone in on herself; she is blind again behind her Snoopy sunglasses.

They cross the great Gatun Lake and it is wide and calm and strange to be in an expanse of fresh water instead of salt sea. The lake is grey-blue and flat and the sky is ash-mauve. All around them are sage coloured hills, low and jumbled together; the trees are purple and birds of prey circle above them. It is very hot, hot like earthquake weather. Still, close, moribund. Like the world might suddenly jolt with restlessness. The sides of the lake are banks of exposed orange pink terraces, cut into steppes, so that the earth will not fall into the water. Official-looking water taxis and small boats zing about; massive tankers, stacked high with containers, sit waiting their turn in the chamber of the next lock; there are herons and cranes at the water's edge and other yachts on the lake. They come across two catamarans lashed together, nesting, waiting for their entrance. The cats are small crafts and when the water empties in the lock, it will be steadier for them this way.

They cross the big pond and he and Eduardo each scan the opposite bank. They have let down the sails, they are motoring. The engine chugs. He thinks of the vast sea on the other side of the canal, the Pacific, the new sea awaiting him. Nine days alone out there. And what of the Galapagos, the enchanted islands awaiting him; they feel mysterious, like shy women.

Up ahead a bridge looms, Centennial Bridge, strung across the dark hump of Gold Hill and another hump on the port side, linking Panama City with the rest of Central America. The canal is infested with legends and stories, thousands gave their lives to building it, most dying from malaria, yellow fever.

Eduardo radios ahead to the *Pacific Queen*, a vessel bulging with tourists. Three hundred or so people are snapping pictures, grilling themselves to a crisp on the top deck. The authorities, he explains, want them to enter the lock chamber behind them. They will be using hand lines, not the silver robot trucks which pull the bigger ships through and run like trams along each side of the canal. They can lash themselves alongside the tourist boat; the other yachts, the cats nesting together, will be included in the chamber.

They follow the *Pacific Queen* in. It is like entering a narrow street of water. On either side there are tracks for the pulley trucks and a guardhouse stands at the end. *Romany* is small inside the chamber, a tiny craft; the Panama Canal will accept any vessel, anything which floats, including human beings. People have even swum through it – for a small fee. There are four catamarans behind them, lashed in pairs. They enter cautiously and pull alongside the larger boat. Tourists stare down at them, the crew throws them lines. Someone on the top deck leans over the rails and takes a picture of Gavin in his sombrero stetson. Eduardo laughs.

Charles Bronson, he says and points at him.

Instinctively, Gavin clasps his middle, realising that he is a bit thinner.

They wait for a while, then the massive steel doors close behind them. The level in the chamber begins to fall as the water is sucked away. The walls of the lock appear like the walls of a submerged fort, glossy with slime. The doors in front of them are immense, bolted with steel rivets in 1914. For a few minutes they are stranded inside an ancient prison of some sort, high walls, gargantuan iron gates. Then the front lock doors begin to open slowly. He and Eduardo throw the lines back to the crew of the *Pacific Queen*. The larger boat starts up her engine and cruises forward and they tag along behind, out of the lock, and back out into the canal. It is still very hot, no breeze. Eduardo receives a call from his wife and smiles into the phone, his face suddenly gone rich and hand-some, his teeth gleaming.

Océan has woken up. She looks impressed.

That was cool, Dad.

Yes.

Where are we going now?

Out. To another ocean.

Her face crinkles with concern. Will we be okay with-out Phoebe?

Of course, he says breezily.

And he means it. They've been sailing for weeks, now. Months. He has claimed it all back, his sailing skill. He can hardly wait to try it alone. They will be fine; they are sailors, about to meet the sea. He has studied the February pilot charts for the Pacific, has a good idea what to expect of the pressure out there, the temperature and the winds.

Before reaching Colón they shopped in a *supermercado*. The boat is loaded with gallons of fresh water and fuel, tins and dried food; the mesh baskets are bulging with yams, sweet potatoes, bananas, oranges, onions, the cooler box stuffed with blue cheese, ham, sausages, even a bottle of champagne for when they cross the equator.

We'll be just fine, dou dou.

She looks at her bandaged leg and nods.

He feels a stab of sadness. Not only has Phoebe left them, but they didn't speak to Claire in Puerto Lindo on the phone. Just Granny Jackie, again, fraught, hopelessly self-pitying and back on the cigarettes. Claire was a little better, she was able to report, just a little. *She knows you've gone sailing*, said Jackie. And he was glad of this. Somehow this makes a difference; she knows they've gone off. She may guess where they're heading.

*

They motor along for another mile. Heat like being close to a fire. Tourists on the boat ahead are snapping pictures of everything. He knows that the Miraflores Locks are the most famous on the canal. This is because they are a double lock; sailors have to pass through two sets of giant steel doors; the locks are like a mini-sea escalator. As they approach, Gavin notices a visitors' centre next to the locks. Troupes of very young men and women dressed in white suits and white caps line the balcony; he guesses they are from the Panamanian naval school. They look glamorous and young, hopeful. He waves at them and a few raise their hands in response.

They follow the *Pacific Queen* into the first of the two locks; they lash themselves to her hull. The four cats follow behind. They wait. The water level lowers and the walls of the lock are exposed and again seem wondrously tall. This is the end of the canal; they are soon to be released into the ·Pacific and back into the salt sea. The Gate of the Americas lies ahead, the archway they will pass under on their path into the southern hemisphere, into the sea where the terrible lionfish originate, where whales roam. The Pacific is the largest of the world's five oceans and named after peace; yet it is ringed by volcanoes and oceanic trenches. Several hundred active volcanoes are studded along the legendary Pacific 'ring of fire'.

Dad, look! Océan points at the air. Hundreds of birds have gathered at the entrance to the second lock.

Ahhhh, says Eduardo. Sushi time.

What do you mean?

All the fish are going to die – I'm sorry to say. They are for fresh-water living. They die when the water becomes salt.

Really? Océan grimaces.

Yes, little girl. It happens every day, all the time. For a hundred years.

All the fish will die?

Yes. The canal engineers couldn't think of everything, says Eduardo. He smiles down at her, but again she's far away.

And yes, Gavin can see hundreds of frigates, gulls, hovering and bickering, waiting for the last lock gate to open into the sea. It gives him an uncomfortable feeling. The huge gates open and they move forward, behind the larger boat. In the second lock they wait, behind the iron barriers, locked in. The birds form a hazardous cloud of beaks, wings and greedy screeches. The naval college students wait and watch. Ahead he can see the slim steel arch, the Gate of the Americas. When he fled Trinidad, he didn't envision this; never thought they would get this far, to the brink of the other side of the world. Now he finds it hard not to grin; a massive urge to laugh grips him. Here I am, here we are. Paco, wish you were here. Océan stands and huddles to his legs.

The second lock gates begin to open. The birds fall as one onto the surface of the sea. Everywhere the silver bodies of fish, floating, bellies up. The larger boat moves forward, but they are not so quick. He is mesmerised by the feeding frenzy. Birds like a blizzard. Gulls and terns dropping from the sky, onto the newly stunned fish. Suzy barks at them, up on deck, snapping and trying to catch them in her mouth. They motor forward and out into the Pacific Ocean. Ahead, to starboard, there is a line of pale skyscrapers, jagged and broken, the modern Panama City. In front of the towers there is a breakwater, the Amador Causeway, lined with traveller's palms. Sixty or so small vessels bob in the water, waiting for their turn to pass through the canal, in the opposite direction; they float in a traffic jam. It is four in the afternoon, the world is all hazy and blue. And the steel archway bends over them like a rainbow.

Eduardo goes below to retrieve his bag from the saloon. A small knot ties itself in Gavin's stomach. *Shit.* Soon they'll be alone. Man, child, dog and boat. Soon it will be his turn to skipper *Romany* single-handedly, for the first time in weeks. Phoebe handed this on to him, helped him to see he could do it alone. His fibres flutter with the thrill of it. *I will be fine*, he knows this, knows it in his entire being. This is a voyage thousands of men have undertaken; others have struck out for these islands ahead, the Encantadas. Many have sailed towards the volcanoes and the black sands in the centre of this vast ocean, sands which crawl with iguanas and turtles. These islands snag in the centre of three major currents and they will be tracking one of them, the Panama, on its path south. To starboard a boat lurches forward through the afternoon haze, the Panama port authorities.

Eduardo turns and shakes his hand.

Good luck, he says. A brief razor-sharp smile flashes.

Any tips? Gavin asks, even though he knows this man has never been beyond this point. He is an expert in the canal, not the ocean.

Do not drink it, Eduardo grins and points to the sea.

Gavin laughs.

The port authority tugboat lines itself up alongside *Romany*. It has an open cabin door to one side. Both boats are travelling slowly. Eduardo lets himself over the safety lines and with a small neat hop, he is aboard the other boat. The pilot waves, and Gavin and Océan wave back. The tugboat peels away from them and he can see that Eduardo is on the phone to his wife again, possibly talking of what is for dinner. Eduardo is a happy man, with a good job and a place in the world. Gavin feels a surge of contentment, as though infected by this man and his goodness. The wind picks up. There are larger boats, container ships a mile out, also waiting their turn to enter the canal, to travel the other way in the sea he's just left behind. He can feel the breeze is strong and beckoning. *Come along now*, it says. Come this way.

Keep still here, mermaid, he says to Océan. Sit here while I go and hoist the sail. Yes, Dad, she says and sits under her hat. Now she knows how to be careful and how to be patient aboard this old boat. Suzy jumps into the cockpit and sits by her side, her tongue wet and pink. They sit and gaze out to sea. He leaves the tiller to the auto-steering, pulls on his gloves and looks up, at the top of the mast, and says to himself that yes, they will be sailing a little bit further.

CHAPTER NINETEEN

THE PACIFIC

Late February, 2011. They've left the Americas behind. Ahead of them, vast open acres of emerald-silver-blue sea – the Pacific Ocean. Already he can feel himself at the edge of things. Sometimes he's okay, sure of himself. And then from nowhere he is anxious, afraid of the sea, engulfed with feelings of cowardice, ineptitude, like they're facing death somewhere out here. Then, he's okay again.

Luckily, the kid and the dog don't seem to notice; Suzy and Océan are fine, like they're off on holiday, sailing towards a good time. Océan seems to have accepted Phoebe's departure: she has left, that was the deal. She may even see Phoebe again one day. Gavin promised to invite her to stay in Trinidad; they could even sail in *Romany* again, maybe. Her glum mood seems to have lifted and she and Suzy look quite mad these days on this old boat. Can a dog's fur grow outwards? Suzy looks

fatter with fur and Océan likes to be close to her and they sit together in the cockpit for most of the day, quiet, under the shade of the mainsail. They swap sideways glances, as though in collusion with each other, in silent conversation, like thugs, up to no good, always. He will make sure Océan keeps her harness on 24/7 for the next nine days; he will too. And Suzy? Should he harness her up in some way, clip her collar to a lifeline? Put her back in the kennel? No, for now he'll just keep an eye on her.

Océan is so different, golden brown, her eyes glistening. Her hair is white-blonde and straggly but he can't bear to cut it. She had the storm of tears when Phoebe left, but apart from that she hasn't cried for weeks, not since the giant parrotfish in Aruba nicked her finger. She hasn't spoken to her mother for months, but recently she sleeps well, eats anything again, not just maccy cheese. He is happy for her; she spreads her happiness to him. She is coping and this helps him cope.

The Galapagos are 848.92 nautical miles away. It will take them over a week to get there. Nine days out of sight of land. Just the sea around them, both alien and natural, sheets of silver-blue, flat and calm for now, spread out like a vast wealth. *Romany* is doing well, why wouldn't she? She too has been released, into her vocation. Phoebe helped him check out the auto-steering system during the trip to Panama so he can more or less sit there, letting the boat sail herself, the winds behind them for now. They are a minute craft in the vast sea. But for some reason, he doesn't feel insignificant. Quite the opposite.

TABANCA

They sail on, all day, that first day, into a powerful dazzling sea, the winds coming from the north and north east, fifteen to eighteen knots behind them and *Romany* flying as fast as she can, sometimes up to seven knots. They are sailing towards the belt around the earth and he can feel his heart expand in his chest, a feeling like being in love again. He can feel hope, for the first time in a year, sailing towards an empty horizon. Clear open sky and sea, the world around him is the biggest he's ever witnessed and even Océan can see that the world is now bigger than anything they've come to before. It has a quietening effect. They both fall into watching as they fly along. And then, just as the winds change, so does he – and he feels fearful again, a clinical aloneness, an awareness of how much peril could befall them if he's not careful. What is out there in this sea of peace – gales, cyclones? And what about when the sun dies, their first night out here, oh Lord.

Love and fear persist all that first day, in equal measures, keeping him alert: good sailor, then bad sailor, good man, stupid man. Suzy and Océan fall asleep. Both start to snore lightly. He wants to sing and wine his hips. Instead, he pees over the side of the boat in his harness. He wants to cry – and lets himself. Tears fall for his son, for his wife who may never fully wake up. His tears aren't salty, like the sea; they are clear, tasteless.

*

At one in the morning the sky is black and lit with stars. Océan and Suzy are asleep in the saloon. They hit a patch of rain which rocks the boat a little – and when they sail through it, he is drenched, shivering. For some reason he turns to look backwards, over his shoulder, and there it is. The moon is high in the sky; there is the disappearing squall, and between the squall and the boat – a perfect hoop. Just like a rainbow, except the seven shades of colour are shades of grey and gauzy light, as though it is a rainbow in negative. A wide delicate arc stretches across the night, each end finishing in the sea. He gazes at it for quite some time as *Romany* ploughs away from it. *I'm with you right now,* he says under his breath. *I am here and you are on the other side of the world.*

The moonbow is so candid in its appearance that he smarts with mild embarrassment. Like he has seen a naked thing, a rainbow before it dressed itself. Out here at sea – this is where rainbows rest before they appear on stage. It stuns his eye, and makes him feel united with the heavens. He gazes at it till they sail out of sight. Perhaps things will be all right.

In the morning, day two, he is restless. Charged with energy from the moon. It is dawn, first light. The sky is like taffeta, the oyster-coloured clouds are low and streaked along the horizon; nothing out here, but them – and sea. There are 733 nautical miles left to sail.

The morning turns into a perfect sunny day. Good winds still steady from the north, a following sea. The auto-steering means he can cook them a breakfast of hash browns and frankfurters in the galley. His hands are suffering, though, splitting again, so it hurts to clench a knife and it stings to slice an onion. He's been forgetting his gloves, the thick moisturising cream. What will it take to smooth them again? *Potato pie, Mr Weald* – it's been over two months now since he left that life behind. All that acid in his gut. Coffee. He doesn't drink half as much these days. He vows to get some sleep early tonight, sleep a couple of hours, and then up. He will only sleep for two hours at a time, max, for the next few days. He is now looking forward to the night sails. What will he see in the blue hours, what else will show up naked?

But soon after breakfast Océan begins to get bored, restless on board the boat in a way she hasn't been before. Cabin fever, it's called. He brings up a pack of cards and they play Snap on one of the bench seats and then they play Patience and this makes her even more bored.

Dad?

What?

Can we make pancakes?

No, sweetie. It's too messy and I don't have pancake mix.

Can we make soupies?

No.

Flapjacks?

No. Look, we are in the middle of the Pacific, we're not going to have a cake bake, okay?

She scowls with impatience.

Would you like a cheese stick?

She shakes her head.

What about some dog chow?

She smiles and nods.

He goes downstairs and brings up the bag of Purina and grabs a handful of the salty lamb flavoured biscuits. He puts down the bag, takes one and nibbles it and says, ummmm, not bad.

Suzy wags her tail.

Come on, he says, let's play a game. He lobs one of the biscuits up in the air towards Suzy and she snaps at it, gulping it in one.

Océan claps. He lobs another biscuit at Océan. She copies Suzy, snapping at it and misses. He throws one up in the air for himself and catches it and crunches it and swallows it down. *Gyaaad*. It tastes awful – like fish food. Oily, full of MSG.

They spend the next hour playing dog chow games, throwing up the biscuits, catching them in their mouths, in their hats, pinging them at Suzy and each other, until the cockpit floor is crumbly and they stink of lamb and Océan abruptly decides she will go and relax downstairs with Grover, leaving him to clear up. This is easy – he gets Suzy to lick the floor clean.

Sailing the ocean seas can be many things, including boring, for a six-year-old. It was easier when they had Phoebe. He realises he misses Phoebe and her guitar, her presence around his daughter, the way Océan looked up to her and the way they fell into a feminine way around each other. He misses female company, a female crewmate. He misses women. He misses his woman; he misses sex. He misses being touched. Maybe Phoebe was right about men escaping to sea. Maybe men don't get enough of women, maybe men love women eternally, and find that quality out here; here there's enough woman to be getting on with. He smells himself – he stinks of lamb-flavoured dog chow and feels sorry for himself, his manliness. This man part of him is unused. He looks out at the sea and thinks, yes, he could jump, certainly, in the right circumstances.

*

The next afternoon, on the third day, the wind drops. Light but insistent winds blow straight at them, from the south; they are sailing into them. There is a two-knot current moving north and he is trying to get south into southerly winds. The sails are useless, flogging themselves. This goes on for hours and so he motors on and off, the sails down. But *Romany* doesn't motor well for long, she chugs like an old tramp, coughing and hiccupping with indignation. Really, they need a gennaker but don't have one stowed. And it is hot, boiling hot, and there they are, like a bug under a magnifying glass. Water, water everywhere and thank fuck they have enough to drink. They are six hundred and sixty miles away from their destination, *Las Encantadas*, the Galapagos. Their

Trinidad ensign hangs like a handkerchief. A sea bird arrives from nowhere and sits on the mast, taking a rest and shitting all over the foredeck. Tiny squid rise up from the sea in flocks, just like flying fish. They rise in zillions and many land on deck. Suzy goes up on the foredeck with her mouth open trying to catch them. Océan has been collecting the squid too, but not in her mouth. A man could go mad out here. He sings to himself, *I could die of tabanca*.

It rains on and off all of the fourth day. Still no wind. The self-steering works on and off. They are wallowing; these are doldrums. Near the equator, the winds from the north and the south meet and mix together, slurring into this negative energy. It is like sailing into a sump of dead air, a morgue zone. No wind. This is what sailors hate most.

They manage to have a picnic at lunchtime, quite leisurely, blue cheese salad, salami and boiled potatoes. Océan and Suzy are bored and restless, both expecting him to relieve this boredom. They try a new game: I Spy, but it doesn't last long. No other boats are in sight. He tries to teach Océan Cribbage, but she loses interest. She slumps across the bench seat in a state she cannot contain in her body; children must be kept active. She is penned in and there is no hope of release.

Four days have gone past and it is getting to him too. Looking out at sea for hours does something to a person's eyeballs. Hallucinations begin, people start to see things. He is seeing elephants, and a steam train puffing across the horizon. Or is he? What are clouds, what is sea? The air boils and turns somersaults. His eyes sting, his hands sting too. Music can help, another adult voice. He switches on the CD player, puts on Erykah Badu, then Billie Holiday and then some Beastie Boys. Océan perks up; she likes the Beastie Boys the most, of course. She laughs and headbangs to the loud shouting music, her bandaged leg something punk, like she might have been in a riot or jumped off stage.

*

Five days in, still no wind. He is worried about fuel and that *Romany* doesn't like to motor for too long, she is labouring. He is beginning to lose his nerve – another thing sailors are afraid of. What has he undertaken? He didn't anticipate this fear when they passed under the Gate of the Americas; it was exciting then, now it isn't. Now he's scared they won't make it, not unless the wind picks up. They are out of radio contact too. He should be scared. *Don't show it*, he tells himself, don't think about it too much.

Is this what he had planned on, quietly, wished for, silently, when they left Trinidad? To be out here, this much out of his depth? Is this the dream he'd conjured all his adult life, this journey, this escape? Why did he want to be out here, in the middle of the biggest sea on earth? Out here he's inside his younger man's dream – and it's nothing like he imagined. It's better and worse. He's not his younger self any more anyway. That young man grew up, became a father, bought a house, made a commitment to a woman, a life as a father. He is another man now since those days with Clive, possibly grown deluded and desperate since the flood. But now he's here, he has to slog ahead. Pray, sing. *It is the mercy*, that's what Crowhurst wrote in his logbook before he went mad and disappeared. He was mad before he started the race, most think. What did he mean anyway? That the sea is merciful, ha ha. Poor man. The sea around him is many things, but not that.

It starts to drizzle. It's hot like hell. If they were on land he would say it feels like earthquake weather.

*

That evening the sky pinks over. Grey and indigo clouds stay still in the sky like towering puffs of cream, like staircases made of foam. Forks of lightning appear miles away, silent delicate veins of gold, fizzing down from the clouds. Océan sits watching too, bedazzled, 'wow'ing and 'oooh'ing and 'ahh'ing, at the storm.

The forks clash and buzz and tangle with each other and yet because they are so far away the tendrils of electricity seem like veins of coral or small pieces of electric crochet, nothing harmful.

The boat is silent, her sails still sagging. There's nothing to do but watch, as though they were sitting at a drive-in movie of the cosmos. They watch for half an hour at least, till the storm runs further away.

And then they are alone again, quiet and valiant, but alone. He props himself in the corner of the rails, legs up. Under his harness he's wearing a grey fleece with a hood and for some reason it feels like a dressing gown. Océan comes to him and arranges herself in his lap and he hugs her tight; Suzy comes mumbling too, sits with her head on his lap. They are all meshed in and it feels safe in the stern, a light breeze now picking up the mainsail and then they are moving, just. All three of them lull into a peaceful slumber in the stern of the boat as she takes them south.

When he wakes, everything is in shades of night. Océan is heavily asleep on him and he pushes her around to make them both more comfortable. Suzy wakes too and thumps her tail for attention. Up ahead, the mainsail is full, thank God; they are sailing again. He checks his watch, then the mileage calculator, and then his heart freezes.

Up ahead, on the port bow, as his eyes begin to focus, he can see the dark shape of a man, struggling with an unruly sail. His first instinct is to go up to help him, but a hot terror in his blood quells this impulse.

The man is hauling down *Romany*'s mainsail; he is wearing foul-weather gear, he is being thrown about by the boat and he is grabbing at the canvas. Suzy whines and he shushes her, clamping one hand on her muzzle.

The lone sailor up ahead is stumbling, gathering in the sail. It must have been a bad storm, something stuck, not coming down; the man must have gone up on deck. And then the sail seems to fall all at once, and the man is

overwhelmed by the weight of it. The boat tips. He drops
the sail. As he rises to steady himself, the boat rocks again,
sharply, and the man is flung, hard, over the rails. It all
happens in seconds, a man's life extinguished.

Oh God, bless his soul, Gavin whispers.

CHAPTER TWENTY

EMBRACE

A blue-footed booby appears on the sixth day, with her exhausted young child. The birds seem more than relieved to see their boat. What are the birds doing out here? God knows. They are four hundred and fifty miles away from land.

The boobies sit on the rails on the starboard bow for most of the morning, shitting heaps of guano, which is full of acid and very hard to remove from the deck. Suzy is beside herself with wanting to chase the birds and so Gavin clips her to her lead in the saloon. Océan cannot believe the blue feet of the birds, or rather bright turquoise. It's like they are wearing kinky boots or designer snorkelling fins, which is in effect what nature has given them.

The baby booby in particular seems utterly content to be on board. It is sitting up there, resting, some of its snowy chick feathers still stuck to its head. Océan wants a closer look.

Dad, can I touch the baby bird?

No. The bird is only small, just like you, and very tired. It flew after its mother, too far out.

Are they lost?

Sort of.

They must be glad to see us.

Yes, I bet they are.

Where are we going, Dad?

Booby Land.

She laughs.

We'll see lots more of these crazy birds when we get to the Galapagos.

Océan nods, she repeats Ga-lap-a-gos out loud and slowly, a new word. She is only now twigging that they are going somewhere special. A big sea trip – and then a very different place. He refuses to tell her much, says 'just wait and see'. But there will be lots of turtles, huge turtles, he says.

And lizards? she asks.

Yes.

The mother bird flies off, looking for fish to feed her child. He becomes anxious, that the mother will not fly back, that she will lose them out here. Six days at sea. They are more than halfway there. They have a passenger now; they will carry it safely home.

What happened to the mother bird, Dad? Océan says.

It flew off to find food.

What kind of food?

Fish.

How does the baby bird know she'll come back?

Because . . . she always comes back. She knows that her baby is here on the boat, where she left it.

But what if she can't find our boat?

She has good eyes. Remember she is flying very high – she can see everything up there.

Océan nods. The baby bird always knows his mother will come back?

Yes.

Oh.

His guts twist at her *oh*. She has never admitted to it, that she is lonely now, without her mother, her baby brother. She squints up at him.

My mummy hasn't flown away.

No, my love. In fact, she's very close to our home.

Sleeping, right?

Yes, it's very natural to go to sleep.

I know.

Even animals curl up in a ball, sometimes, to protect themselves.

Like hedgehogs?

Just like hedgehogs.

Phoebe wasn't sad, though.

No.

People come and go, don't they, Dad?

Yes.

They sail on, into the haze. He hasn't lied to his child. It's true they'll see her mother again. *She knows you've gone sailing*, Jackie said. And Claire would be pleased they sailed out here, this far; he'd told Claire all about his dream of the Galapagos. He contemplates the big brown wave, roaring down the hill, the memory still enough to raise his skin in bumps, changes the way he breathes. Why didn't he think to gather them all up that night, leave the house sooner? Was it his fault, their son drowned, is that the unmentionable truth? They should've evacuated the house, got out. It's hard to remember what really happened, the *crack* of the garden walls. What happened? It doesn't matter: that's the truth.

Six days' sailing and he's had very little sleep. Océan and Suzy have been sleeping, but he's not been able to let go completely, not for more than an hour at a time. He slumbers, generally, from 4 to 6 a.m. He stinks, they all do.

On the seventh day this happens:

Dawn, calm sea. Gavin has a mug of tea in his hands; he is climbing the stairs to the cockpit and his head is fuzzy. Something isn't right, and he feels it in his marrow; something isn't right at all. Suzy, he can hear her whining in distress.

Instinctively, he glances behind him, towards the starboard bow, his eyes tracking the lifelines. There, caught up in the meshing, is Suzy. Her body is twisted up, half-over the rails; she is dangling overboard.

Suzy, he cries. He drops the mug. Her hind legs have become entangled, like she was climbing over the side. Was she trying to get to the baby booby, chase after its mother?

Suzy, he shouts, no, dear God, no.

Suzy kicks and struggles at his words. He races to the foredeck, arrives just as Suzy has begun to loosen herself.

No! he shouts.

But Suzy has pitched herself over the side. She falls into the sea with a frothy splash.

He stares, aghast.

Océan, he screams. Come upstairs, NOW.

He runs back to the cockpit.

The child dashes out from the saloon.

What, Daddy?

He grabs her and stands her upright in the cockpit.

Suzy has fallen into the sea, he says, gibbering. I want you to stand here, very still and point at her, do you understand? POINT, straight at her, wherever she is and do not move. Do not lose sight of her.

Océan is crying, she nods, she says yes, Dad, is this my job?

Yes.

Suzy is panicking in the sea, paddling after them, some distance now opening up between her and *Romany*.

He is shaking. He lets the main and the jib fly, all the while shouting at Suzy, *keep swimming*, shouting God knows what, for this is like the blind panic of the brown wave all over again. His heart is hammering. He is crying too, he realises, tears of wild terror.

Océan is standing rigid, pointing.

He jumps into the cockpit and turns on the engine. It coughs. He cranks it again. *Come on*, he shouts, come on!

And then the familiar chug starts up and he drives the boat forward and then around 180 degrees, and all the while Océan is pointing and shouting *Suzy*. When the boat has turned he can see the dog still paddling towards them, her head up above water. He slows the boat right down, one, two, three, very slow now, easy, easy.

Océan, you must move now, out of the way.

He puts the engine in neutral. The boat slows so it's almost stationary. Suzy is paddling towards them, and he knows that all will be in the snatch, his hold on her. He reaches down, over the lifeline, so he is more than half over the side, ready to grab her, pick her up just like he picked up that dying iguana on the road in Curaçao: one hand on the scruff of her neck, one hand on her rump. He will lean and pick her up in one. She is swimming straight at him, head up, her eyes on him and only then can he see the tears in her eyes. She's crying, making such agonised sounds, that he begins to pray, for her, and for himself.

Océan is screaming for her dog. Then Suzy is right beneath him and he lunges and grabs her by the scruff of the neck, his right hand like a vice. He smashes his left hand on her rump – and heaves. In his imagination, this should be enough. But Suzy is wet. And she is heavy, a lot heavier than an iguana. As he lifts her from the water, she begins to writhe and gnash her white shark's teeth, growling with her own panic. She goes into a storm, thrashing, her legs striking out in the air, trying to reach the deck, or something solid, but she wrenches so hard she arches up and out into the air.

She drops back into the sea.

Océan is wailing and screaming out over the deck, *Suzy*.

He spots Suzy, pointing his finger at her, revving the engine, driving forward again, flipping the boat around. In moments, he's heading right back at the dog again.

But this time, Suzy is gone.

Suzy, he shouts, but she's nowhere, not on the leeward side of the boat; she's disappeared.

Then he sees, her, paddling now towards the stern, weaker, but on the windward side. Again, he puts the engine in neutral.

Suzy is swimming towards him, their eyes are locked.

Come on, he says to her, keeping his eyes on hers. Come on now, girl, don't panic this time, do this one thing. Stay calm.

This time he reaches half his body down the side of the hull and hugs her to him in an embrace; like this he scoops her up and out of the sea, in one tight clinch. But Suzy's fur is slippery, sodden with seawater, and she is tired and she is old. He squeezes and she whimpers in pain and he realises she's hurt herself, maybe even broken something in her fall. *Suzy*. He relaxes his grip but he cannot hold her for too long like this, and she cannot hold onto him. She groans in his arms. He tightens his grip again and whispers her name. But the sea sucks her out of his arms and away from him. She struggles, kicking her legs, as if not to save herself but to kick herself free of him, to say *let me go now*. He is hauling her up through the sea but she is wheezing, shivering with shock and fatigue. He hangs onto her by her front legs, hurting her, and she squeals, and he pulls at her fur, pleading, saying, *Suzy, now, come on, Suzy*. But she's been injured in the fall overboard, she is losing her fight. *Suzy*, he cries, but she slips free and he is left with the phantom of her in his arms, his hands empty. The sea closes up on her, swallowing her; in moments she disappears downwards into the blue waves.

CHAPTER TWENTY-ONE

SONG

The baby booby's mother flew back. She arrived with a small silver fish in her mouth and proceeded to tear it up on deck and then regurgitate it, feeding it back to her child. They watch with a half-hearted interest, mute after Suzy's plunge into the sea. Neither of them have slept since the accident. They can barely look at each other. He is a foolish man after all. Sailing by the seat of his pants. He shouldn't be out here. Clive is a good sailor. Clive and he should have come out here, years ago, as young men. That would have been different.

More birds are appearing from nowhere, so they are not too far away now. Gulls, frigates, more tiny squid. There is an atmosphere, a tang in the air of land, of something up ahead. They have enough food and water to get them there, enough fuel, just, but they've lost the spirit of things. Neither of them can eat either. Océan has been sobbing since Suzy drowned, sobbing on and off in spontaneous spurts. Her dog has disappeared into the sea and he is unable to console her.

She looks at him, her eyes reddened, full of remembering and trying to understand, like she's had enough now. She is trapped aboard this boat.

Dad? she says.

Yes, dou dou.

I'm sad.

I know. You look sad today.

When are we going to get to this new place?

Soon.

How soon?

In two days.

Then we'll get off the boat?

Yes.

For how long?

For however long we want.

And there'll be turtles there?

Yes. Galapagos is the Spanish word for turtles.

I don't like turtles.

You've never even seen one.

Well, I don't like them.

You *might* like them. These islands are special. Even Herman Melville went there once.

Who's he?

He's a writer, he wrote *Moby Dick*. Remember him?

The white whale?

Yes.

Captain Ahab, with his wooden leg.

Yes.

Ahab tried to kill the whale and got killed himself?

That's right.

We never saw a whale, did we?

No.

Dad?

Yes, dou dou.

When can we go home?

Home?

Yes.

Where is home for you, my turtledove?

Home is our house, in Trinidad, where we live.

What about *Romany*?

Romany is a *boat*, Dad.

I know.

Dad?

What?

Little baby Alex died in the flood.

Yes.

Then Mummy went away.

Yes.

Then *we* went away.

Yes.

Suzy went away, yesterday.

Yes.

I just want us to go home. Please. Stay in one place. It's just *us* now.

I know. I'm sorry.

I want Mum to wake up.

Me too.

I feel weird, Dad.

So do I.

I'm feeling sorry for everything.

It is the sea, my love. It makes you do that.

What, Dad?

The sea makes you think about everything.

Océan looks away, out to sea. She nods at something, distracted with her loss, like she doesn't want to look at him ever again, like he's in the way of her vision. He is beside himself. Océan no longer trusts him, he can tell. His staff didn't trust him either, only Petula did and she was too trusting of everything. Now his child has the same composed faraway look, like something too much has happened. He didn't want to catch what his wife had, his staff didn't want to catch what he had. Now his child has the same reaction. The equator looms and they should be celebrating this voyage as they sail into the southern hemisphere. Instead there's a solid grief in his chest: 247 nautical miles to go before they cross the equator. So what?

*

The wind picks up and they sail for hours. Océan sleeps and weeps. The sea is massive and there is a sense of its grand entitlement. The sea owns 70 per cent of the world and the sea has taken Suzy. It is simply untroubled for now, for a few hours. It owes them nothing. Gavin feels this keenly, for the first time in his life. He has had a romantic attachment, notions about the sea, but these are fantasies. Now, he is aware that the sea isn't interested in him – and yet he's fascinated with her. The sea has no feelings towards him whatsoever, and yet she stirs unfathomable moods in him. The sea doesn't care, cannot care, one jot, for him and his boat, his child, his dog, and yet they've been held mesmerised. At best, the sea is an accomplice to his restlessness.

Even so, the sea has always reminded him of qualities he knows humans to possess. It is shifting, and prone to moods. It's as if he is floating on a giant mirror and the sea's purpose is only to reflect himself back. Who the fuck is he, after all? Who does he think he is to have come all this way, this far away from land? *You're not safe,* she whispers.

A silent desolation descends. For hours, the sea throws him into meditation. *ABC,* one, two, three . . . corn birds in the trees. He should be in his hammock, at his pink home, except it rains too much these days, no trees now on the hill above his home. Everything is jumbled up, inside and out. The world isn't what it was: too much damn rain these days.

Océan comes up, with Grover, to stare at the sea. He hugs her in his arms, and they gaze out at this big rolling space of dispassionate sea.

I don't like it any more, Dad.

I'm sorry.

I don't want to be a sailor any more.

I know. Maybe I don't either.

I am alone now.

No you're not.

Yes I am.

He hugs her tight and says: this feeling will pass eventually.

There's no need for talk and nothing to talk about, either. They are quiet together for miles of open water. They clip along at five knots, the main and jib out, the craft eager to please. They notice very little. Lots of blue, which sometimes changes to violet and purple and sometimes it looks a little frosted. The breeze shifts around from time to time and he trims the main. He can feel a strain in his vision from fatigue and from the salt spray and the air starts to bend. The air starts to boil, shapes loom.

And it's precisely at this moment, when he cannot peer out to sea much more, when, up ahead, the sea parts.

A tail fin splits the surface.

Océan points, *Daddddd*! she shouts, and jumps up out of his arms.

His heart thumps. He rushes to the port rails. They both gaze hard.

Then the sea is quiet again.

Dad, did you see it? She is jumping up and down, crazy with excitement.

Did he see it? Did he ever. It was astonishing.

Yes.

What was it?

A tail fin, he says.

It was big, Dad.

Yes it was.

Where did it go? he thinks to himself. It was a large tail fin. This could be trouble, for a tap from the hips of a whale can splinter a small boat. He cranes his neck and stares at the sea, searching for a shape, anything beneath the surface.

Nothing.

He shivers because the flash of the tail fin he saw was white. He's *sure* he saw it, a white tail. He rubs his eyes and suppresses the urge to cry.

Dad? says Océan. Did you see that the tail was white?

He looks down at her; his throat is dry.

Yes, dou dou. Yes, I did see the tail was white.

They stare ahead, port side. He doesn't say anything. But he feels a mixture of guilt, awe and fear snake up his back. He goes into the saloon and gets his binoculars.

Did they really see a tail?

There's a splash, to starboard now. Fifty feet away, the sea parts again. Then they see a creature rise upwards like a tower from the sea, gigantic, like a spaceship. But it's sleek and has a fluted stomach, ridged, like the hull of a dinghy. It has an enormous mouth, yes, like the gullet of a pelican; and a tiny eye next to it, quite blue. And it has wings, this creature, or maybe they are oars; they are fretted – no, they are giant flippers. And the chin of the beast has buttons, maybe, barnacles or crustaceans. It seems to be up on its tail, rowing itself backwards in the air, smiling and saying *here I am*. And the creature is completely white. White all over, like milk. White like peace.

And then it's gone.

Dad, screams Océan. Was that a *whale*?

He has tears in his eyes. Yes, darling, that was a whale.

Was it Moby *Dick*!

He laughs. Yes. Well, I'm not sure. Maybe.

Was it Captain Ahab's whale?

No, he stammers, not *that* whale.

But was it the same whale?

Oh, God, he cannot think straight. No, well, yes. I don't know, I really don't know what kind of whale it is, darling. Look! He points.

The white whale has surfaced again, this time half-in and half-out of the sea. It sort of bobs up and down and then it becomes clear; the whale is looking directly at *Romany*, its eyes fastened on them standing there in the cockpit. The whale is studying them, curious.

He waves at it. He actually waves at the whale, because he knows it is looking right at him.

Océan waves too.

He remembers when his children were born, what that was like; he feels engulfed in this natural serotonin surge of love, of bliss. It is rarely so freely and spontaneously released. Only occasionally, here and there, in moments of a long life. This love is something the beast knows about. It is nodding.

And then there's an almighty sound, a sonar moaning, and it is coming from the whale: its song.

Is the whale trying to say something?

Yes.

What?

Whales sing, my love, they sing to each other, to find each other in the sea. They mostly talk underwater, but sometimes you can hear them from boats too.

And is the whale trying to sing to us?

Maybe.

The whale bobs lower in the water, its eye on them still, and it continues its low moan, harp-like, somewhere between the mewing of a kitten and the wailing of a banshee. It is a humpback whale, male, as only the males sing. It dives, flamboyant and powerful, nosing the water with its head and arching into the sea, picking up its tail in the air, like a horse might kick up its heels, slapping the water on the downturn, and then it is gone. Gavin has a sense that it hasn't vanished or fled. They can hear the whale's song to its mate, *where are you*?

The whale trails *Romany* on her voyage south, and he and Océan are enthralled as the whale, mostly gentle and slow, but now and then mischievous, takes off to the side and flips its huge body out of the dark placid sea, creating a splash which rocks the boat. It glides closer again, tracking them. The albino whale stays with them for quite a while, swimming past, singing and wailing like a cat or a man driven mad by grief.

INDEFATIGABLE

CHAPTER TWENTY-TWO

APPLE OF SODOM

They arrive in San Cristóbal, the easternmost of the Galapagos Islands, in the early afternoon. Soft rain falls in veils from under the sheet of cloud. There are many other boats moored in the harbour, a small fleet of visiting yachts and fishing boats, and he throws out the anchor near the back of them.

They're tired. Worn from the wind and sea, from the sun's daggers; it has been relentless out there, and, despite the light rain, it is all of a sudden much hotter the closer they get to land. Both have turned another shade of bronze, both have that look in the eye of gazing outwards, a look only sailors possess. Both speak less.

The capital of the Galapagos archipelago is here, Puerto Baquerizo Moreno, and Gavin knows they are strict on customs, so they must go through straight away to declare themselves. But they don't get off the boat immediately.

They sit in the saloon and wait out the rain; they eat a small meal of cheese and bread, salami.

The cabin still stinks of dog. Suzy's white hairs are everywhere and her smell is still in their nostrils. Her bowl is still on the floor. Over the last day or two they have grown downcast and listless with each other. This will take weeks, he realises, weeks to come to terms with the loss. Pets usually grow old, get put down; then there are talks, quiet, stoic words. Months pass. The child may want another pet at some point. But Suzy fell and disappeared, into the sea. It shocked him too, his old dog, the dog who survived the flood, who's been with him for over a decade, many times aboard this intrepid boat. He hasn't been able to say much to Océan. It all happened so quickly, and yes, it is partly his fault, for not harnessing her up.

Animals fill the gap between man and God. It's only been two days: but Suzy's disappearance has given them a dread of going forward. What can they trust now? The sea? This boat? Can Océan trust him? Can he trust himself? Are they safe together any more? Outside, the land is flat and black. Black like hell crusted over, sharply spiked and gnarled. The *apples of sodom*, that's what Melville said of these isles; that they were hideous. Yet this is where they've ended up; this is his destination, a long-held fantasy. Another archipelago, this one at the centre of the world, snagged up on three major currents, currents so strong that when the first visitors arrived here by sea they thought the islands were adrift.

He inflates the dinghy and lets it over the side.

Look, Dad, says Océan. Seals.

Yes, dou dou.

They're everywhere in the sea. Chubby, whiskered, unafraid, affable in their demeanour. Their fur is slick and black-brown with a golden tobacco-coloured hue. They're like dogs. Like Labradors.

He drops Océan over the rails into the dinghy. She is lighter, as though half the weight, half the child. Now this is all that's left of his family or so it feels, there's no guarantee Claire will revive her spirits. It's just him and the kid, and even she is half herself. She sits quietly in the dinghy and watches the seals scoot about in the sea. He'd hoped she'd marvel at this world, be impressed, spellbound, enchanted even; instead, she's miserable, barely there at all. She's had enough. There are abandoned boats and barges for the seals to lounge on and many are lying about, lazy, relaxed, not a care in the world. They've arrived at a spot on earth where all animals are safe, protected from man. It's *their* island. But Océan doesn't care.

Gavin rows them towards the shore with their papers in his bag. On the jetty seals are packed up into crevices, snoring and snuffling and curled up on planks, not the least bit disturbed by passing human feet. They are so relaxed they look dead, asleep with only their moustaches twitching. Océan looks at them with vague curiosity; he looks at his daughter with intense guilt.

Immigration and customs is on the quay, manned by the Ecuadorian army. Three men sit at the entrance in khaki uniforms and aviator sunglasses. They don't speak English. They see him through to the office indoors. There, another Ecuadorian soldier stamps his passport, stares at his papers and gives them permission to be on the islands for two weeks.

You bring no fruit with you?

No.

No animals?

No.

Océan stares, her eyes glassy.

No animals?

No.

Okay, then. You can visit the other islands too, two weeks.

They leave and walk together along the malecón. No Suzy pulling between them on the lead. Everywhere there are seals, 'lobos', sea wolves, as they are known in the Galapagos. Seals lying inert all over the pavement, in front of shops, in front of the bank, along the seafront, under the awnings, flopped into flowerbeds, lying on park benches, and spread out flat, flippers splayed, under a big child's playground, all ropes and slides. From under the ropes, a lone young seal chases two children around the climbing frame. They are wild creatures and the children are careful of them. Lobos bite each other and children too. Seals are in the street, lolloping after humans walking by, trying to catch up with humans on bikes. The seals are either snoozing, or up on their front flippers, back arched into an S; but the humans keep their distance.

Further up, there is a beach and he can smell the seals and hear them before he sees them, a colony, hooting and barking; hundreds spread along the beach and the rocks around, mothers canoodling with their pups, and juvenile males gadding about, and they're snuffling and burping and barking and lying about like a pack of relaxing vaga-bonds. The two of them climb up onto the sea wall above the beach and look down onto the massive tribe. The sight and the stink of them, their small but urgent cries, their heaving mass make him fall silent. He feels a strong pull to go down there and lie down next to them.

Are they a family, Dad?

Yes, sort of. There are many mothers and fathers and brothers and sisters here, but yes, they are all related, like cousins.

Does everything have a family, Dad?

Yes.

Birds?

Yes.

Trees?

Yes. Everyone is related, my love. Everything on the planet is related to everything else.

How?

It's complicated. But trust me, we all have something to do with each other. Seals and humans have a link. Look at them; can you see what I mean?

She gazes out onto the snuffling pack, hordes of crea-tures comfortable with each other, slumped on top of each other.

Yes, Dad.

They are like us and we are like them.

Am I related to a seal, Dad?

Yes, you could say that.

Was Suzy related to a seal too?

Maybe.

Does the Pacific Ocean have a family?

No. But the sea is water. We are made from water. So again, it's related.

So the sea is related too?

Yes.

And Suzy was made from water?

Yes.

She gazes out onto the pack of sea wolves. They seem happy, all huddled close. They seem many good things: safe, familiar, at home.

I am sad, Dad.

Me too.

My body hurts, Dad.

That is called sadness.

What is sadness?

A feeling, my love.

It hurts, what is it?

I don't know. But I feel it too, though. I think it comes from God. Nature. There is a source, some-where, of emotions, and we all get them from the same place.

The white whale we saw, Dad, he looked sad.

Yes, he did.

Is Suzy with the white whale now?
Yes, I think she is.

*

Days pass. They stay on the boat, row to shore, potter about. They don't go anywhere to begin with. It is early March, and the days are long and intensely hot. And yet, slowly, he can feel it happening, a dawning, descending sense of enchantment. Here, things are different. It is peaceful in this small harbour, it is quiet and the land is flat and the sky is translucent; huge sea turtles paddle past, nonchalant, on their way to another spot. Seals duck and dive about their boat. In the water, everywhere, there are iguanas, black fancy crested marine iguanas, drag-ons, monsters, snaking about in the sea.

By very dint of being alive, aware, by the fact that they have continued on, living, breathing, that the sun keeps arriving every morning, they begin to harmonise with the earth, reconcile with their loss. Losing Suzy was losing part of themselves, their experience of being together. Her physical presence is missing; it is mysteri-ous for Océan, for him too, something impossible to understand and it is as though the world is folding them into its mixture. Understanding is not the point.

He takes *Romany* for a sail east, towards a small cove, La Isla de Lobos. The cove is shallow, surrounded by black volcanic rocks, home to another colony of seals; he anchors and doesn't throw down the ramp. It is their first swim without Suzy. They are very far away from Trinidad. And yet he must face Océan. Be a man, a father for her, still. Show her that he won't die on her.

Come on, sweetie, he says. Let's go for a swim, shall we?

He spits in their masks to clean them. They climb down the stern ladder into the sea.

In the sea, they plunge their heads downwards. There are rocks, and lots of reef fish, shoals of sergeant majors and parrotfish and trumpetfish; reef fish but no reef, just rocks. He holds onto her hand as they head closer to the shore. On the bottom of the sea floor they see iguanas, sitting there, resting. Fish and lizards in the sea. Big fat-bodied lizards on the sandy bottom, just like the one that climbs his mother's coconut tree. And in the sea, on the surface, they see legs, the black hind legs of the iguanas, kicking and scuttling through the water. They can see the tops of their bodies too, the bizarre conquistador helmets, as they plough through the aquamarine water. Then there are the lobos, three of them, swimming alongside.

Océan squeals. *Daddy!* She clambers onto his back in a mixture of panic and delight.

The seals are young, friendly, and playful; they are curious too, and all of a sudden they are surrounded. The seals swim so fast they are like torpedoes, slippery and agile. They come right up to their masks. One pokes its snout straight into the glass of his mask. They stick their funny laughing faces up close.

Ha, ha.

Océan is still hiding behind his back. But they are eager to play, like puppies. One jumps straight out of the sea and plants a kiss on her cheek.

Daddy, she shrieks with glee. The seal darts away, pleased with its stolen kiss. Océan rubs her cheek and scowls, like she has got something back, her spirit. Like she wants to chase after the seal.

He doesn't move. More seals join them and for a few minutes they are at the centre of a lively party, the seals jubilant and splashing, making fun. Then he takes his child and swims along some more. Some of the seals join them, tracking their course. It is hard to know which creature finds the other more interesting, the seals or them. He and Océan are silent, all this is new, they don't know what to think; but the Galapagan seals have met humans many times, they seem openly amused.

And then the seals are gone. It's so shallow he can stand up. He stands in the water and takes off his mask and looks upwards to see chaos in the air.

Look! He points up.

The sky is choked with frigates, their scarlet red chests puffed out like balloons. There must be forty or fifty flying through the air, so many he guesses it is their mating season. They look like old-fashioned aeroplanes, held in space by virtue of the air in their necks; like they are floating around on bags, like they are an early or rare version of a creature of flight, a paper bag bird. On a rock nearby stands a quizzical-looking bird, white-chested with turquoise flippers. The booby's feet are spectacular, dandyish; how could anyone have matched those feet to such an ordinary creature? And it is there and then that he is overcome with a peaceful and reassuring feeling. *All is well*. Right there, in the water, gazing up at the skies which are whirring with birds. He sees it, feels it, the presence of God.

And yet the young Darwin sailed here too, on board a vessel called the *Beagle*. Like Gavin, he was in search of answers, and yet Darwin concluded it was unlikely there was such a thing as God. He decided that the world came about as a series of accidents, without design or purpose, over millions of empty unrecorded years. The earth is old. Left untouched, it simply evolved, the strongest surviving, adapting, no meaning, no romance, no God – but how? How did Darwin look up and behold these skies and think there was no art here, no divine alchemy?

Gavin puts his hand to his chest. It's hard for him to find his heart. It is hiding behind his lungs, lodged between two ribs. He and his daughter have lost their bearings. They drowned too, a bit, when the dog drowned. Her leg is still healing from the fall weeks ago, a pearly red crust. The pink slave huts of Bonaire, the white hills of salt, they float in a haze. Slaves who never went back to Africa. Bones of coral hanging on a string in front of a pink house on the beach in a hidden archipelago off the coast of Venezuela. Wild donkeys brought by the Spanish in Curaçao. Slaves traded along with rum, sugar, spices. Humans for sale. The Panama Canal scooped by workers from the Caribbean, dying in their hundreds from yellow fever. Man severed two continents to get what Man wanted. Man sells other men, cuts continents in half, steals hundreds of thousands of helpless tortoises to eat, extinguishing entire species. It feels like he cannot get home now. He has come apart; he has lost something he never knew he had, some notion of innocence, a belief in himself. He wanted to see the world, but it has flashed him an evil grin. The brown wave knocked him for six, took his wife, his son. The ocean gulped his dog. They should go home now, but he cannot face sailing back. He could sell *Romany* perhaps, auction her off, even give her away.

And what if Claire hasn't woken up? What if they return to a wife and a mother who is still swamped, waterlogged with grief?

They leave San Cristóbal eventually, and sail to the island of Floreana where the sands are black. There is a famous hotel on the beach, metres from the sea, art deco in style, the Wittmer Hotel. There are some tiny wooden huts further along, eco-cabins for tourists; there is water here, too, rainwater collected in a lake in the centre of the island. They take the dinghy to the jetty and walk along the black beach. The sun rains down on them and the sand is prickly and fiery with heat, like fibreglass, like space dust. Up ahead, a big iguana is on its way towards them. They both flinch. There is no Suzy to restrain but somehow she is present.

Suzy, Océan says quietly as if testing the word for life. The reptile seems indifferent to them and this doesn't seem natural. He is tempted to do something bad, like scare it, run after it with a stick.

They hitch a ride up to the highlands in a truck with bench seats, an old banana truck from Ecuador. There used to be so many tortoises on these islands that visitors had to climb over them. But the whalers stole them all. Some ships took as many as five hundred in one go. The whalers carted thousands off and ate them. Man slaughtered all the tortoises on these islands in order to slaughter most of the whales in the sea. Now Floreana has no more giant tortoises. What they have is a small hopeful corral, up in the mountains, a corral made of concrete, walled off, and eighty or so turtles, brought from other islands, a mixed bunch. The tortoises here are safe.

Océan is impressed. She stoops to examine one.

The beast resembles an elephant trapped under a huge antiquated army helmet; it looks tired. Its forelegs are scaly, like a dragon's, its limbs, neck and head look sculpted from brown mud. It has slanted beady black eyes, like it is hiding under its own eyelids.

Dad, is this a tortoise?

Yes.

Will it try to kiss me?

No.

Can I kiss the tortoise, Dad?

Okay.

She bends forward and tries to kiss the tortoise on the forehead, but it quickly pulls its head into its shell with a hiss, startled.

What happened?

It's hiding. I don't think tortoises kiss, not like seals, so it didn't know what you were trying to do.

Can I kiss it on its shell?

You can try.

She leans forward again and this time puts her lips on the armour-plated hide. The tortoise has buried itself in its own flesh, under its own roof.

Again a flutter in his chest, that feeling of being lost. Of having lost something he will never get back. He has never felt so empty or dumb, like he is learning how to walk again.

There are other people milling about in the corral, also visiting this exotic out-of-the-way zoo. Like them, they've come to look at the animals, peer into their eyes; they're trying to see their own creature in these creatures. But these animals do not give them magical looks. The animals chew on cabbage leaves and cactus and carrots and barely glance upwards.

Gavin notices an older man sitting on a wall. He has silver hair and a silver goatee and he is wearing a sailor's Tilley hat pulled low. The man looks gentle and sad. A younger man is with him taking pictures of the tortoises. They are father and son, comfortable and proud to be together, or so it seems. The man speaks in a soft American voice. He must be sixty, the son in his twenties. Again Gavin projects and tries to imagine what it would have been like to be father to a son, to be a guide, an example. Now, he knows. He has fainted on his daughter, lost her dog, brought her to look at tortoises which don't want to be kissed. He is still overweight. His hands are still peeling and he cannot think of what else to do now.

The man smiles at him. Gavin senses it's okay to sit next to him. He feels the need to be fathered himself; is that what all this God business is about?

That your little girl?

Yes.

Pretty. Did she kiss that turtle?

Yes.

Heh, heh. My son loved it here.

Gavin picks up on the use of the past tense, but this is confusing. The man's son is taking photographs.

He used to come diving here, loved the sea around these islands. It was a kind of spiritual home for him.

Oh.

That's why we're here.

Gavin doesn't know what to say. He shows the man that he is listening.

We came here to scatter his ashes in the sea.

Oh. I'm sorry.

We did it yesterday. He died just before his birthday. Motorbike accident.

That's terrible. My sincere condolences.

Yeah. The three of us travelled everywhere together. Now it's just the two of us.

Jesus.

Yeah. Tough. Very tough. Especially on his mother.

Did she go to sleep?

Yes.

CHAPTER TWENTY-THREE

CUYE

It's late afternoon when they sail into the island called Indefatigable. It is hot, hot like when the poui trees start to explode in the hills, like when fires erupt of their own accord all around Port of Spain. They've been travelling for almost four months. They are as salty as the sea, but they are weary, the opposite of indefatigable.

As with San Cristóbal, there are many yachts moored in the harbour, Puerto Ayora, a small community afloat. There's also a large fleet of white cruise boats of all sizes, some luxury, some economy, those licensed to take the tourists around the islands. Lobos have stuffed themselves into cubbyholes and transoms and onto the low aft decks of these cruise boats, turning them into mini loberias. There is a high rock wall port side, and as they arrive, many boobies stand in their blue socks observing their arrival. He and Océan are so tired that he thinks that for a few nights they'll go and stay in a hostel in the small port town. And so after they moor, as the sun begins to withdraw, he packs a small bag of clothes.

*

Later, they walk out into the town. The main road hugs the coast and curves along the bay and up on the right, they find a small fisherman's wharf. As they pass, the fishermen are bringing in the day's catch, dozens of silver black wahoo, long sturdy fish, almost like tuna. Some of the fish are being filleted on the stone counter; inside their flesh is a deep earth-red. The fishermen slice off the fish heads and throw them to pelicans and lobos and marine iguanas gathered around them. They see a pelican and a marine iguana vying for the same fish, the iguana with half its body inside the head. They see a seal, waiting, head cocked, as a man guts a fish. Massive pelicans sit, wings outstretched, on another counter, others are perched up in the mangroves. One or two are walking around with their gullets opened like umbrellas. The air is full of seal barks and bird cries and the stink of newly dead fish; the ground seems to be moving with animals. They don't stop, but walk past in a mild blueness. These islands have got the better of them. In the last few days they've swum with manta rays and sharks, walked long white sand beaches crawling with iguanas. Everywhere there is a cactus which grows like a tree, and tame finches, colonies of seals, penguins and rare birds. Everywhere they have witnessed wild animals and reptiles going about unafraid of man, even happy to be around him.

They turn left and thread through the back streets and end up near their hostel, finding themselves in a long open street with many kiosks and makeshift stalls like open-air restaurants, selling barbeque this and that. The air is pungent with smoke and grease and the avenue has a lively festive feel; they sit ravenous at a table and order barbeque chicken and chips. Océan rests her head on the table. He sips a cold beer and lets his mind wander. Soon it will be carnival. His sister Paula will be coming back to Trinidad for that. He thinks of his old mother Audrey, how much he dislikes Jackie. Clive, Paco, Petula. Has Petula missed him? Who got his old job? How is Josephine? What must the neighbours think: actually, of all people, they would understand. It all feels like a long time ago. He's been checking his heart less; he has maybe even lost a few pounds. He got here on his old boat *Romany*; who would have thought?

Suddenly, Océan jerks up her head. Daddy, what is that?

Next to them, an Ecuadorian family is dining. One of the waitresses has brought out a platter; on it, quite clearly, there is some sort of roasted animal and a lump of distaste emerges in his throat at the sight, for he instantly recognises it. From the kitchen, another waitress brings out a platter too, on it the same animal, the size of a small rabbit, and the family all oohh and aahh at the delicacy as it's laid down before them. The two small creatures have been dipped in batter and deep-fried to a crisp.

Errrr . . . he stops to ask one of the waitresses in broken Spanish, *Qué es eso . . .*

Cuye, she says.

Ahhh. *Cuye?*

She nods.

Qué es?

Guinea pig, she says loudly and emphatically.

Océan flashes her eyes. Guinea pig, Dad?

Yes.

What is that?

It's an animal, like a rat or a . . . hamster.

They are eating it, Dad?

Yes.

Yuck.

Well, that family likes it, it's considered special here.

But why?

Well, why not?

I don't understand, Dad.

What don't you understand?

Why do we eat some animals and leave others alone?

I don't know. Good question. Ask the Prime Minister of Ecuador.

Why don't we eat seals or penguins?

Some people do, but not here. Here they are protected.

Why aren't *hamsters* protected?

Guinea pigs. And I don't know why they aren't protected.

It doesn't make sense, Dad.

No. It doesn't. He fears an argument, that she will

out-question him again. He says: Now eat your chicken and chips.

But she's gone off her chicken. She picks at the chips, watching the family pull apart the guinea pigs. One woman, the mother, chomps on the head, others fight over the twiggy legs.

I bet Mummy wouldn't eat a guinea pig.

No she wouldn't.

Can we call her again soon, Dad? Tell her about Suzy?

Okay, we can try tomorrow.

Minutes later she has her head on the table again, asleep. He cannot help thinking about Suzy. They wouldn't eat Suzy. He didn't know what to expect of these islands; he didn't expect to see fried guinea pigs or to lose his dog on the way here. To be so goddamn weary. This island was named after a famous British warship, HMS *Indefatigable*, a ship which took many other ships with its heavy guns in the Napoleonic wars; it marauded the seas for decades, that's the story Gavin read as a child, a brave boat – but it ended up in the scrapyard.

He carries his daughter back to their hostel room and lays her on the single bed and he cannot remember getting undressed or even going to bed himself, he is so tired, tired from so much sea.

*

In the morning, he wakes to a sense that something is wrong. Océan is sleeping on her stomach, face down, drooling into her pillow. He opens the bedroom door and stands on the balcony and looks up at the sky and he is enough of a sailor to know a bad sky when he sees one. The clouds have gathered as if to talk, low and tightly bunched, grey and lilac.

He wakes Océan. They get dressed, go upstairs to the dining area and eat warm bread rolls with jam and fried eggs. He checks his watch. It is 9 a.m., Friday, 11 March. There are other guests in the dining area, young couples, feral-looking backpackers with deep tans and nose rings. The lady cooking the eggs is young, friendly. Océan is dozy. But something isn't right. He lets her chew and hum through her breakfast while he feels a flicker of foreboding up his back. This feeling is unusual, a call, but he cannot pinpoint where from. His spine, his flesh, his cells are tingling.

They go downstairs and out onto the street and it's then that he sees, yes, things are different. Army vehicles everywhere, young men in combat fatigues standing with loudspeakers. In the square, where there was a floodlit volleyball game the evening before, a crowd has gathered and soldiers are giving orders. He cannot understand what's going on; everything is in Spanish. But clearly, something important is happening. He enters a shop selling tours.

Habla Inglés? he begs.

Yes.

What's going on? he asks.

There's been an earthquake, says the young man behind the desk.

An earthquake? And then it all makes sense. Of course. It's been hot, too hot for weeks. Too hot in the ocean on their voyage across. An anxiety out there at sea, the electrical storm, the boobies flying too far out. Signs. Things weren't right. And the white whale. Was it lost?

Yes, sir. An earthquake.

Here?

No. In Japan.

But Japan is on the other side of the world.

Big wave coming. Very bad.

A wave? His stomach constricts, hot terror blossoms in his chest, his face. A *wave*?

Big wave. Tsunami.

Jesus Christ.

Coming here, this way, soon.

In how long?

We don't know. Hours, maybe.

He must phone Claire. He must run, fly.

Everybody must go up, they are saying. To the highlands.

But I have a boat, in the harbour.

The army will tell you what to do. You must take it out to sea. So it will not crash onto the port.

Gavin laughs. Tears spring in his eyes.

You okay, Mister?

No. His stomach has turned to mush. No, I'm not.

Océan has been standing next to him, holding his hand, listening. She has gone white.

A wave, Dad?

Shush, dou dou. Come on now, he says and he runs with her towards the square.

In the square he stops a young soldier with a gun and gabbles in his broken Spanish about his boat, asks what he should do. The man points him in the direction of another soldier, older, with a clipboard, who seems to be taking down the names of boats and it's then that an idea seizes him. No, he will not register his boat with the army. Nothing like that. A much better idea has struck him, a solution to all his weariness.

On the quayside there is a frenzy of activity, fishermen and yacht owners shouting and jostling, some trying to get water taxis out to their boats; people are being ferried from the Finch Bay Hotel which sits on the rocks. Tourists stand on the quay with their bags, a queue of maxi taxis and pickup trucks waiting to take them up to the higher ground. He goes to the end of the pier. He has tied his dinghy to one of the many jetties there. All around there is an atmosphere of human urgency, so much so it has affected the animals; the pelicans wander about on awkward toes; the seals have all vacated their platforms. The water is choppy.

The outboard motor is attached to the dinghy, so they spin out to *Romany*. Half the private yachts in the harbour have fled, along with many of the white cruise boats for tourists. A small fleet has already headed out to deeper water. *Romany* sits there, where he left her. Patient. Old. Pretty. How long has he owned her, twenty years? She was found. The poor man who owned her last, the poor,

poor sailor, lost over the side. *Tabanca*, how much grief that sailor must have caused his family, how much grief has he, Gavin Weald, caused his family? How much grief has his wife caused him and Océan? They draw alongside *Romany* and he lashes the dinghy to the stern. He helps Océan on board, then heaves himself up too.

What are we doing, Dad? she asks.

We're going to pack.

Pack?

Yes.

Now?

Yes. Just what we need for now, my love.

He opens the hatch and they both go down into the saloon. From the V-berth he takes the two black canvas bags, now empty, that he packed when they left the pink house in Trinidad. They go about trying to gather the clothes that are supposed to go into the bags. But instead, they find that these clothes no longer exist. They are either soiled or have disappeared. They seem to have no clothes at all, just what they are wearing and what is back at the hostel. There are a few stray extra garments in the saloon. And so they pack one bag between them: two or three T-shirts, some underpants, his flip-flops, Océan's pink frilly skirt, her flippers and mask, their bathing suits, a handful of shells they've been collecting, a feather from the young booby. Grover, Mr Ahab, the stuffed iguana.

He decides to tidy the saloon, make up the V-berth, leave the bedding, leave all the tins and the food in the cooler and the charts and the maps and the VHF. He washes up and stows away the plates. He mops the floor.

He goes up onto the foredeck and pulls the anchor. By now, *Romany* is one of the few yachts left in the small harbour. He turns on the engine and takes her out, heading to where he can see that the other boats have moored, and his heart begins to thud, because he knows now the best thing to do. Everywhere, skippers are heading back in to land in their dinghies; he waves at two or three, everyone with bags, everyone leaving their boats to the giant wave which is arriving, a massive bulge of water heading east around the surface of the earth. They have anchored and are hoping to get their boats back later, tomorrow, maybe, after the wave has passed. He takes *Romany* out to the edge of the flotilla and turns her around. He stops the engine and lowers the bags and his camera down into the dinghy. In the saloon he opens his logbook and writes:

I bequeath this boat, Romany, to the man or woman who finds her. She is a good boat and I have owned her for twenty years. She was found adrift and I return her to the sea. I did not drown. I have not gone mad and jumped overboard. I am a sailor but have no more use for this fine vessel. I give her to whoever finds her with my best wishes and sincere gratitude for all the years she has given me. She can handle the high seas and will take you wherever you please. I leave the engine keys, maps, charts, all that is in the lockers. Bon voyage!

And then he and Océan are in the dinghy, leaving *Romany* afloat, awaiting the giant wave which will carry her to her new owner. Océan doesn't realise what he's done and as he leaves the boat unanchored he doesn't look back, but instead feels a flourish of pride, knowing this will be a good thing to do; that this is a fitting way to end this love affair. Oh, goodbye *Romany*, goodbye and how much I have loved you. It is the end, the end of their romance, of his time with this small boat.

*

In Puerto Ayora there is chaos in the streets. Hundreds of tourists are trying to get taxis up to higher land. He and Océan thread through them to their hostel, which is closing its doors and evacuating its residents. Two or three hours now before the wave is due to hit. No one can say how bad it will be, though there are rumours it is sixty miles long, travelling as fast and strong as a train. No one can say how much damage it will cause. CNN news footage of Japan and the tsunami's wreckage is already flickering all over plasma screens, shocking images of a massive wave spilling over bridges, tankers floating in it. A wave roaring into a town, demolishing houses and buildings, churning up all in its wake, people screaming on the roof of a building.

The earthquake happened out at sea, a mile or so off the coast of Japan, sending a wall of water west, a wave which engulfed the coastal city of Sendai, reducing it to matchsticks. But also, it sent a larger wave east, travelling across the Pacific, heading for Hawaii and the US and South American coasts, hitting the Galapagos well before the mainland. Hours left. A giant wave is on its way. He can feel heat on his neck, in his chest. Sweat on his palms. Océan is going into a state he's seen before, a silent terror. After the brown wave she went like this a lot, a cold sweat, then the screaming. Her eyes are full of tears. She cannot believe it. Neither can he. *A wave, Dad, a wave*, she keeps murmuring. With their few bags, they go downstairs and speak to the panicked woman on reception and she says there is a bus coming for the guests, to wait for it in the lobby.

In the highlands of Indefatigable the bus stops at a roadside restaurant in a small village. The passengers unload their bags. They will wait out the tsunami here. There are crowds of people milling about, dozens of vehicles laden with bags and pets and furniture. Everyone has come up here, all the tourists in the town and anyone else working or living there. Below Puerto Ayora is a ghost town, no one there. He leaves their bags with the hotel staff in the café, takes Océan by the hand and walks up the road in order to get away from the crowds. Crowds will panic her; crowds will only make her more aware of what is going on. They walk north, up a small tarmac road. The sky is still low and sullen. Everywhere the intense dry static heat has burst. It is humid now, and quiet. He can feel a sadness in his chest, the sadness which has been with him now for over a year, which has never left him, which will not go away. He has tried to leave himself, leave his home, outdo his past. But here it is again, aiming straight for him. Another wave, this one worse, travelling from those cold waters of Japan.

They turn right and find themselves on a lonely tarmac road. They pass by some trees full of white egrets and beneath them they can see the enormous wizened shells of two hundred year old Galapagan tortoises, hunkered in the shade. They walk on, up the road, and soon they come to what seems to be some kind of farm entrance. No one is about. There is a gift shop, rows of bathrooms, a changing area with lots of gumboots. The place seems deserted.

Helll*ooo*, he calls. But the farm keepers and tour guides have all disappeared, most likely to tend to their families. This is a park, he realises, a park for tortoises, high up. He reads a notice. Five hundred tortoises are roaming wild on the estate. It is forbidden to walk here without a guide. But Océan is now too upset to walk any further. No one is here, so he goes behind the café barrier, swipes two bottles of water from the fridge and leaves the money on the counter. He finds two pairs of gumboots for them and says to Océan: we are going for a walk.

She nods. A wave, Dad, is all she can say.

He piggybacks Océan into the green leafy park. It isn't long before they come across the tortoises. Lone, solitary beasts, humps wandering about in the long grass, big humps, oval, grey and brown, with frilled spoilers on the back, blind and mysteriously legless. Where on earth are they going? Each tortoise seems purposeful, marching towards some destination further away, another pasture, another part of the field. Here and there, beneath a tree, a hump; in the shadows of a thicket, another hump, walking somewhere. They are like scholars walking across an Oxford quad, ruminating, heads down. Where are they going? These creatures are hundreds of years old; so big they weigh up to two hundred and fifty pounds. It is hard for them to get around, but this doesn't seem to stop them. In the long grasses, half-elephant, half-garden shed; they have work to do.

Gavin and Océan find a shady, slimy pond. The surface is pea-green. In it are three black humps: tortoises wallowing. He sets Océan down, on her feet, and they sit nearby, under a tree. It is then that they see the biggest tortoise of the lot, not in the water, under a shrub. It has folded its legs under itself and laid its head on the ground; so tired it looks, tired of itself, its house on its back, its own caravan. It looks deflated and fed up, too heavy to heave itself into the water. The tortoise is looking at them with tender eyes. They look back.

What is it thinking, Dad?

I think she is tired. Having a rest.

She?

Yes. I imagine it's a she-tortoise. Don't you?

I guess. Is she tired like Mum?

No. I think she is just old and heavy.

Why did God make crazy creatures, Dad?

Like what?

Like fish that can fly and the white whale we saw. And that giant turtle which can't move.

I don't know. They are one-offs. Like he was trying out designs.

We *did* see the whale, didn't we, Dad?

Yes.

I'm going to tell all my friends when we go back to Trinidad.

Me too.

Will they believe us, Dad?

Probably not. Some creatures people will believe in, like black swans or giant tortoises. But other creatures are just too unbelievable; they are from books or fairy tales, like unicorns or white whales. They don't really exist.

But we saw a white whale. It was true! We saw it with our own eyes. I love the white whale, Dad.

So do I.

It was our friend. It came when Suzy died. It came to take care of us.

Yes.

Now the giant tortoise is here to help us too.

He laughs. The tortoise doesn't look the least bit help-ful. It looks fatigued. Unhappy with its hump.

Can we go home now, Dad?

Yes, my love.

I'm scared of the wave, Dad.

So am I.

Will it knock everything down?

I don't know. It might.

Is it the same wave that took baby Alex?

No. It's another wave.

Another wave?

Yes. I'm sorry, dou dou. But they happen every now and then. They happen when it's too hot, or when it rains too hard and there's no trees. They are natural.

Will the white whale die in it?

No. The white whale will dive underneath it. It will be fine.

There are tears in her eyes, of incomprehension. The tears sparkle and make her look prettier.

They sit there for some time, by the pond, in the shade, next to the wallowing tortoises, waiting for the giant ocean wave to pass below. And when it does, an hour later, everything goes quiet, and they notice that the ancient tortoise has vanished, it has stumbled away into the long grasses.

CHAPTER TWENTY-FOUR

JOUVAY

Early evening they return to Puerto Ayora to find that very little serious damage has been done. Only two of the evacuated seafront hotels have been badly hit. One, right on the rocks of Academy Bay, has been invaded by the wave and smashed up, attracting many onlookers. No one has been hurt, luckily. He doesn't care to take a peek. He knows what it will look like. The wave swept into the streets and the square, but it didn't devastate, nothing like Sendai. And the animals, it seems, all took to cover. No yachts or cruise boats seem to be lost. He imagines *Romany* out there somewhere, soon to be found. The wave will have pushed her east, towards the coast of Ecuador; she will be found again by fishermen, or perhaps the coastguard.

The restaurants are opening their doors on Charles Darwin Street. At one, Rincón de Alma, he bribes the owner with a fifty-dollar note to use the phone. He finds that his heart is leaden and his hands are damp when he punches in his mother-in-law's number. This is his last attempt. He whispers *we'll be okay, whatever happens, we'll be okay*. Océan stands beside him. They are at the back of the restaurant, down some stairs, in darkness, between the kitchen and the *baños*. In the kitchen, the chef is frying fish. The phone rings. Once, twice. Three times. Then, it's Jackie.

Hello?

Hello, Jackie, it's Gavin.

Oh. It's *you*, she says.

Jackie.

Don't Jackie me like that. Wait one minute. I'll get her.

A lump emerges in his throat. Heat in his face, behind his eyes.

Seconds pass.

Hello. A shy voice. His wife's voice. Thinner, unsure. Gavin?

Tears run down his face. Yes.

It's me.

Thank God, he whispers.

I woke up.

When?

Oh, I don't know, a week ago, I guess.

I'm so glad.

Where are you? she asks.

I'm on an island. It's called Indefatigable.

The Galapagos. Ahhh, you went there, at last.

Yes.

And is it good? Have you seen the tortoises?

Yes, we've seen tortoises.

Did Océan like them?

She did.

Is she well?

Yes.

Are you well?

I'm fine.

Gavin, I want us to sell the house.

Good.

Let's put it on the market as it is. I don't want to go back there.

Neither do I.

We can sell it for whatever we can get. My mother says she will release some funds, help us buy another house.

Good, thank her for me. That's very generous.

It's carnival here soon. Your sister is here. She's nice. I've always liked her.

Me too. She's bossy, though.

She's been here a lot. Reading to me, talking, cheering me up. She'll be playing Jouvay, in a mud band.

Maybe I'll join her.

Are you coming back?

Yes.

When?

On the next possible flight.

Gavin, I'm sorry. I just . . .

It's okay. I'm sorry too. I ran away.

Did it help?

Yes. Running away helped.

How?

The sea, you know. It gets you thinking. I thought I was separate. Me *against* the world. I wanted to escape that house, everything. But really, I'm part of it all, the earth, the sea. I can't get away.

I've been so sad, Gavin.

I know you have.

I wish you were here.

Me too. I'm a stupid bastard, Claire.

I love you.

Yeah. I love you back.

Can I speak to Océan?

He hands over the phone and feels her little body go rigid.

Mum?

And then she is talking to her mother, weeping and talking, about giant tortoises and the white whale and telling her all about Suzy, about how she fell off the boat.

*

It is 4 a.m. in St James, when the rain falls down from the sky. Thousands of people in the band, most daubed with cocoa mixture, mud, or paint, many now well past the point of remembering their own names. People in a state of intoxication, jubilation. This is dirty mas, dark mas, the opening to Trinidad's yearly festival which celebrates the fight of the flesh. This is Jouvay, *jour overt*, the opening of the day, of carnival, two days of celebration – and he is black, slick with mud and paint and wearing a cowboy hat with winking lights. There is a pouch of rum slung round his neck. He is Bacchus, he is Dionysus, he is a drunken sailor man, a wild man, a lover man; he is home, back, a person from this particular island, lush and green and fertile, Trinidad, the end link in the chain of this long and dazzling archipelago. They all are, these Trinidadians, a people living at the end of the chain, only six miles from the mainland of South America, spitting distance from the coast, a small island with the same mountains.

Thousands of Trinidadians are out in the road. It is 4 a.m. in the streets of Port of Spain and they have gone mad. Everyone is wining their arses and chipping down the street, drunk and happy on red rum and grinding up on everything, human and otherwise, leaving behind their ordinary lives for a while.

The rain dances down from the night sky and turns every person into a slippery wet brown statue. Arms in the air as the rain comes down. People open their mouths to catch the rain. Women jump on men, wrapping their legs around the men's hips. Men open their arms to receive the women. The rain is like wine being poured down their throats, men and women jammed up on each other in the road. Calypso in the air, the music of the steel pan, sweet calypso music booms from the trucks which accompany them down the road, and the sound of thousands of feet scraping the pavement. The air is full of sex and love.

There are people dressed up as birds, men dressed as angels, women as prostitutes, the whole band is meant to be dressed as cowboys, but there are devils too, jab jabs, a man dressed as a donkey, another man dressed as a robberman, the outlaw of carnival. At one point, the whole band slides into another band jumping up in the road in the opposite direction and there is a clash of joy as they collide. An invasion takes place, everybody kisses and greets this other band, cheering each other on into the night. His sister Paula is so intoxicated she can barely stand. He props her up and says, are you okay?

I'm fine, she says. Clearly she isn't, clearly she's beyond herself.

Look. He points. Above them is the southern cross, the constellation of stars he looks out for every year at this time of the night. Every jouvay he looks up and orientates himself to this cluster of stars in the sky; every jouvay he passes under this cross.

Paula looks upwards and says: I remember seeing those stars with you years ago, for the first time, on *Romany*, remember?

And he does remember, those years ago, his younger self. And he goes on down the road, in the flow of winking cowboy hats, and the rain falls down harder now, rain like wine, raining down on them, washing them. And the band moves together as one, everyone with their hands in the air, greeting the sweet, sweet rain.

ACKNOWLEDGEMENTS

On 19 December 2008, my brother's home in Perseverance, Maraval, Trinidad was badly flooded. While this was the starting point for this novel, the rest is pure fiction.

Between December 2010 and the end of March 2011, I embarked on a journey, mostly by boat, west out of Port of Spain, Trinidad, towards the Panama Canal. I met many people along the way who all helped me with this novel. In El Yaque, Margarita I would like to thank Johanne, William, and Rudolpho at Casa Rita. Thanks to Hank Lim and his boat *Further*, for his patience and the chilli dogs. In Bonaire I would like to thank Deidre Pederson, fellow Trinidadian, free diver, owner of the *Woodwind*, also Pahle and Petrie Hausmann for their knowledge of the island which they so generously shared. In Curaçao, Michael Newton and Howard Newton, cousins, who showed me so much of the city and the island; also Lonny Stoutyesdykin for our stroll down Booty Walk; also Raoul Granja, Ronald Pinkeur and Bertie Con and his boat *Timeshare*, for a memorable trip around

Spanish Water. In Aruba, thanks to Brenda Jansen and Freddy Noorlander for being so kind to me over Christmas, for taking me to see the south of the island. Thanks to Theo Shoemaker for his good company aboard the *Ildiki*. Also thank you to Captain Rufino, in San Cristóbal, the Galapagos, for jumping with me into the shark infested seas around Kicker Rock. Thank you, also, Sarah-Helena Barmer, muse, and Lee Winters, for the sailing tips. Both of you, excellent sailors.

I would like to thank my mother, Yvette Roffey, once again, for giving me a place to write and call home. Thanks to Victor Blackburn for a better scar. Thanks to my brother, Nigel Roffey, for tracking down his old boat, *Romany*, for a lifetime of boat trips and sea adventures in Trinidad.

Also, the earthquake which devastated Sendai, Japan happened on 11 March 2011. Carnival in Trinidad took place on the 7th and 8th of March 2011. For the purposes of fiction I have altered these dates. I would also like to thank my editor at the time Francesca Main at Simon and Schuster UK for making this a better book; also Maxine Hitchcock and Clare Hey for their dedication, and my wonderful agent Isobel Dixon at Blake Friedmann, a great team. Finally, I would like to thank my editor at Penguin Group (USA), Allison Lorentzen, for her eye for detail and creative input in editing this novel for American readers.

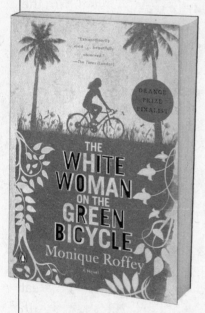